T0243587

STORMING THE IVORY TOWER

HOW A FLORIDA COLLEGE
BECAME GROUND ZERO IN THE STRUGGLE TO
TAKE BACK OUR CAMPUSES

RICHARD CORCORAN

BOMBARDIER
BOOKS

Published by BOMBARDIER BOOKS
An Imprint of Post Hill Press
ISBN: 979-8-88845-827-3
ISBN (eBook): 979-8-88845-828-0

Storming the Ivory Tower:
How a Florida College Became Ground Zero in the Struggle to Take Back Our
Campuses
© 2024 by Richard Corcoran
All Rights Reserved

Cover Design by Jim Villaflores

This is a work of nonfiction. All people, locations, events, and situations are
portrayed to the best of the author's memory.

Post Hill Press
New York • Nashville
posthillpress.com

Published in the United States of America
1 2 3 4 5 6 7 8 9 10

To the *New York Times*, the *Washington Post*, the *Tampa Bay Times*, the *Sarasota Herald-Tribune*, and so many of their sister publications.

Without their boundless hubris, steadfast dedication to avoiding self-reflection, and unshakable commitment to ignoring any fact that does not support their predetermined narrative—not one chapter of this book would have been possible

CONTENTS

FOREWORD

For years, conservatives have bemoaned the capture of America's universities. They wrote books, hosted panels, and furrowed their brows. But we have entered a period in our history in which complaint is no longer enough. We have identified the problem and discussed it to the point of exhaustion.

Now, we need action.

Richard Corcoran is a man who exemplifies this new spirit of politics. He is not satisfied with the fact that he believes in the right ideas; he wants to see those ideas manifested in the real world. As a legislator, education commissioner, and public-university president, he has learned how to wield power and orient institutions toward the true, the good, and the beautiful—the great transcendentals of the West.

The story in *Storming the Ivory Tower* is not one of dry abstraction. Corcoran is actively engaged in this fight, leading the effort to reform Florida's most left-wing public university, New College of Florida, and restore the classical liberal arts education that inspired its founding. This requires conflict and controversy, which he has confronted with remarkable candor.

At New College, Corcoran has worked to abolish the DEI department, terminate the gender studies program, and replace useless bureaucrats with mission-aligned leaders. He has implemented the vision of Governor Ron DeSantis, who provided the impetus for these reforms. He has fought the press—and won.

Florida has become the blueprint for red-state governance. And, as the president of New College, Corcoran has demonstrated the promise of no-holds-barred reforms.

We are in deep trouble in America. Our institutions have been captured by poisonous ideologies and our culture has been set adrift. If there is hope for restoring the principles of our country, it will require a project of institutional recapture.

This is not an easy undertaking. There will be trials, challenges, and failures. But there will also be victories and triumphs. This book is an honest look at the project of reconquest and, in time, will prove to be a valuable guidebook for others who want to follow the Florida model.

As a trustee of New College, I have been in the trenches with Richard Corcoran and watched him work. He has shown grace under pressure and a refusal to compromise on principle.

I hope *Storming the Ivory Tower* will show readers, including those in higher education, that all is not lost. The spirit that is required is courage, which leads to action. If New College can be rescued, so can other institutions.

This is only the beginning.

—Christopher F. Rufo

PREFACE

This is the story of how New College of Florida, an institution that had been on the verge of closure, was transformed in just a few short months.

On the surface, it is the story of a battle.

However, on a deeper level—like all great battles—it is about much more than that. It is the story of what we were fighting for: the power and beauty of a liberal arts education.

While in the modern world that may not strike many as a particularly inspiring mission, once upon a time, a liberal arts education illuminated the world, bolstering the new and radical concept of self-government. In fact, the liberal arts emerged in concert with the first glimmers of hope for the possibility of such government—around 400 B.C. in ancient Greece. In many ways, the concepts of self-government and a liberal arts education go hand in hand because almost as soon as the outlines of self-government began to take shape, a perplexing question emerged: How could people self-govern given the fallible nature of humanity?

The consideration of this dilemma weaves through the conversation of the centuries, including Plato's *Republic*, Locke's *Second Treatise on Civil Government*, and *The Federalist Papers*.

In 2005, it was echoed in David Foster Wallace's famous commencement speech at Kenyon College when he spoke about the power of the liberal arts. Humans, Wallace said, have a "default setting"—a desire to put our selfish interests first.

> *[E]verything in my own immediate experience supports my deep belief that I am the absolute center of the universe; the realest, most vivid and important person in existence. We rarely think about this sort of natural, basic self-centeredness because it's so socially repulsive. But it's pretty much the same for all of us. It is our default setting, hardwired into our boards at birth. Think about it: there is no experience you have had that you are not the absolute center of. The world as you experience it is there in front of YOU or behind YOU, to the left or right of YOU, on YOUR TV or YOUR monitor. And so on. Other people's thoughts and feelings have to be communicated to you somehow, but your own are so immediate, urgent, real.*

Wallace was merely saying in modern terms what Socrates, Plato, and countless others had considered in earlier times. This is why the liberal arts are worth the fight. They are helpful in equipping humans for self-government, both personally and politically. The purpose of the liberal arts is to force us to think critically: to have perspective, to be aware of long-term consequences, to look beyond ourselves and at a larger picture. These abilities are desperately needed in today's world of AI, propaganda, and endless ways to entertain ourselves into oblivion.

The story that follows is about our experience storming the ivory tower. However, I hope it can also serve as a roadmap for others who might want to follow. A liberal arts education—one which allows for open dialogue and civil discourse, free from indoctrination—is a powerful legacy to leave for future generations.

"Education...means emancipation. It means light and liberty. It means the uplifting of the soul of man into the glorious light of truth, the light only by which men can be free."
—*Frederick Douglass*

CHAPTER 1

The Greatest Threat

Don't you see that the whole aim of Newspeak
is to narrow the range of thought?
—*George Orwell,* 1984

On May 19, 2023, the graduation speaker at New College of Florida, Dr. Scott Atlas, walked up to the podium to begin his remarks. The sun was just beginning to set over Sarasota Bay, off which the campus is located, and guests were seated near the water under a large white tent. Behind Dr. Atlas on an elevated stage, faculty and administration wore their academic regalia. The event looked like many college commencements taking place around the nation that spring. However, when Dr. Atlas had accepted the invitation to speak from me—the recently appointed interim president, we had both known that it would be anything but typical.

Shortly after he began his remarks, yells from the audience of "Murderer!"[1] and "Go f*** yourself!" would result in police entering the crowd to stand quietly, scanning the rows. [2] A chorus of boos and jeers continued throughout Dr. Atlas's six-teen-minute speech.[3] He stoically read from his script, stopping rarely, except once toward the end, when many of the several hundred in the audience stood up, turned their backs on him, and chanted, "Wrap it up!" for more than a minute,[4] forcing him to pause as the noise became overwhelming.[5]

• • •

New College was at the center of a national firestorm and had been for four months, ever since Florida governor Ron DeSantis appointed six new trustees to its board. At the time DeSantis had made the new board appointments, enrollment hovered at around 650 students, and the university—one of twelve in the Florida system—had struggled for years with enrollment and retention.[6] When a seventh trustee was chosen by the governing board of the Florida university system shortly after DeSantis named his new members, these seven now formed a majority of the thirteen-person board. Attempting to stabilize the floundering college, they quickly began making changes, including choosing me as interim president.

The goal was to return New College to its mission of providing a traditional liberal arts education. This included a recommitment to free speech and civil discourse, essential components of teaching students to think critically. Many of the university's enrollment and retention issues arose from a cancel culture that permeated the campus, known for its radical leftist ideology.

The parents and students waiting for Dr. Atlas to begin his speech had signed on to be part of the college long before the current transition that was taking place. As a result, they had been steeped in the ideological conformity of the "old New

College." They had also been fed a steady stream of media disinformation about the purpose of the changes and the reasoning behind the decisions that were made in the weeks between the new board appointments in January and this picturesque graduation evening.

When I looked out at the crowd from my place on the stage as Dr. Atlas prepared to speak, I wondered how they would react to someone who did not align with their ideology, a distinguished medical doctor who had been a chief of neuroradiology at Stanford, along with serving as a professor for twenty-five years at the University of California, San Francisco and the University of Pennsylvania, among others.[7] However, most importantly to this audience, Dr. Atlas had served as a COVID advisor to President Donald Trump. According to ABC News, during his tenure, Dr. Atlas had "called on schools to open, endorsed the return of college football, raised questions about mask wearing and spoken out against lockdowns."[8]

In his calm, academic manner, Dr. Atlas began his speech with the following:

> *You are a very special group for many reasons—especially because you endured the craziness of the COVID pandemic.... What excites me the most about New College is its stated commitment to "free speech and civil discourse." This is the most urgently needed change in America today—restoring both civil discourse and the free exchange of ideas.*[9]

At the back of the tent, reporters from around the nation were packed into a roped-off area along with numerous television cameras. This group of legacy media outlets had been spinning a false narrative that the purpose of DeSantis's appointment of the new board members was to make the college into a conservative institution.[10] Though the reporters at the event and the crowd in front of us were not receptive to Dr. Atlas's message of free speech and civil discourse, I knew there was another audience, the people who would be watching as the commencement was reported upon around the nation and world. The question implicit in this speech—as well as in what was happening at New College in general—was much bigger than this graduation, much bigger than New College, much bigger even than universities in Florida: What would be the future in the United States of free speech and civil discourse in higher education?

● ● ●

According to the mainstream press, the governor's act of changing the leadership of the New College board was an attempt to remake a progressive public college into a conservative institution, which apparently included—according to the framing of the media—marginalizing those who identified as LGBTQ and stifling free speech. Judging from the article in *Rolling Stone* on the day of the graduation ceremony—entitled "Inside the Fight to Keep a Florida College Queer" with the breathless subtitle "Ron DeSantis staged a hostile takeover of tiny New College, an LGBTQ oasis. Then, students dug in,"—they were intent on continuing this storyline.[11]

If one was a student or a parent of a New College student in the spring of 2023, the national press hung on one's every word, eager to confirm this spin on the move by Gov. DeSantis—a favorite boogeyman of the national media. The narrative of the press was embraced by a cohort of current NCF students and faculty as well as alumni, eager to see themselves as the brave fighters defending freedom and defying the "fascists."[12]

As part of signaling their opposition to the change, students had held an "alternative graduation" with a progressive speaker the night before the commencement but, to get their diplomas at a ceremony, most were begrudgingly attending this one. During tonight's event, students were still proudly playing to the media as they had the previous night, with one student handing me a copy of *1984* as they walked across the stage to receive a diploma and another wearing a hand-decorated mortarboard: "We will not be silent. We will not be good. We will not behave."[13] There was a flavor of youthful melodrama about it all, but the parents at the event—who were the loudest and most disruptive of any of those present—did not have youth on their side to explain their behavior.

It was undisputed that New College was home to radically left-leaning students, confirmed not just by the national media but—unlike the rest of their fictional story—actual data, including from a 2019 survey by an outside consultant hired by the college itself which revealed a student body that self-described as 3 percent conservative, 11 percent moderate, and the rest liberal or very liberal.[14] These students existed not just in the ecosystem of New College but in the current environment of higher education in the United States, a system that was often intolerant of viewpoints that did not follow the prescribed ideology of much of its leadership.

In a 2023 national survey, 63 percent of college students indicated that "shouting down a speaker to prevent them from speaking on campus" was acceptable; 45 percent agreed that "blocking other students from attending a speech" was acceptable; and 27 percent agreed that "using violence to stop a campus speech" was acceptable.[15] Another 2023 survey of college students showed similar results. Conducted annually, the poll showed that "for the first time in the history of the poll, more students support shout downs (46%) than oppose them (45%)."[16]

In the spring of 2023, it was nothing less than righteous in the eyes of the New College community to shout down a distinguished medical doctor because he had argued during the pandemic for what were now accepted approaches. In his speech, Dr. Atlas noted that he was passionate about health policy, not politics. "My position was never political. It was solely to help the American people—you may wonder why my political party voting registration, a matter of public record, is never mentioned in the press—think about that. Maybe it doesn't fit their narrative?"[17] The audience might have had trouble digesting this point, as many seemed more intent on blocking out his words with their disruption. The reality was that by May 2023, many experts agreed that the responses Dr. Atlas had supported during the pandemic had been proven by a review of data in the aftermath.[18] Even some of the biggest former proponents of the repressive policies—such as California governor Gavin Newsom[19] and teacher union president Randi Weingarten[20]—would soon accept the reality that the lockdowns opposed by Atlas at the time had not been the panacea they had once believed.

However, tonight, at this graduation, many NCF students, parents, alumni, and supporters around the nation were basking in the media adulation of their fight to prevent "fascism," bolstered by stories from the *New York Times*, the *Washington Post*, CNN, MSNBC, and more. The narrative, however, was nothing more than expert gaslighting, a textbook illustration of why the public no longer trusts the press.

• • •

It was simple data that resulted in the governor appointing a new board majority: plummeting retention rates, enrollment numbers, and test scores. The media often ignored this reality or brushed by it as if too busy to be bothered to give it much attention. While it might be inconvenient for their preferred narrative, the numbers showed that it was likely New College would have been shut down in short order by the Florida legislature if not for DeSantis's intervention. In fact, the legislature, in a last attempt to salvage the college in 2017, had given approximately $10 million to the institution to move enrollment from 857 to 1,200 in five years.[21] In January 2023, enrollment was around 650.[22]

Begun in 1960 to be a liberal arts college with a unique and individualized program, New College had initially been well-known for its outstanding students and stellar academics. In the last ten years, however, it had become a hotbed of despotic cancel culture, a fact that had been documented by the student newspaper, the *Catalyst*, as well as by other sources, over the years.

As early as 2014, an article in the *Catalyst* noted the issues with the culture. According to then dean of students Tracy Murry, "campus climate is one of the largest challenges that administration seeks to improve in regards to retention."[23] She stated that "[campus climate] is the biggest issue that we're dealing with…. The constant thing that I hear is that it's such a negative environment. I hear that if you throw out an idea that other students will rip it apart instead of weighing options—people's first reaction is a negative reaction to anything."[24]

That environment would only get worse. In an article on March 6, 2019, in the *Catalyst*, Associate Provost Suzanne Sherman bluntly addressed the retention issue to the student reporter in the following manner: "I think what the whole community needs to work on is improving our interactions with one another so that students feel like they do belong."[25] Then president Donal O'Shea echoed this in an article on March 14, 2019, discussing that an outside consulting firm had found that the "social climate [can be] challenging." O'Shea said that some students reported in surveys that "they couldn't make a friend, and the Forum wars didn't help. You'd have somebody, and something wasn't going well for them, then they'd have this flame war on them, and that'd be the last straw."[26]

The "Forum wars" were named for an online student discussion board called the Forum. When interviewing students in focus groups, over half mentioned the Forum as being an issue.[27] According to the paper, O'Shea pointed to the "particular toxicity of communication on the Forum, where he believes students struggle to empathize with their peers on the other side of the screen." O'Shea noted in particular the "challenges facing those with different political and social values than the majority of the student body."[28]

Sounding a note that would be echoed by Gov. DeSantis in January 2023 when he appointed the new board members, O'Shea continued to expound on the campus culture stating that "[w]e pride ourselves on being a very liberal place, but the result is that students who are more conservative don't really feel welcome here. They keep their mouths shut. If you don't fit in, you're ostracized. Students who are religious, sometimes they report feeling unwelcome."[29]

In a March 28, 2019, article, O'Shea referenced the fact that the school had surveyed students who left prior to graduation to see why they left.[30] He stated that "[t]here [were] bad quotes from students and there was one student who said, 'I got called out here and then I got cancelled'...By cancelled I guess she meant that she wasn't welcome at [a social event called] walls or something—and it sounded awful.'"[31]

However, one of the students quoted in the article appeared to support the bullying in the Forum, showing there might not have been a desire to change at the student level. "The Forum could be a valuable tool for students to hear perspectives from peers that they may not come across on campus...Call-out culture can be harmful,' thesis student Bianca Persechino said in an email interview. 'However, this does not mean it can't be improved somehow and [that it is] not still beneficial. Many alums on campus look back on that stuff in a positive way, expressing how it made them grow.'"[32]

To improve the retention rate, as well as test scores and the enrollment rate, President O'Shea had asked the Legislature in 2016 for money to raise metrics and received approximately $10 million in the 2017 and 2018 sessions to improve these, with the understanding that such data would begin moving in a positive direction. However, at the Feb. 26, 2019, board meeting, President O'Shea dropped a "bombshell" that the college had begun the year with over 800 students but would likely be below 800 for the next school year—and that the retention rate had dropped "precariously."

"This place is on fire," Trustee John Lilly told the paper.[33]

"We had promised the state that we would grow to 1,200 students [by 2022]," O'Shea said. "We hired a lot of new professors and things like that. We're probably okay for a while, but we have to turn that around. We promised them we'd grow; we'd better do it."[34] The inference was that there would be consequences at the state level, which was understood by those with a knowledge of the governing body of the state university system—the Florida Board of Governors (BOG)—and the legislature. These entities had expectations and a fiduciary duty to the public.

In 2017, total undergraduate enrollment was 838. In 2018, it was 808, and the downward trend continued, with 703 in 2019, 646 in 2020, 633 in 2021, and 671 in 2022. In addition, retention rates also continued to be poor. Before the "bombshell" board meeting in February 2019, O'Shea had already hired a firm to, according to the *Catalyst*, "find out what was depressing retention rates."[35] The Art & Science Group surveyed students who left. According to the *Catalyst* in an October 2019 article, the survey showed "the bulk of the problem comes from the perception of New College's social atmosphere as unwelcoming."[36] A spokesperson for the Art & Science Group delivered the bad news, stating, "When we look at current students, we see levels of satisfaction that are lower than we expect to see in these studies…And indeed, at least 40% of [current students] now feel the expectations they had upon arriving here have not been lived up to. 54% of them have thought about leaving—about 30% of them seriously."[37]

However, it was not just the president, the associate provost, and the outside consulting firm noting the cancel culture being a significant problem in the retention and/or enrollment rate(s). The *Catalyst* itself took a poll to which 82 students responded—and found similar trends to what the more scientific poll by the Art & Science Group had found. More than 74 percent of these had thought about dropping out.

"According to the poll, some of the answers that were obtained state the difficulty of making friends and finding a crowd to fit into, the lack of respect between students' opinions, a feeling of being attacked and not having a voice on campus and the feeling of being very isolated," a reporter for the student newspaper wrote. "Given this is a small campus and a majority of students are required to live on campus, any toxic environment can feel hard to escape."[38]

One student interviewed by email for the article stated that "I've seen the smallest of issues be made into horrific ordeals and bigger issues be torn apart in ways that are totally useless...[That does] nothing but confuse the issues until nothing is clear and everyone gets hurt."

The Art & Science Group report noted other issues with the social culture that were chasing away would-be students. Commissioned by NCF to research its market placement and issues, the firm found that admitted students (of whom many opted not to attend) indicated that adjectives strongly associated with New College social culture were "politically correct," "druggies," and "weirdoes."[39]

This political correctness resulted in a groupthink that pervaded the campus. In a 2019 article entitled "Hot Takes on the Retention Rate," one interviewee, alum Joy Feagan who had graduated in 2012, noted that part of the problem was "this school is so much weirder than other places." She continued that when "mainstream students get here, they still get freaked out by how weird it is and a lot of them dip. Because even though it's not as weird as it used to be, it's still pretty f****** weird."[40]

As one of the new trustees noted, it was a problem that needed to be addressed if the college was going to stop its downward trajectory. Needless to say, the "politically correct"/"druggie"/"weirdo" niche is fairly narrow, the exact opposite of a slogan any rational organization would adopt if it was trying to appeal to a broad swath of students and parents.

• • •

When DeSantis appointed the new trustees in January 2023, he made it clear he was choosing these individuals to ensure that New College would meet its founding mission to provide a traditional liberal arts education, which included recommitting to the goals of free speech and academic excellence. It was a public college, and the taxpayers would no longer be funding parts of its program that were merely leftist propaganda projects, such as DEI. There were two different issues at play: the suppression of free speech through leftist propaganda projects—such as Critical Race Theory (CRT), DEI, and gender studies—and the enrollment/retention rates linking back in part to the cancel culture. These two problems were merely different branches of the same tree, interwoven, their roots deep in the soil of radical liberal closemindedness.

To ensure this was not a mere performative exercise, DeSantis chose trustees who had a fierce resolve to accomplish his goals. The fact that recapturing a public university had not been done elsewhere in higher education was an indicator of the Herculean effort that would be necessary. In 2016, the *Washington Post* ran an article about a study which found that in higher education, "liberals outnumber conservatives by roughly

5 to one," also noting that among the public, "conservatives are considerably more prevalent and have been for some time."[41]

Among liberal arts colleges such as New College, the ratio was even worse. In 2018, researchers reviewed the political affiliations of professors at fifty-one of the sixty-six highest-ranking liberal arts colleges. It revealed a desolated landscape. Thirty-nine percent of the colleges did not have a single faculty member on staff that identified as Republican, and an additional 39.2 percent had "so few [Republicans] as to make no difference"—resulting in an astonishing 78.2 percent that had in essence no Republican viewpoint represented on the faculty that was teaching the next generation. If the other 22 percent are added back into the calculation—excepting West Point and Annapolis—the ratio across the institutions found that for every eight Republicans there were one hundred Democrats.[42]

This had resulted in a predominantly "leftist groupthink." As researchers noted in 2009 based on their study of groupthink in academia, "In hiring a new member of the department, most existing members will tend to support candidates who share their fundamental beliefs, values, and commitments…In academia, the beliefs are deep seated and connected to selfhood and identity. For that reason, protecting and preserving them have high personal stakes" meaning there is a powerful "existential significance of ideological beliefs."[43] The authors used the following example.

Suppose a department must hire a new member, and 51 percent of the current members share a broadly similar ideology—say, social-democratic progressivism or conservatism or classical liberalism/libertarianism. Moreover, they believe that

> one must broadly conform to that ideology to be
> a good colleague and a good professor. What hap-
> pens? The department members hire someone like
> them. The 51 percent becomes 55 percent, then
> 60 percent, then 65 percent, then 70 percent, and
> so on. As Stephen Balch (2003) and others have
> noted, majoritarianism tends to produce ideologi-
> cal uniformity in a department.[44]

DeSantis knew from personal experience how rabidly and unfairly the radical Left would struggle to keep their conquered ground in education, with a hefty assist from the media.

Therefore, it was logical to choose from the small group of conservatives in and around academia who were vocal about their commitment to ensure free speech and civil discourse in the nation's system of higher education.

It is important to remember that, at this moment in time, the view that education had been ideologically captured was not widely accepted, despite data showing otherwise. At the very least, even if people agreed that the Left controlled much of education, it was not seen as a problem by the liberal elite. For example, in 2016 in response to data that showed faculty voting records revealed that professors were far more politically liberal than the nation in general, *New York Times* columnist Paul Krugman dealt with the subject as follows:

> [W]hat's really happening here? Did professors
> move left, or did the meaning of conservatism
> in America change in a way that drove scholars
> away? You can guess what I think...Overall, the
> evidence looks a lot more consistent with a story

*that has academics rejecting a conservative party
that has moved sharply right than it does with a
story in which academics have moved left.*[45]

Such shoulder shrugging and dismissiveness about the capture of academia was about to change. The reactions by administrators, students, and faculty on campuses to the Hamas attack on a peaceful music festival in Israel on October 7, 2023, shocked the nation, including many moderates and liberals.[46] The fallout resulted in a much broader coalition joining this call for a reboot of higher education and a return to the ideals of free speech and civil discourse.

However, in January 2023, it was only a small but passionate group who was sounding the alarm, and it was from this group that DeSantis made his board choices—not to create a conservative institution but to signal a renaissance of freedom of speech and respect for others' viewpoints in public higher education that would prevail despite what would be a vigorous assault to prevent it.

• • •

While the media tried to avoid as much as possible any direct reporting on the "why" behind the change in direction, the governor, the board, and I did our utmost to get the message out. From the very beginning, on January 3rd, three days before the governor announced the new appointments to the New College board, Gov. DeSantis stated in his second inaugural address that "we must ensure that our institutions of higher learning are focused on academic excellence and the pursuit of truth, not the imposition of trendy ideology."[47]

Then, on January 6, the day of the announcement of the new board members, DeSantis press secretary Bryan Griffin sent an email to members of the press.

> *New College of Florida is a public institution with a statutorily stated mission of "provid[ing] a quality education." Unfortunately, like so many colleges and universities in America, this institution has been completely captured by a political ideology that puts trendy, truth-relative concepts above learning. In particular, New College of Florida has reached a moment of critical mass, wherein low student enrollment and other financial stresses have emerged from its skewed focus and impractical course offerings.*[48]

On January 31st, DeSantis gave his first public comments on the board changes. He was holding a press conference to announce his legislative priorities relating to higher education for the approaching legislative session. In the press release before his public remarks, the first sentence plainly stated the governor's focus: the legislation would "further elevate civil discourse and intellectual freedom in higher education, further pushing back against the tactics of liberal elites who suppress free thought in the name of identity politics and indoctrination."[49]

In his speech at the press conference, he emphasized that he wanted to "elevate civil discourse and intellectual freedom" by stating that he would stop any agenda in higher education that was "hostile to academic freedom" in Florida including any agendas that "impose ideological conformity to try to provoke political activism."[50] He put this in a larger context stating that there was a "debate going on [around the country] about what is the purpose of higher education, particularly publicly funded higher education systems." He was particularly concerned that there was now a focus on "impos[ing] ideological conformity."

> *I think you have the dominant view...to impose ideological conformity to try to provoke political activism...That's not what we believe is appropriate in the state of Florida. Instead, we need our higher education systems to focus on providing academic excellence, the pursuit of truth, and to give students the foundation so that they can think for themselves. Now the former approach is dominant throughout the country particularly with respect to academia.*

The governor then drew the focus in tighter, to New College—located just five miles down the road from where the press conference was being held—the tiny college that had been the subject of outsized attention in furious press coverage in the last three weeks since he had appointed the new board members. He laid out the picture as he saw it:

> *[New College is a] college that the Legislature thought about just moth-balling or folding it into UF or USF...[I]t's not been able to have the enrollment that you would want, the test scores... [I]f it was a private school [it would have been closed but]...what are you gonna do? But this is being paid for by your tax dollars, and I can tell you I've talked to people who live in Sarasota*

who didn't know what New College was...and
in Florida statute it's supposed to be our premier
honors liberal arts college...and yet nobody even
knows what it is.[51]

At the press conference with the governor was Chris Rufo, one of the newly appointed New College trustees. Rufo was not there to talk about New College but to address his research related to higher education. These findings had in part informed the drafting of the governor's proposed legislation.

While each of the new trustees to the New College board had conservative ties, Rufo had drawn the most ire because his research had started a national discussion about the ideological bent of many public institutions, including those in higher education. In a speech in early 2022 at Hillsdale College, Rufo had discussed his findings about the "march through the institutions," defined as a "militant liberalism" that invaded federal government bureaucracies, K–12 schools, and universities as groups of young leftist activists from the 1960s entered public life. These liberal acolytes had then implanted their orthodoxy into these institutions, effectively attempting to silence other viewpoints. Rufo concluded that such "private political activism" should be vigorously opposed and that the government should stop funding unbending orthodoxy in public entities, including universities.

These are public universities that should reflect
and transmit the values of the public. And the
representatives of the public, i.e., state legisla-
tors, have the ultimate power to shape or reshape
those institutions. So we have to get out of this
idea that somehow a public university system is

a totally independent entity that practices academic freedom.[52]

His point was not to make public institutions reflective of a conservative viewpoint but to set them free from "militant liberalism."

While, like the governor, Rufo was at the January 31st press conference to speak about upcoming legislation relating to higher education in Florida, Rufo had already addressed the New College issue, first by tweets on January 6th when his appointment was announced and then by voluntarily meeting directly with the faculty and students at two meetings on campus on January 25th.[53] The tweets on January 6th had been wildly misrepresented by the media. In the tweets, he was jubilant that his ideas to keep out "militant liberalism" were being realized at a public college, exactly what he had said needed to happen at his Hillsdale speech just one year before. The press mostly interpreted his tweets to mean that he wanted to make New College a conservative institution rather than throw out the groupthink that was rotting the higher education system in the US.

Rufo pushed back on this interpretation immediately. At the public meetings on January 25th with the faculty and students, he spoke with a reporter and voiced a similar message to what the governor had previously stated.

[W]e're not going to try to suppress your opinion. We're not going to try to stifle debate. We're not going to try to create one orthodoxy to replace another.

He was so clear on this in his two meetings with students and faculty that one professor, Diego Villada, left the meeting saying, "I hope that they do what they said they're going to do in terms of open conversation, open dialogue and that everybody is welcome at the table." However, he conditioned his statement as well: "I am only cautious that zealotry will be over independent thought and independent academic freedoms." [54]

One parent of a New College student echoed such thinking when she stated she would not believe Rufo. "Absolutely not," she said. "He's a great speaker. You know what, I am too. I can stand here and get you guys engaged in a grocery store line and you'll like me just as much as we all liked him in there. We can all chameleon ourselves to whatever it is that certain individuals we're speaking to need to hear." Basically, Rufo could tell them exactly what the governor said, and they were going to have an opposite opinion. Facts were not going to matter over their feelings.[55]

The press generally drove right over the governor's and Rufo's clear remarks, instead claiming that the goal was to set up a conservative university at New College. The media occasionally also tried to draw the same inference from the fact that another new board member, Matthew Spalding, worked at Hillsdale College. While Hillsdale is a private university that has religious ties and an affiliation with right-of-center academia, Spalding from the beginning of his tenure took pains to explain the difference between Hillsdale and New College. He pointed out the obvious- that Hillsdale is "a private, Christian college" that accepts no government funds, while New College is public and funded by taxpayers. He then spelled this out further to make sure there was no confusion, promising "[t]hat will not change."[56]

At the first board meeting with the new members on January 31st, Spalding stated the following near the beginning of the meeting:

> *Some have said these recent appointments amount to a partisan takeover of the college—this is not correct...[T]his [is] a public institution [and] acts in accordance with the laws of the state of Florida, passed by legislature representing the people of Florida. A well-constructed program of students in liberal arts teaches one how to think, not what to think. It liberates the mind from prejudice and nar-row-mindedness, but also political ideology, parti-san dogma or whatever methodology is academi-cally evoked. It's not a takeover, it's a renewal.*[57]

The audience full of faculty, students, and alumni laughed at his statement.[58] Following the lead of this group who thought such plain statements laughable, members of the community opposing the changes were busy giving interviews to the press about their personal opinions of the board change, often assert-ing that it was about "fascism." The press doubled down with their framing using these unsupported opinions.

The media also occasionally threw in statements that had been made based on the governor's original announcement of the board members from the Florida state education commis-sioner, Manny Diaz, and the governor's chief of staff, James Uthmeier. Both had briefly mentioned that New College could be the "Hillsdale of the South." Rather than calling these two individuals and asking what they meant by the correlation with Hillsdale, the press often assumed that these statements meant

New College would become a conservative, Christian institution. Both men, if the media had bothered to follow up with them, were clearly pointing to the fact that New College could, like Hillsdale, be a successful liberal arts college focused on providing such a curriculum, which had been the original mission of NCF. In addition, Hillsdale was very successful on measures such as enrollment, retention, and fundraising, unlike the failure that NCF currently was in all three metrics. In fact, to believe the media's common framing of these statements, one would have had to suspend disbelief and think that they were directly contradicting their own boss—the governor of the state—as well as board members Rufo and Spalding.[59]

When I was appointed as interim president, I made sure to articulate the goal in plain, simple terms because the press seemed intent on ignoring it. I had read the governor's comments as well as those of my board members. There was a clear, delineated game plan, and I agreed wholeheartedly with it. In my first public comments when asked about my vision for New College, I stated the following:

I want to ensure that the Chicago Principles are followed because "without a vibrant commitment to free and open inquiry, a university ceases to be a university." These were adopted by the University of Chicago's Committee on Freedom of Expression in 2014 and have since been adopted by many colleges around the country, including the Florida university system in 2019. It is important that higher education is not dominated by a self-aggrandizing few who want to co-opt the education system to

*force their personal beliefs on other people's chil-
dren. That is the opposite of what education is for.*[60]

To turn a public college into a private one catering to a specific niche was not the point, no matter how many times the media tried to frame it that way. In fact, *it was the exact opposite of
what was intended.* While private Christian colleges are an important part of the higher educational landscape, New College
is a public institution that provides a different option in the
marketplace. My conversations with reporters began to feel like
they were following a page from the Ministry of Truth in *1984*
that used slogans such as "freedom is slavery." I would state our
goal was to ensure free speech at a public college. The resulting
articles or segments would state the complete opposite: that our
goal was to destroy free speech at a public college. For the press,
it was a simple task to find any of the "old New College" crowd
that sat in the audience at board meetings to state unsupported
opinions that tracked with the media's preferred narrative.

As I pointed out frequently in interviews during this time,
there is a difference between an opinion and a fact. Despite the
determination to ignore our messaging, we kept repeating the
vision we had for New College—a public college would exist
with a commitment to free speech and civil discourse and not
be the ideologically captured institution that most universities
had become.

•   •   •

From the time of the new board appointments in early January,
the campus had been swarmed by state, national, and even

worldwide media. The choice by the board to appoint me to be interim president did nothing to tamp down on this attention.

Until the board chose me as interim president, those who wanted New College to stay as it was held out hope that this would be a blip on the radar. They knew that while having a strong board was the first step in transforming an institution, an effective leader on the ground was also a key component to effecting change. They were correct. Both were necessary to make a systemic change in higher education, and the fact of this needed alignment was one of the reasons such an experiment had never been accomplished.

When Michelle Goldberg wrote an opinion piece for the *New York Times* on January 9th entitled "DeSantis Allies Plot the Hostile Takeover of a Liberal College," she cast Rufo and Spalding's appointments as dire indicators for "the most progressive public college in the state." Adding, "[n]aturally, Gov. Ron DeSantis…wants to demolish it." She wrapped up on a happier note though by stating the following:

> *[R]eplacing one culture with another can be harder than anticipated. New College students may not go quietly. Steve Shipman, a professor of physical chemistry and president of the faculty union, points out that tenured professors are covered by a collective bargaining agreement, which makes it hard to fire them unless there's cause. People like Rufo "are making statements to make impact," Shipman said. "And I really don't know how viable some of those statements are on the ground." We'll soon find out.*[61]

Another reporter agreed with this assessment shortly thereafter. "A public college is not a weak target...to challenge an entrenched bureaucracy...I am curious as to how it will turn out."[62] The inference was clear: good luck trying to change the "entrenched bureaucracy" with edicts from a board meeting.

On January 31st, following the DeSantis news conference where he gave his first public remarks about New College, the new board held their first meeting and chose me as interim president. No one had seen this turn of events coming, and the press buzzed with it when word got out around noon just prior to the 3 p.m. meeting, likely resulting from an internal email from the law and consulting firms that I had founded a year prior that had gone out late that morning to staff. The announcement had informed employees that I would be leaving to be interim president at New College. I had had private conversations a few days prior with Trustee Spalding about the possibility of being interim president, and, knowing the composition of the new board, we both felt confident that my name would meet with approval from a majority.

State Rep. Anna Eskamani, an Orlando Democrat, spoke at a rally before the meeting, and she had heard the news through the political grapevine. Eskamani led a chant to "reject fascism and protect freedom," wrote a reporter for the *Tampa Bay Times*, "[t]hen she dropped a bomb: Okker [the current NCF president] was to be replaced by Richard Corcoran, the former education commissioner and Florida House speaker."[63]

While I was not nationally known, the board members—and the state press—knew me well: from my term as Florida House Speaker from 2016 to 2018, from my time as a competitor to DeSantis in the 2018 Republican primary for governor, and from my role as his chosen education commissioner from

Dec. 2018 to May 2022. When one of the main political blogs in Florida empaneled a group of Florida political insiders to choose the Politicians of the Decade at the beginning of 2020, I was number two between US senator Rick Scott (number one) and US senator Marco Rubio (number three).[64]

In an article widely disseminated on media platforms immediately after my appointment, the reporter described my role as education commissioner in the following manner: "Corcoran took on schools, teacher unions, the courts and even the federal government in the battle against COVID mask mandates and closed schools during the pandemic. Corcoran also penalized school districts that defied the governor's order by withholding salaries."[65] Forcing schools to open during COVID and fighting mask mandates were my most current touchpoints in politics. However, the main reason I was chosen between Scott and Rubio as number two Florida politician of the decade was because of my track record as Speaker from 2016 to 2018, along with my role in the Republican Party in earlier years as House Speaker designate.

In reporter Matt Dixon's book released in January 2024, *Swamp Monsters: Trump vs. DeSantis*, Dixon describes the way I was viewed by the press in the 2018 primary for governor where I originally jostled with DeSantis for the conservative lane based on my time as House Speaker. According to Dixon, DeSantis in the primary was trying to capture the "conservative role in the Florida GOP primary that had been long filled by Richard Corcoran…Corcoran was seen as a pugilistic, rock-ribbed conservative."[66]

"Pugilistic" is typically a negative term and was in line with the way in which my fights were often described by the press and my opponents. In an article from 2017 about my speakership entitled "How Richard Corcoran Stormed Florida's Capital and Made Some People Angry," the reporter labeled me a "bare-knuckled political brawler."[67] Another wrote, "Controversy doesn't scare him, and tough fights don't intimidate him…[H]e will bloody your nose if need be. He knows how to work a room or twist an arm."[68]

What was missing often in these articles was my why. While the fight was sometimes against Democrats, when I was Speaker and Speaker designate more often it was challenging those in my own party who would not fight for the principles on which they ran, a party that had held the reins of power in both the legislative and executive branches of state government for two decades. When I was championing ethics reform as House Speaker, most of the Republican-led state Senate opposed the reforms. During this fight in 2017, I spoke at the same event as a powerful state senator, a Republican, who was against the measures. In front of the seven hundred-person crowd, he gifted me a set of red boxing gloves. "I've been up there 22 years, and he has flat picked more fights with more people than anybody I've ever seen before."[69] He did not mean it as a compliment, but I took it as one.

For most of my political career, it was not looked upon favorably in general to fight against Republicans in one's own party, though Donald Trump has recently changed the thinking on this. However, prior to Trump and his gradual reset on this mindset, these fights could be complicated—and dangerous. I had to be creative and strategic. I had to get my message out and form alliances. The press wrote often about my tactics, with the *Tampa Bay Times* stating in a profile piece of my speakership that I was the "most unpredictable force in Florida in decades" and "a fearless political marksman who uses laws, rules, tweets, videos, lawsuits, and sheer nerve to lay waste to what he calls a 'culture of corruption' in Tallahassee. Senators, judges, lobbyists, college presidents, teachers and business owners are all among his targets...Some can't stand him, but they can't ignore him."[70]

I had a history of winning complicated battles against long odds. When I dropped out of the Florida governor's race in 2018, the Florida Squeeze Blog—a progressive news source,—wrote about the following about my time as speaker.

> *It's difficult to not admire and respect Corcoran even in a begrudging manner. He's changed the game in Tallahassee with his force of will and courage in his convictions. He's made it clear how comfortable so-called conservatives have become with the same government that they detested before they were in power. He's put the fear of god into Tallahassee-based lobbyists. Progressives need a Corcoran of our own in Florida. Someone who understands how to obtain and exercise power yet has enough courage in her/his convictions to not let power force an unwise compromise. Simply put, we need an elected official or strong candidate for high office willing to buck the establishment but unlike so many who have run before, actually knows how to work the system to garner power. Democrats and progressives can learn a lot from Richard Corcoran. We don't like where he stands, but unlike so many in a corrupted process based upon cronyism at least he does take a stand.[71]*

My point in saying all of this is that I agreed with the reporter's assessment: "A public college is not a weak target."[72]

Changing an "entrenched bureaucracy" was going to be an enormous battle, and the temptation to compromise would be powerful. However, I was all in. This was a fight that meant something. The greatest threat we faced as a country was in the arena of education, because the leaders in both K–12 and higher education were intent on indoctrinating students into a radical ideology rather than teaching them to think critically.

The playing field might have changed now that I was in academia—but not the game plan. As I said when I was Speaker, "I tell the members all the time, fight MMA [mixed martial arts]—not ninja. My philosophy has always been: I'm going to tell you exactly what I'm going to fight for. And we'll get into an octagon, and we'll fight it out."[73]

• • •

Between the board appointments by DeSantis in January and that graduation night in May, New College had come a long way in just over four months. We were working hard to recruit new students and were succeeding so well that we set a record for enrollment that coming fall. On September 13, 2023, I tweeted out that "Under the new board, NCF is setting a record pace in growth! Fall enrollment #'s are in, & we significantly increased new students (346 this year v. 269 last year) & total enrollment (747 this year vs. 689 last year). Look for next year's #'s to be even greater!"

To achieve this rapid turnaround by the fall, we had done away with liberal passion projects such as DEI and gender studies, and we were starting a series of public debates on campus about important issues called the Socratic Stage. We had also instituted student discipline for violent or destructive acts. In addition, we were recruiting new faculty to serve the growing student body, and we were expanding student life, including increasing dorm and food options and improving the buildings and meeting spaces on the campus. We were also starting a sports program and had begun the process of being accepted into the National Association of Intercollegiate Athletics (NAIA). By the fall, we would be competing in six sports. We also revamped the recruitment office and updated the marketing and strategic plans. Finally, we were building community partners which would reap rewards in less than a year as we obtained nine waterfront acres free-of-charge from the county and began the process to own rather than lease key parts of the campus from the local airport.

The fact that so much had been accomplished in so little time was because New College had the most important elements of changing any public higher education institution: a governor who takes the lead and appoints board members who share his vision, board members who then focus on the mission and are not intimidated, and a president with a track record of not backing down to challenges. We all felt the power of the moment. The reality was we were "over the target"—a phrase we often said to each other—and the progressive Left knew it.

Leftwing academia did not want to lose their iron grip on higher education. As a *New York Times* opinion piece darkly predicted on January 9th, three days after the new board appointments, if the new board prevailed, "it will set the stage for an even broader assault." DeSantis echoed this, concluding during his press conference on January 31st, immediately before the first meeting of the board of trustees where they would choose me as interim president, with these words: "I think you're going to see some really positive results very quickly at New College, and I think this will be able to build off of the momentum that we have in higher education."[74]

• • •

We were intent on reversing the incursions on free speech which had occurred on campuses as a result of factors including DEI bureaucracies, radical leftist groupthink among many faculty, and departments based on so-called "social justice" theories, such as gender studies.

If we succeeded, it had the potential to up-end public higher education.

Dr. Atlas, an academic who had also navigated the political world, understood what was at stake. New College was an experiment that, if successful, would hopefully spread across the nation. We wanted to set students and faculty free—not just to express themselves but to learn to respect others, to wrestle with questions and not fear them.

He concluded his remarks by drawing out the lens broadly, framing the issue facing higher education, which was the greatest threat to the country that he termed "the world's beacon of freedom."

> *I fear for our students and our country. Without permitting, indeed encouraging, open debate, we might never solve any future crisis...Let's be clear...well-intended statements on "Academic Freedom" are of little value...Many faculty members of our acclaimed universities are now dangerously intolerant of opinions contrary to their favored narrative...We cannot have a civil society if it's filled with people, led by people, who refuse to allow discussion of views counter to their own.*[75]

This final statement—as with much of the rest of the speech—was somewhat difficult to discern. Most of the audience was loudly yelling, "Wrap it up!" and "F** you," standing with their backs turned to the stage.[76]

CHAPTER 2

DEI

*All animals are equal, but some animals
are more equal than others.*
—*George Orwell,* Animal Farm

On February 16, 2023, President Biden signed an executive order mandating that federal agencies establish agency equity teams to implement "equity initiatives" within their agencies.[1] In this executive order, Biden referenced previous such orders—including one signed on June 25, 2021, entitled "Diversity, Equity, Inclusion, and Accessibility in the Federal Workforce"—to demonstrate how his administration had "embedded a focus on equity into the fabric of Federal policymaking and service delivery." The current executive order was extending such overreach further.

On February 28, 2023—a mere twelve days later—the board at New College of Florida, which oversaw one university with around 650 students, voted to abolish its DEI program.

The signing of the executive order on February 16th received little coverage, while the action of the New College board on

February 28th was reported on extensively at the time, as well as referenced frequently for months afterward, by the legacy media.

It was mind-blowing—the intense media attention on the board action at tiny New College, but hardly a mention in the press about the executive order. By any rational criteria, these two events were worlds apart in their scope: one closed a DEI office at a small college and the other further entrenched the philosophy behind DEI into the major agencies of the U.S. government.

With the executive order on February 16th, Biden had effectively weaponized the federal bureaucracy by in many ways making agencies arms of the DEI movement. As Rich Lowry wrote in the *New York Post*, Biden's order was the "most radical act [he] has undertaken that almost no one is talking about." It was a "push for so-called equity so shockingly far-reaching that, not so long ago, a woke diversity officer wouldn't have attempted it at even the most progressive liberal-arts college. Biden is pushing to make the federal government a frank instrument of…radicalism."[2]

The president's takeover was accomplished quietly with the stroke of a pen. It was not voted upon. It was not broadly communicated. It was pure, unadulterated "policy capture," a scenario in which policy making is utilized to serve the interests of a minor group.

The order appeared innocuous. The last thing proponents of the concept of "equity"—the "E" in DEI—wanted was for someone to turn on the lights to see what it meant in practice.

However, there was one thing that might result in a broader conversation about what that executive order did—a discussion about what DEI with roots planted in the radical philosophy of critical race theory (CRT) meant in practice.

This was the conversation that was happening at New College about shuttering its DEI office. Therefore, the changes the board was making must be discredited and those involved disparaged at every opportunity.

• • •

At 12:02 p.m. on January 6, 2023, shortly after the new trustees of the New College of Florida had been announced by the office of Florida governor Ron DeSantis, board member Christopher Rufo tweeted the following:

> *We are now over the walls and ready to transform higher education from within. Under the leadership of Gov. DeSantis, our all-star board will demonstrate that the public universities, which have been corrupted by woke nihilism, can be recaptured, restructured, and reformed.*

The basis of this tweet was found in Rufo's recent writings, in which he had exposed, in part, how the philosophy of CRT was being promulgated in public institutions, including K–12 schools. While K–12 education had received the lion's share of the news coverage recently regarding the use of ideas based in CRT, DEI programs were another way in which the radical Left was sowing seeds of ideological orthodoxy based on ideas within the theory throughout public institutions. The DEI bureaucracies that had been proliferating in the public sector, including universities, had become a Trojan horse driven right into the heart of the nation's institutions.

When Rufo had originally highlighted that underlying premises of CRT were being advanced in K-12 schools, some jumped to defend against this claim by pointing out that CRT was not explicitly taught in K-12 classrooms, which was typically true. However, the philosophy behind CRT often influenced aspects of K-12 education. Similarly, beliefs within CRT were rampant in DEI offices. First, in DEI offices, "equity" was typically promoted rather than equality, resulting in systems that explicitly favor certain groups to the detriment of other groups. Second, limitations on free speech were often advanced through the use of speech codes and other mechanisms. Both of these concepts link back to ideas propounded by scholars who were instrumental in the development of CRT.

In 1993, several CRT academics delineated "defining elements" of critical race theory in an introduction to a book entitled *Words That Wound: Critical Race Theory, Assaultive Speech and the First Amendment.* While the book itself is comprised of essays by some of the most important thought leaders in the development of CRT, it is the introduction—co-written by the book's essayists—that is of particular interest as it contains one of the clearest answers to the question "What is critical race theory?" To explain CRT, the scholars listed several defining elements. The first "defining element" was that CRT "recognizes that racism is endemic to American life. Thus the question for us is not so much whether or how racial discrimination can be eliminated while maintaining the integrity of other interests implicated in the status quo such as federalism, privacy, traditional values, or established property interests. Instead we ask how these traditional interests and values serve as vessels of subordination." The second "defining element" of CRT was that the theory "expresses skepticism toward dominant legal claims of neutrality, objectivity, color blindness, and meritocracy. These claims are central to an ideology of equal opportunity that presents race as an immutable characteristic devoid of social meaning."

Academics who have studied the CRT movement have remarked on its antipathy to the American legal system and its supporting documents. Constitutional scholar Maimon Schwarzschild states that CRT proponents are wary of "American constitutional government, the Bill of Rights, neutral principles of law, and the goal of government without regard to race or colour" because they believe that these "are all instruments of racial subordination and camouflages for white supremacy."[3] Another scholar similarly noted that "[c]ritical race theories attack the very foundations of the liberal legal order, including equality theory, legal reasoning, Enlightenment rationalism, and neutral principles of constitutional law."[4]

On the spectrum of legal theories, CRT was and is radical in nature. It is not unusual, however, to have theories pop up in academia that stretch boundaries. Originally, the discussion of CRT followed the typical path for new ideas within the academy, as scholars fleshed out ideas related to it in journals. For example, in 1993, one academic who responded directly to the essays in *Words that Wound* was Henry Louis Gates, Jr., the W.E.B. Du Bois Professor for the Humanities and chair of the Afro-American Studies Department at Harvard. Gates questioned the position of CRT scholars as to the First Amendment. He was concerned about the implications of placing further strictures on free speech in the hope of combatting racism. Gates noted that it was an expansive vision of the First Amendment— not a narrow one like that proposed in *Words That Wound*—that had led to successes in the fight against racism.

The larger question—the political question—is how we came to decide that our energies were best directed not at strengthening our position in the field of public discourse, but at trying to move the boundary posts...The struggle with racism has traditionally been waged through language, not against it; the tumult of the civil rights era was sponsored by an expansive vision of the First Amendment...And it is this concrete history and context that make it so perplexing that a new generation of activists...should choose the First Amendment as a battlefield.[5]

Gates' response to ideas propounded in *Words That Wound* occurred within the academic arena through a scholarly article. Unfortunately, such opportunity for reasoned critique on the underlying belief system of CRT is not designed to occur within DEI offices, which generally operate as mere conduits of parts of the CRT philosophy, including the understanding of the First Amendment by the authors in *Words That Wound*. While the authors admit that at the time the book was written, in 1993, that the "debate has deeply divided the liberal civil rights/civil liberties community and produced strained relations within the membership of organizations like the...ACLU," in DEI offices, it would be difficult to learn anything about this analytical discourse as the CRT viewpoint often dominates as to speech and equity with little pushback.

In addition, DEI offices typically uncritically embrace CRT's skepticism as to equal protection. Schwarzchild notes that traditionally in America the view of equality is based on the understanding that people have "equal natural rights to life, liberty, and property", and the role of government is to "ensure these rights through the impartial rule of law, with equality of civil opportunity, but without venturing to ensure equal or identical outcomes in life." He contrasts this with CRT and its "rejection of equal opportunity, 'colour-blindness,'...or equality before the law regardless of race." DEI offices tend to follow, uncritically, the underlying philosophy of CRT in this regard. Therefore, instead of equal protection, the notion of "equity" tends to be inserted in DEI offices, again functioning as mere carriers of an idea in radical opposition to the traditional understanding of equal opportunity. Harvard's DEI office is an example. It provides a Glossary of Terms which defines "equity" as "fair treatment for all, while striving to identify and eliminate inequities and barriers."[6] In a blog on Harvard Business Publishing's Corporate Learning website, the difference between "equity" and "equality" is described by an author in the following manner.

> *Equity is different than equality—if I am helping all employees reach the top shelf of the supply room, I would give everyone access to the same height ladder, regardless of how tall they are. The problem with treating people equally is that not everyone has the same needs. In this case, some may not be able to reach the top shelf with the provided ladder, while others may not need to use one at all! Compare this to "equitable" treatment. When I am treating people equitably, I strive to eliminate barriers and overcome past inequities—I would give the tallest people the shortest ladder and the shortest people the tallest ladder so everyone can reach the same height.[7]*

In the last 10 years, DEI offices have been used to build a fiefdom within the public sector, spreading these radical ideas through administrative bureaucracies. Parts of this basically untried theory were thereby embedded somewhat wholecloth into these institutions, which often enforced complete obeisance to a philosophy that in many ways undermines modern constitutional thought. When Rufo exposed this issue, his writings immediately connected with the public. Suddenly seemingly inexplicable things made sense: the cancel culture, shouting down speakers on college campuses, safe spaces. The assault on free speech was not arbitrary. Neither was the subtle undermining of the idea of equal protection through the elevation of certain groups to the detriment of other groups.

The movement to institute DEI bureaucracies worked as a subterfuge for implanting CRT's radical legal theory into public institutions. It happened with a rapidity that was astounding. To achieve this, three prongs had been utilized in concert. First, language was coopted such that the public perception of the definition of terms used differed from that within a radical theory. Second, the administrative bureaucracies of public institutions had been enlisted to embed such ideas, protectively cloaked by linguistics, into the practice of the organizations' structures. Finally, any attack on this overreach was defended by calling those who challenge it racist, sexist, homophobic, and/or fascist.

However, Rufo did not merely report on the problem. He posited a solution. Rufo's plan to counter the successful assault by a radical group to take over public sector institutions was as follows: public universities are public institutions; public institutions are funded by state legislatures; state legislatures should use the power of the purse to eradicate incursions on free speech by DEI bureaucracies and any other way that these insidious ideas were trampling on the freedoms provided under the Constitution.

On January 6th, the date Gov. DeSantis appointed the board members, Rufo's intellectual theory was now about to become reality.

Therefore, the message of Rufo's tweet was clear. The takeover was to restore free speech and civil discourse on college campuses, to stop the promulgation of radical liberal ideology that had become orthodoxy at these institutions. The problem was it was imperative to the Far Left that Rufo's tweet and any other messages about the changes at New College should be *misunderstood* in order for their power to remain unchallenged.

New College, with its rampant cancel culture which—based on the data—chased students away, was a powerful example of how putting into practice the philosophy of CRT affected students and faculty who did not wholeheartedly embrace whatever was the approved ideology of the moment. With its small student body, there was no place to hide if the current political orthodoxy was not adhered to, magnifying the issue—and showing to the world just how repressive and authoritative such belief systems were.

It was not hard to see why the radical Left knew the issue must be reframed immediately, why Rufo's tweet—and any other actions or words by the trustees, the governor, or myself—must be wrongly construed. Therefore, Rufo's tweet was translated by the press to mean that *Rufo* wanted to curtail free speech. The largest mouthpieces of the national and local press were soon filled with such explanations about the motives behind what was happening at New College, following the fascist narrative about stifling free speech and not providing equal protection to marginalized groups. The problem was that it was DEI itself—not those wanting to remove the entrenchment of a radical philosophy from the administration of a public college—that was guilty of undermining free speech and equal protection.

• • •

The press had been busy between January 6th and January 31st with its stories about how DeSantis and his appointed board members wanted to make New College a conservative university. The press signals were jumped on by the detractors of the changes on the ground. At the first opportunity to be heard—the board meeting on January 31st—one of the public commenters put the radical Left's message plainly:

> [The New College community should] force the
> unjustifiable to justify their every slimy move.
> Protect the next victims. Claw, bite, and scratch
> until violators have no face left to save.[8]

This characterization by one of their own of their behavior was apt: they would truly "claw, bite, and scratch" trying to make our message unrecognizable. They believed they were righteous for using such tactics because we were "unjustifiable," "slimy," and "violators." Such language, opinions with no facts, was their modus operandi.

The board's first target would be abolishing the office that administered the DEI programs at New College, the Office of Opportunity and Inclusive Excellence (OOIE). The governor and board members had signaled that DEI was in the crosshairs, and its supporters, both local and national, were rounding the wagons.

STORMING THE IVORY TOWER

While the press tended to buy the messaging of the proponents of DEI in the lead-up to the January 31st board meeting and other subsequent meetings, in a few months, questions would be raised on a larger stage about DEI. Following October 7th and the response within academia, DEI would be unmasked. In fact, after the response within higher education to the events on October 7th, even many liberals and moderates would signal their disgust with the aims and practices of DEI bureaucracies. One of these was billionaire and hedge fund investor Bill Ackman, a supporter of the Democratic Party who had given to Democrats Barack Obama and Pete Buttigieg, among others.

On January 3, 2024, Ackman would tweet out his findings about the link between DEI bureaucracies and the responses within higher education to the Hamas attacks. He charged that "the root cause of antisemitism at Harvard was an ideology that had been promulgated on campus, an oppressor/oppressed framework, that provided the intellectual bulwark behind the protests." He pointed the finger for this straight at the DEI program.

> *The more I learned, the more concerned I became, and the more ignorant I realized I had been about DEI, a powerful movement that has not only pervaded Harvard, but the educational system at large. I came to understand that Diversity, Equity, and Inclusion was not what I had naively thought these words meant. I have always believed that diversity is an important feature of a successful organization, but by diversity I mean diversity in its broadest form...What I learned, however, was that DEI was not about diversity in its purest form, but rather DEI was a political*

advocacy movement on behalf of certain groups that are deemed oppressed under DEI's own methodology. Under DEI, one's degree of oppression is determined based upon where one resides on a so-called intersectional pyramid of oppression where whites, Jews, and Asians are deemed oppressors, and a subset of people of color, LGBTQ people, and/or women are deemed to be oppressed.

Ackman was shocked to find that "equity", as the term was utilized generally by DEI bureaucracies, was different than the traditional concept of equal protection. "Under DEI's ideology, any policy, program, educational system, economic system, grading system, admission policy…that leads to unequal outcomes among people of different skin colors is deemed racist," he wrote. Therefore, "any merit-based program, system, or organization which has or generates outcomes for different races that are at variance with the proportion these races represent in the population at large is racist under DEI's ideology." Ackman explained this as follows.

*When one examines DEI and its ideological heritage, it does not take long to understand that the movement is inherently inconsistent with basic American values…**The E for "equity" in DEI is about equality of outcome, not equality of opportunity…** DEI is inherently a racist and illegal movement in its implementation even if it purports to work on behalf of the so-called oppressed…it is the lack of equity, i.e, fairness, in how DEI operates.*

Ackman also homed in on the attacks on free speech, which linked back to the belief system of CRT and essays such as those in *Words That Wound*. He noted that "certain speech is no longer permitted," resulting in such things as "microaggressions", "trigger warnings", and "safe spaces." These were all related to the "trauma" that words caused which were basically "words that are challenging to the students' newly-acquired world views." According to Ackman, speakers and faculty "with unapproved views are shouted down, shunned and cancelled." A member of the Harvard community indicated to Ackman a concern that "[t]here is no commitment to free expression at Harvard other than for DEI-approved views."

Finally, Ackman also pointed out what those on the New College board already knew. There was a high cost to challenging the DEI orthodoxy.

> *Why, you might ask, was there so little pushback? The answer is that anyone who dared to raise a question which challenged DEI was deemed a racist, a label which could severely impact one's employment, social status, reputation and more. Being called a racist got people cancelled, so those concerned about DEI and its societal and legal implications had no choice but to keep quiet in this new climate of fear. The techniques that DEI has used to squelch the opposition are found in the Red Scares and McCarthyism of decades past. If you challenge DEI, "justice" will be swift, and you may find yourself unemployed, shunned by colleagues, cancelled, and/or you will otherwise put your career and acceptance in society at risk.*

Ackman would release his letter on January 3, 2024. However, this was January 31, 2023, months before October 7th when the response within academia to the Hamas attacks would shock the nation, revealing the danger that DEI orthodoxy posed to higher education. It was January 31st, 2023, and the board members at New College were standing in the harsh spotlight alone, the only public university leaders willing to confront the uncomfortable truth about DEI.

• • •

At the pre-meeting rally on January 31st, the data points for why New College was in this precarious position were writ large. The documents presented annually to the governing board of the state university system, the publicly available budgets, the 2019 outside consultant's report, even the internal focus groups and articles from the student newspaper, the *Catalyst*, had revealed the issues resulting from the college's radical leftist groupthink and harsh demands for adherence to a specific ideological orthodoxy. Such hard data though merely reported the numbers in black and white; here, in the bright sunshine of a Florida winter day, the issues leaped to life in the content of the speeches, the handwritten messages on the signs, and the overall hysterical tone of the rally, completely untethered from the facts.

About one hundred people attended a rally beforehand where many protestors held signs with messages such as "Jesus for Diversity Equity and Inclusion," "Equity is not a trend. It's a value," and "Are we too woke, or do you need to wake up?"[9]

The first speaker was X Gonzalez, an alumnus who had graduated in May 2022 and was returning for the rally to support the students. X began by stating that "the claim that this is to help New College to become better is bulls***. Nobody here knows better than the students what needs to be fixed on this campus, and it sure as f*** isn't this." They, X's preferred pronoun, listed "some of the things I learned at New College," voice shaking with rage throughout much of the comments.

> *I learned how New College's reaction to COVID differed from DeathSantis's.... I learned how a fascist dictatorship or authoritarian leader can break down a society by pouring out propaganda encouraging students to stop trusting facts, science, and the news. I learned how a fascist like DeSantis can come into power and try to tear apart this state's healthy and functioning institutions with claims that they were full of corruption while replacing those institutions and local leaders with some of the most corrupt and vile people this planet has to offer. I learned how these small-time corrupt leaders will do anything they can to get what they want at the expense of the people they are in charge of. I learned why a* fool *like DeSantis would try to destroy anyone saying nay to his white supremacist values, his cries to protect children and homophobic and transphobic rhetoric.*[10]

The irony inherent in these statements appeared lost on the speaker and listeners.

These students, and those on the steps in front of them holding signs, seemed to believe completely that the school was "targeted...because of our marginalized student body" though this was unsupported by any fact—except that the press kept repeating what the students and other supporters were saying. The financial, enrollment, and retention issues over the years were not a secret, unless you were a New College student, faculty member, or alumnus at this rally.

Florida State representative Anna Eskamani and former state representative Carlos Guillermo Smith, both Orlando Democrats and two of the most liberal members ever to serve in the state House, spoke next. Unlike the students, they did not have the defense of being unaware of issues that had plagued New College at the legislative level for years.

Eskamani, passionately yelling into the microphone, asserted that "I fight like hell for the needs of everyday people and against this fascist regime. I am here today to stand shoulder-to-shoulder with each one of you in the name of academic freedom and against political interference through a classroom...[W]hat happens at New College can happen anywhere. No institution is safe from the erosion of democracy."[11]

According to Eskamani, the goal was not to stabilize a university that had struggled for years with enrollment and retention but to "take over our schools and not allow for there to be critical thought and freedom of expression." While data or facts were nonexistent, she was not going to let facts affect her feelings.

Finally, former state representative Carlos Guillermo Smith spoke, giving a speech almost interchangeable with Eskamani's messaging. Guillermo Smith was here to prevent a "hostile rightwing takeover."

> *The new appointees of New College...are not here to improve higher education. They are not here to improve student enrollment. They are here to*

launch a hostile rightwing takeover of our state colleges and universities and New College is their first test. It's their first trial run. Your campus is next.... DeSantis' claims of indoctrination [are false].... He wants total political censorship and control.

It was simply disingenuous for state representatives who worked in the legislature for years to claim this. It was no secret why New College was in trouble. As if to underline why the college was running off would-be students, the rally put an exclamation point to the governor's reasoning.

● ● ●

Inside, the Sudakoff Center's auditorium was packed for the main board meeting. With the large amount of faculty, students, and community members wanting to attend, many were unable to find seating and were left watching the meeting on a livestream at locations around the campus. Inside, protestors carried signs reinforcing the messaging of the speakers outside including "Keep diversity, equity and inclusion" and "NCF is public—not the Christian Hillsdale."[12]

Twenty-three speakers spoke during the public comment section at the beginning. Limited to one minute each, the speakers had signed up beforehand, including three members from the Party for Socialism and Liberation,[13] a local activist known for her support of Far Left educational policies,[14] and president of the Democratic Public Education Caucus of Manasota.[15] No one spoke in favor of the changes.

A theme arose from these speakers that mirrored the rally beforehand: namely, there was a right-wing conspiracy to silence students and create a conservative institution. In addition, abolishing DEI, clearly a part of this "conspiracy," would mean the board was racist, sexist, and anti-gay.

Watching the meeting unfold, the public commentors appeared to be at a different event than the board meeting that followed. One speaker who was with the Party for Socialism and Liberation claimed, "DeSantis has made political appointees that are clearly sexist, racist, and anti-gay."

> *You come here to a progressive school to try and shut out and destroy the schooling that they have here. You've been appointed because you will enact the racist, sexist, and anti-gay agenda DeSantis wants to create here at New College. The people and the students will not stand idly by while fascists try to change this school into something that it's not. You will answer to the people, and the people will make themselves known.*

A speaker, who identified herself as a Cuban-American, agreed, stating that "what DeSantis and these trustees are proposing has more in common with dictatorial regimes than it does with any of the values that make America the country that saved my family so many years ago." Like others, she spoke in favor of DEI programs, stating that "to abolish DEI programs and dictate what can and cannot be taught in an institute of higher learning, is opportunistic, shameful, and cowardly."

Another member of the Party for Socialism and Liberation who spoke stated that she was "here to reject fascism, reject white supremacy, reject homophobia, and reject the privatization of public education. We reject the focus on Christian, fascist, conservative ideology to promote capitalism."

Another speaker, who identified herself as a Sarasota resident, said that "[t]his is the dystopian universe in which we now find ourselves."

> *Fortunately, we have this younger generation. They cannot be fooled, and they're not falling for the nonsense being pushed in Dear Leader's culture wars. These are the students of New College of Florida. These are the students who actually do believe in diversity, equity, and inclusion. These are the students who will fight against policies that seek to disenfranchise individuals on the basis of their sexual orientation.*

The conflating of abolishing DEI with racism, sexism, and homophobia threaded throughout the remarks. Assistant Professor of Theater and Performance Studies Diego Villada spoke about the "wellbeing" of his current students if DEI was abolished.

> *I rise today in opposition to initiatives...namely, the abolishment of DEI training and programming...I am a professor. I am primarily concerned with the wellbeing of my students. To that end, I feel compelled to share that there are more things in heaven and earth than are dreamt of in your philosophy...Many students came here to feel safe and access the education that is their right as Floridians and the impulse to make this a place where race, intersectionality and DEI are banned*

indicates to them that you want everyone to be the same, to be like you...I guarantee you that DEI programming initiatives make me a better teacher.

The inference was clear: wanting to ban DEI meant that "you want everyone to be the same," that the board was racist and sexist and homophobic.

● ● ●

All thirteen trustees were present. After brief updates, Trustee Spalding made a motion to adopt a resolution to affirm the board's commitment to the mission of New College. Spalding went straight to the point, answering the hyperbole and misinformation of the press, the rally, and the public speakers.

"Some have said that the recent appointments amount to a partisan takeover of the college," Spalding said. "This is not correct."

Rather than be relieved at this plain statement that told them their fears were unfounded, the audience met this statement with derisive laughter. Spalding continued by iterating what the governor, the BOG, and the trustees had been saying to the press ad nauseum.

It's not a takeover. It's a renewal...[to] ensure New College is strong and true to its long-standing mission so that it may grow and flourish as a unique institution within the state of Florida university system. I think we should all embrace that purpose and with that in mind as a recognition of our responsibility and a sign of our good faith to adopt the resolution.

The resolution was as follows:

The board of trustees reconfirms its commitment to the distinctive mission and supporting goals of New College as adopted, promulgated in Florida law and pledges to uphold, maintain, and insist on that mission in any and all governance and educational reform efforts.

Spalding stressed the importance of this in case anyone in the audience or the press missed it.

I think that is a signal that is needed right now in this community, in this college...our commitment is to abide by the mission of this college. It's got a good mission. It's got a great history. I think we are missing an opportunity not for us to immediately commit in a general way to the mission of this college.

Another board trustee agreed. As a trustee who had been on the board prior to Gov. DeSantis's recent appointments and a New College alum, Ron Christaldi stated that "I appreciate Trustee Spalding's comments, and I echo it. It's a sentiment that I feel as well. I'm inclined to be supportive of it.... I think it's timely for Trustee [Spalding] to raise that because we've seen a lot in the media trying to tell us as a board what we [stand for]."

Chris Rufo, whom many of the nefarious intentions had been ascribed to, agreed as well, stating, "I share Trustee Spalding's sentiments."

Though the board could not vote on it because it was not a read-ahead on the agenda, the trustees indicated their approval of Spalding's statement, with not one dissenting voice. The press did not report this. Giving time to this discussion in their reporting would interfere with their attempt to gaslight the public about what was really going on in higher education. The parents, students, and community members apparently did not hear it as well—or did not want to hear it.

Rufo then introduced his motion. It had four parts: abolish the OOIE, ban use of DEI statements, ban mandatory diversity training, and prohibit identity-based preferences. Underlining the point of his recent research, he stated, with "diversity, equity, and inclusion the whole meaning of the word 'equity' is to actually create separate standards for people based on their identity categories. This goes against the founding mission of the college. It goes against the will of Florida voters. And against the stated vision of the governor and the legislators."

The crowd booed loudly.

New trustee Mark Bauerlein—an English professor for almost thirty years at Emory University—jumped in, specifically addressing the audience in his role as an academic. "You must understand that for many, many people in Florida and in this country, DEI is experienced as coercive and oppressive." This was met with derisive laughter from the audience.

"You can disagree with that, but you have to acknowledge many people experience it as that." Again, the audience voiced disagreement.

"This is a public university. Now a concrete example of a practice is requiring a faculty DEI statement," he continued. Here the board chair, a member from before the changes, asked the audience, which was continuing to voice dissent, to be respectful.

"This is a McCarthyite litmus test," Bauerlein continued. Again, the audience vocally disagreed. This was something Bauerlein, as an academic, felt strongly about as someone who had experienced this personally.

> *To require [professors] to add a non-academic, non-research-oriented criterion to their work, to their research...is a form of coercion. Peer review cannot survive if an equity criterion is included in it.... I'm happy to talk with you about the peer review process, and the way equity can come in and it just skews things. It starts to poison the process. I've seen this many, many times in a long 35-year academic career.... In hiring committees, I've been behind the closed doors, I've done peer review of manuscripts for presses, and I've judged people for promotions, and tenure. The operations of a university are very fragile things, and one must set up the guidelines carefully.*

The board was amenable to the substance, but, as the proposal was originally drafted for legislative texts, they agreed it would need to be adapted for a university. The board and Rufo agreed to give staff time to prepare a draft policy specifically based on the structure of the current New College office and Florida law to present at the next meeting.

The meeting moved on quickly with Spalding recommending that I be made interim president, and the board voting in favor, with one dissent by the student body representative.

How did the press report it? The main takeaways for readers of the mainstream press were that the board members were "conservative," and they had "ousted its current president," according to *Politico*, "with the idea of overhauling the liberal arts college in Sarasota into a more conservative-leaning institution."[16]

For those following the meeting in the press, there would be little to no mention of Spalding's resolution and the board's agreement. In addition, the general silence about Rufo and Bauerlein's points about DEI was deafening.

This meeting was a shot across the bow. However, it was a powerful one. The press and others had wondered if change would happen. Would the board stand up to intense outside pressure? Then, even if this first major hurdle was met, how would the board ensure their will was implemented on the ground?

This meeting showed that the board had held steadfastly to its asserted goal of returning New College to its mission with its discussion moving forward with the abolishment of the DEI office, despite virulent disagreement. They had then swiftly installed me as interim president, someone with a track record of achievement even in complex and challenging situations. Things had suddenly become much more serious in the minds of those who opposed the changes.

Therefore, at the next meeting on Feb. 28th, the radical Left would bring in more firepower to protect DEI, gender studies, and other radical leftist sacred cows. One thing I realized in my years fighting this group—they firmly believed if they yelled the loudest, they would win. Typically, this crude tactic worked. However, New College had just caught lightning in a bottle— the governor, the legislature, the board, and now an interim president—were all in agreement and willing to fight for free speech and civil discourse.

We would not cede that ground, as so many before us had done.

• • •

Apart from the board changes at New College, DeSantis was fighting against DEI and the radical Left's stranglehold on education in other ways as well. In late December 2022, just days before he appointed the New College trustees, he had asked universities and colleges to turn over to his office the budgets for how much they were spending on DEI initiatives. On January 31st, he filed HB 999, which would bar public higher learning institutions from supporting DEI initiatives. HB 999 would be voted on—and passed—during the legislative session that began March 7th.

As they did with his decision to appoint new trustees at New College, the media tried to paint him as a dictator intent on stifling free speech. The legacy press was following the play-book it had when DeSantis had challenged the radical Left's incursions into the K–12 arena: repeat ad nauseam that DeSantis was a fascist dictator who was racist, sexist, and homophobic. The New College protestors had followed this lead at the first board meeting on January 31st. This road map continued at the second board meeting on February 28th.

Rufo's motion to eliminate DEI and its accoutrements was front and center on the agenda. I was now interim president, and there was a full meltdown taking place among the media that was reporting on New College prolifically both nationally and internationally.

The press was specifically focused on this meeting for two reasons: for one thing, it would be the first time I would speak officially to the campus community, and, for another, the DEI proposal had worked its way through official channels since the last meeting and was now ready for a vote.

The drama started at the rally beforehand, which was attended by approximately two hundred people. Despite the fact that the entire message of the last board meeting was that the board of trustees intended New College to continue as a public university and increase free speech protections, the speakers at the rally and the meeting acted as if this never happened. It was not a secret: the new trustees had deliberately stated at the last meeting and in the press that the point was *not* to make the college Christian or stifle free speech; however, this was as effectively ignored as Biden's order expanding DEI programs would be. The criticisms leveled at DEI by Rufo and Bauerlein at the last meeting were also unanswered, both at this rally and generally in press articles of major outlets between the previous board meeting and the board meeting currently taking place.

In fact, one speaker at the meeting, a parent of a New College student, spent his entire time bemoaning "the stated goal of this board to make NCF the Hillsdale of the South…I have no problem with Hillsdale opening a southern branch in Florida…. If there's enough Floridians to support Hillsdale down here, then Hillsdale should buy some land and open themselves a campus…. Instead, Hillsdale is taking an existing college with existing students and mooting its foundation to fund their expansion into Florida."

This father was a sincere and concerned parent. Who could blame him if he had read some articles and thought Hillsdale was opening a campus in Sarasota? Despite the fact that Spalding, Rufo, myself, and others had repeatedly stated that New College would remain a public institution following the laws which applied to public institutions, that Hillsdale was established to be an institution with a different vision, the legacy media seemed to have little interest in explaining this differentiation to the public.

Prior to this February 28th board meeting, while the crowd at the rally outside was larger than that at the January 31st rally, the speeches tended to be centered on the same types of messages. Sam Sharf, a current student, spoke at the rally stating, without a fact in sight, "We have witnessed harrowing incursions on academic freedom, akin to authoritarian regimes around the world. These trustees, new president, and governor have made it clear that they are waging a war on academia's most marginalized…These people are fucking fascists."

Not only was the crowd outside at the rally larger than at the previous meeting, inside there were forty-nine speakers, more than twice as many as last time, as well as the addition of several speakers who wore long red gowns and white bonnets, á la *The Handmaid's Tale*. According to the Catalyst, "The topic those delivering public comment expressed with the most frequency was an overwhelming disapproval of Corcoran."[17]

Thesis student KC Casey stated that he would "like to be one of the first students to welcome our new president by letting you know that you are in fact not welcome here." This was greeted with loud cheers from the audience. "We do not welcome you here because you do not reflect the values of the New College community."

My past as education commissioner was the main basis for the dissent. Carol Lerner, leader of the liberal local organization of Support Our Schools, which lobbied for a liberal radical agenda in K–12 schools in Sarasota, stated that parents and students in the K–12 arena were concerned about my appointment.

"Parents and students witnessed Corcoran's pushing privatization schemes on K–12 education," she said. "They watched as Corcoran banned books, distorted history, including black history, and attacked LGBTQ plus students...K–12 high school students and parents understand that Corcoran's dystopian plans for New College will be replicated."

Robin Williams continued the attacks but added in jabs at DeSantis and the rest of the new trustees.

> *You can be a bull in a China shop, Corcoran, shattering academic freedom...While DeSatan yells "freedom state," he'll ban courses and majors at universities and tenure for professors...You, Corcoran, and your distrustees pushing Christian nationalism and privatization are looting public coffers with Hillsdale-connected classical education grift.*

The pinnacle of these comments came toward the end when an NCF student dramatically stated, "You are here to deliver us all onto our demise under your fascist regime. I hope you enjoy the blood on your hands. History will judge you harshly."

As the NCF student's statement only took up thirty-five seconds of the allotted minute, the student spent the next twenty-five seconds leaning over the podium and glaring at me while doing hand motions that used the pointer and middle fingers to point at their own eyes and then to me, yelling, "I see you there! You can't hide from me! You can't hide!"

This was typical of certain NCF students. It was a campus where students had run the show, and few to no guardrails were placed on behavior. In a sense, the NCF student's conduct was a direct result of the adults who had been on the campus beforehand refusing to apply any rule of law to student conduct no matter how egregious.

However, while they were a student, the adults in the room offered no guidance on appropriate civil discourse. Hitler was a favorite theme. One parent of an NCF student stated, "To the newest trustees, to the interim president, and to your puppet master Governor DeSantis, I simply remind you of this: silence is complicity. Hitler did not and could not have acted alone. He relied on the cooperation of many people and the silence of even more. Know this ladies and gentlemen, we won't be complicit, we won't be cooperative, and I can promise you we won't be silent."

Another commenter professed his "moral outrage" at "what the seven of you appointed by the governor have set out to do here." He then used a historical reference to Martin Luther King, an insinuation that there was an underlying racism to the decisions such as one to eliminate DEI.

When Martin Luther King said that the moral arc of the universe is long, but it bends toward justice he did so to warn us of sycophants like you. To inspire the kind of resistance that we see erupting on this campus right now. And to remind those that have been victimized by your brutality that it looks like you have the opportunity to wield your power for this day, the long arc of history will grind you into dust and they will win this battle and you will be remembered for the sycophants that you are. That's what history does.

Many explicitly mentioned DEI, including one student who stated, "Students on the whole are not in favor of reforming or abolishing the Office of Outreach and Inclusive Excellence and are not concerned with its existence or actions." Another student, representing the admission student employees, agreed. "As student ambassadors in the admissions department, we oppose the changes proposed by this board as well as the comments made by the newer members of the board," she stated. "We foresee that your presence and changes will negatively impact our admissions and retention efforts."

Once the final public comment had been delivered, the audience broke out into a chant of, "Shame on you. Shame on you. Shame on you."

•   •   •

During these board meetings, when commentors dissented with ending DEI initiatives, they tended to focus their statements on challenging the motives of those who supported the measure. Facts were almost nonexistent. This was because—if the goal was actual diversity—data related to New College's DEI office generally supported abolishing it.

According to an article in March 2017 in the student newspaper, New College had recently hired its "first official Director of Diversity and Inclusion."[18] From 2017 forward, the percentage of Black students enrolled continued to hover around 3 percent and the percentage of Hispanic students also remained around its 2017 number of 18 percent of the student population based on data published in New College's annual Fact Books.[19] In addition, in August 2022, the New College Board approved a report entitled the "New College Equity Report" based on data from 2020-2021. According to the report, the percentage of bachelor's degrees awarded to Black and Hispanic students had declined since the DEI office began. For the 2015-2016 cohort, 4.7% of degrees were awarded to Black students and 18.8% were awarded to Hispanic students. For the 2020-2021 cohort, 2.5% were awarded to Black students and 12% were awarded to Hispanic students.[20]

New College followed the trend in higher education of ignoring the data which pointed to the fact that DEI offices often did not achieve their stated goal of combatting bias—and appeared even in some research to work against it. A report published in *Anthropology Now* in September 2018 by Frank Dobbin, a professor of sociology at Harvard, and Alexandra Kalev, an associate professor of sociology and anthropology at Tel Aviv University, was entitled "Why Doesn't Diversity Training Work? The Challenge for Industry and Academia."[21] The authors had spent a decade spreading "the message that diversity training is likely the most expensive, and least effective, diversity program around." They felt like they hit a brick wall with both employers—who worried about the optics of discontinuing such training—and in higher education. The authors were particularly confused by the resistance to following data in higher education. "That colleges and universities in the United States persist in offering training to faculty and students, and even mandate it (29% of all schools require faculty to undergo training), is particularly surprising given that the research on the poor performance of training comes out of academia. Imagine university health centers continuing to prescribe vitamin C for the common cold."[22]

The $8 billion DEI industry[23] thrived in higher education and beyond, even though research often showed that most DEI programs in existence accomplished nothing at best or, at worst, exacerbated problems of bias toward others. In 2022, in the *Annual Review of Psychology*, researchers reviewed data on "diversity training goals, limitations, and promise." According to the authors, "we are far from being able to derive clear and decisive conclusions about what fosters inclusivity and promotes diversity within organizations."[24] In addition, in 2021, the *Annual Review of Psychology* studied 418 experiments that examined "methods for reducing prejudice."[25] The authors found the following.

> *Although these studies report optimistic conclusions, we identify troubling indications of publication bias that may exaggerate effects. Furthermore, landmark studies often find limited effects, which suggests the need for further theoretical innovation or synergies with other kinds of psychological or structural interventions. We conclude that much research effort is theoretically and empirically ill-suited to provide actionable, evidence-based recommendations for reducing prejudice.*

In 2022, William Taylor Laimaka Cox published a peer-reviewed article about the "state of DEI trainings currently being implemented in the world...and assessments of their efficacy." According to Cox, the "overwhelming consensus is that (1) DEI trainings are largely non-scientific and not experimentally tested, (2) the limited but consistent non-experimental evidence suggests that at worst they cause more problems for organizational climate, and at best they are ineffective at creating lasting, meaningful change, and (3) experimental tests of their common components lead to more negative outcomes than positive outcomes related to bias, diversity, inclusion, and equity."[26]

In fact, evidence sometimes seemed to show what was seen at New College—DEI initiatives can be counter-productive. As Dobbin and Kalev noted after three decades of research, "studies show that this kind of force-feeding can activate bias rather than stamp it out." In January 2023, journalist Jesse Singal, the author of a 2021 book entitled *The Quick Fix: Why Fad Psychology Can't Cure Our Social Ills*, wrote an opinion piece in the *New York Times* about the fact that "[t]here's little evidence that many [DEI] initiatives work." Singal stated that the "history of diversity training sessions is, in a sense, a history of fads. Maybe the current crop will wither over time, new ones will sprout that are stunted by the same lack of evidence, and a decade from now someone else will write a version of this article."[27]

Singal's observations highlight that—just like at New College—ensuring evidence exists before implementing DEI programs simply does not often appear to be a priority for DEI supporters. The wind in DEI's sails rather seems to be the powerful feeling of superiority—like that expressed by those in the audience at New College board meetings in early 2023. The often unspoken or—in the case at New College board meetings—spoken belief was that those questioning DEI "wanted everyone to be the same, to be like you." However, if one were to rely only on data and not look at these personal statements of self-righteousness—the data would appear to show that it was DEI's supporters who were actually supporting blatant financial waste at best or, at worst, perhaps even exacerbating bias.

With the current focus on DEI, there has been in the last year or so a push to find evidence-based approaches. The purpose of Cox's 2022 article was to posit how to fix the "pervasive failures of the DEI industry." Cox noted that there had recently been requests by "[n]early every major scientific organization (e.g. NIH, NSF, AAAS) [to institute] experimentally-tested, evidence-based approaches to addressing bias and promoting diversity." Cox's observation—that much of the demand for research-based approaches has come from "major scientific organizations"—is interesting. Why did this push not arise initially years ago from those in the movement itself? Given the lip service such activists pay to wanting to combat bias, this seems to be curious behavior. In fact, it points to a more important question. Are they promoting DEI because they want to combat bias? If that was the purpose, surely they would have been passionately seeking out best practices.

In the introduction to *Words That Wound*, the CRT academics wrote that "[o]ur colleagues of color..needed to know that the institutions in which they worked stood behind them." Professor Gates quotes this in his essay in which he refutes some of their ideas. Gates puts in italics their phrase *"needed to know that the institutions in which they worked stood behind them."* Gates notes that "I have difficulty imagining that this sentiment could have been expressed by their activist counterparts in the sixties, who defined themselves through their adversarial relation to authority and its institutions. And this is the crucial difference this time around. Today, the aim is not to resist power, but to enlist power." The disinterest in proof of the efficacy of DEI programs which inject CRT philosophy into their structures seems to point to what could be the real end: the enlistment of power. In essence, this is what they have accumulated—the power to indoctrinate the best and brightest in the nation, with little oversight. Or little need to show that they are actually combating bias rather than perhaps propagating it.

• • •

Rufo submitted two motions.

The first was to eliminate the OOIE office. The motion passed 10–3. Voting against it were the student and faculty representatives and one board member who had been on the board for years prior. The other three members who had been on the board previously turned out to be in support of our vision to move the college forward and were glad to have the backing of additional new members.

Rufo then made a second motion to authorize me to follow through on the steps recommended in Proposal 1, inclusive of eliminating the OOIE and making any necessary personnel decisions. This motion was also approved 10–3, with the same three voting against it who had opposed the first one.[28]

Originally, the second motion had been put forward to follow the recommendations of an internal report that related to eliminating the DEI office. However, this report had not been provided by me. It had been compiled by Brad Thiessen, a member of the New College faculty who had been chosen by the board to serve briefly as interim president during the four weeks in February in which I was wrapping up loose ends at the companies I had founded.

Per the board's request at the January 31st meeting, Thiessen had spent the last four weeks reviewing the college's DEI program and considering how to eliminate it. His report recommended transferring the only full-time DEI employee, Yoleidy Rosario-Hernandez, the school's dean for diversity, equity, and inclusion initiatives, to another position within the university, suggesting she be moved to the position of associate dean of housing and residential life.

During the meeting, Rufo made the motion to eliminate the office but wanted to specify in the language that I, as interim president, was "authorize[d]...to make necessary or appropriate personnel decisions." Rufo understood that there would be on-the-ground decisions that the board would not be present for and did not want to tie me to any specifics in the report. He worked in the moment to find the correct wording to ensure the motion gave me the scope of power needed. I knew where he was going, and I suggested wording for the amendment to the motion as the board discussed it.

"I think we can fix the motion to say that you guys are voting, moving to authorize the president to follow through on the steps recommended in Item One, inclusive of eliminating the office or making the personnel decisions necessary," I said, referencing "Item One" in Thiessen's report entitled "Abolish DEI Bureaucracies." It offered proposed "next steps" once the DEI office was abolished and included the recommendation to "Direct the Interim President to eliminate OOIE and transition staff to new positions." The language I recommended gave me much more flexibility, and Rufo amended the motion to include the suggested language.

On March 3rd, I chose to fire the dean rather than transition her to a new position. This is an example of the synergy when a president and board are aligned. A different president might have merely moved Rosario-Hernandez to a new position. I was present day-to-day in management. I knew where the board wanted to go; therefore, this was the call to be made.

Rufo, Spalding, Bauerlein, and the rest of the trustees were passionate about achieving the governor's mandate. However, they could not be there for the myriad of day-to-day decisions that would ensure the intent was carried out. This is how bureaucracies undermine boards that want to make change. When this happens, the board might win the vote—but in the end will not make powerful, systemic change on the ground. When there is synergy between the board and a strong CEO, the board's stated goals will not only be accomplished, but they will also be thoroughly instituted across the organization.

• • •

After all the noise of the public comments, the rallies, and the intense media pressure, the board showed why DeSantis had picked them. They were unmoved by the hysteria and misinformation.

This may seem like a small thing. However, it was the first university in the nation to do so. Even after Oct. 7th and the shameful exposure of the racism and exclusionary practices of DEI departments, how many boards have done away with these offices? Even in Florida, not one of the other eleven public universities eliminated DEI until forced by law. That is why the vote that day, while quiet, was a shot heard round the nation. At last, a university had stood up and called DEI what it was—an attack on free speech and equal protection.

However, the board was not finished sweeping away the institutional mechanisms that enabled speech suppression. DEI offices were not the only way in which the radical left stifled dialogue on campuses. These administrative bureaucracies often worked in concert with other recently developed programs that had been designed to purvey so-called social justice rather than open and honest inquiry.

Gender studies departments were one of these apparatuses. Beginning in the 1990s, these programs had quickly proliferated in higher educational institutions, and, through their self-proclaimed "interdisciplinary" nature, they often served as experts within institutions on the subject of sex and gender. If concerns were raised about lack of dialogue about critical concepts in such departments, gender studies programs could look to DEI offices to protect them. They were two of a kind in their origins and belief systems: speech suppression over open dialogue; equity over equality; feelings over facts; social justice over science. Therefore, New College's gender studies program was next in the board's crosshairs in its mission to ensure that—at one public institution at least—ideas would not be sacrificed to the demand that no debate should occur on certain intellectual issues.

CHAPTER 3

Gender Studies

The American Conversation is an argument, after all, and way worse than our fear of error or anarchy or Gomorrahl decadence is our fear of theocracy or autocracy or any ideology whose project is not to argue or persuade but to adjourn the whole debate sine die.[1]
—*David Foster Wallace*

In July 2020, Bari Weiss—an opinion editor and center-right columnist at the *New York Times*—resigned her position at the newspaper. In her resignation letter, she charged that "intellectual curiosity—let alone risk-taking—is now a liability" at the publication.[2] Weiss, however, had no plans to drop out of the conversation. In June 2021, she launched a podcast, *Honestly*.[3] A month later, one of the first stories it ran was entitled "Med Schools Are Now Denying Biological Sex."[4] She introduced the segment with the following.

> *Some of you may find [this] story* shocking *and* disconcerting *and perhaps even* maddening*. You might also ask yourself: How has it come to this?*

*How has this radical ideology gone from the rela-
tively obscure academic fringe to the mainstream
in such a short time?...*
*So far, it has taken root in some of our leading
medical schools. Some. Not all. But I'm left thinking: What state will American medicine—or any
other American institution—find itself in after
being routed by this ideology?*

A few months later, in November 2022, more than 150 academics met at Stanford to discuss the state of academic freedom in higher education. Professors from many institutions including Duke, Harvard, Princeton, and UCLA presented their concerns about free speech on campuses. Several sessions focused specifically on the sciences.[5]

Biologist Luana Maroja, a professor at Williams College, was one of the speakers on the topic of "Academic Freedom and STEM". Maroja was concerned that "authoritarian ideology" was affecting the hard sciences. She spoke of a "censorious, fearful climate [that] is *already* affecting the content of what we teach…the most fundamental rules of biology from plants to humans is that sexes are defined by the size of their gametes …In humans, an egg is 10 million times bigger than a sperm. There is zero overlap. It is a full binary. But in some biology 101 classes, teachers are telling students that sexes—not gender [but] sex—are on a continuum."[6]

In the spring of 2023, Olivia Krolczyk, a student at the University of Cincinnati, received a zero in her gender studies class because she used the term "biological women" in a paper. When Krolczyk filed a Freedom of Speech complaint with the university's Office of Gender, Equity, and Inclusion, her professor, Melanie Rose Nipper, confirmed the story. Speaking to a local paper, the professor affirmed why she believed the grade that she had given to Krolczyk was valid.

> *Although Nipper said she agrees classrooms should be places for debate and discussion, that ends when "you are, intentionally or unintentionally, participating in a systemic harm of some kind." She cited transphobia and white supremacy as examples... When a student uses "an outdated terminology," Nipper said she feels it is necessary to correct those mistakes.[7]*

The office enforcing DEI beliefs originally reprimanded Nipper, but then rescinded the reprimand. Krolczyk was shocked. As she told the *New York Post*, a conservative media outlet, "UC is affirming that professors will have no consequences for failing students with dissenting opinions...they will not uphold a student's rights to free speech and will take no action to ensure that the educators hired are acting in a professional manner."[8]

While these stories were often not covered by the mainstream press, the reality about the lack of free speech in academia as to new and radical definitions of "sex" and "gender" in higher education was not unknown in August 2023 when the New College board took up a discussion of its gender studies program. However, the public generally would not have known this from the mainstream media coverage of the board meeting, even though trustees had alluded to the ideological capture of such departments.

When Weiss resigned from *The New York Times*, she had noted in her resignation letter that there were "unwritten rules" for career advancement as a reporter and editor.

One of the first rules was to "Never risk commissioning a story that goes against the narrative."

Given this unwritten rule, it was logical that—while the mainstream media had effectively ignored the ideological capture of academia as to radical new definitions of "sex" and "gender" on a national scale—its editors and reporters *did* have time to cover the decision by the New College board to consider dismantling its gender studies program.

Or, at any rate, their preferred narrative about it.

● ● ●

Two and a half hours into the August 10, 2023, board meeting of the New College of Florida, Trustee Christopher Rufo pointed out to Trustee Amy Reid, the faculty member on the Board as well as the director of the college's Gender Studies Program, that it was acceptable to have a constructive debate about an intellectual issue.

"If your discipline cannot be subjected to rigorous criticism, if you take it as a personal slight, I think that is a sign not of the discipline's strength but of the discipline's weakness," Rufo stated to Reid.

Outside, the temperatures in Sarasota were in the mid-90s with 70 percent humidity, which translated to a heat index of around 118 degrees. Inside, tempers were growing heated as well, as a debate about terminating the gender studies program dragged on.[9] This motion, if passed, would make New College the "first public university in the country to tackle this department."[10]

Rufo, who had brought the motion to direct me as interim president to investigate abolishing the program, argued that the discipline of gender studies was not part of the traditional liberal arts and, thus, not in line with the mission of the college. First and foremost, this was the crux of his argument to terminate the program. However, Rufo also noted that these types of programs have "strayed from [a] scholarly mission in favor of ideological activism," pointing out that the option of choosing to no longer provide a major is not uncommon for universities where this has occurred, citing similar moves recently by the University of Chicago and the University of California, Berkeley.

Trustee Reid asserted that the discipline of gender studies— which had only been in the academic arena since the 1990s— was a part of the traditional liberal arts. Other board members quickly dismissed this claim. According to Trustee Bauerlein, as "an independent disciplinary formation," gender studies should not be a separate discipline at New College. He supported rigorous academic debate on intellectual works around gender within other disciplines, but it did not make sense "as a matter of disciplinary structure" to offer it as a standalone major.

At this point, Reid became incensed stating that many other colleges offer gender studies programs and then addressed me directly, charging that there had been "attacks" on gender studies. This comment related to the fact that I had sent out to board members an opinion piece, authored by an alumnus, that had been published in the local paper. The article discussed how New College was becoming a beacon of free speech and civil discourse—and how it had been an ideologically captured institution prior to the recent changes by the board.

In the article, alum Robert Allen Jr. noted that "before the implementation of the changes 39 [of the approximately one hundred faculty members were] affiliated with gender studies. Yes, 39."[11] This meant that, though the college only had one full-time professor who taught gender studies, thirty-nine used their disciplines as direct-support organizations of the program. According to Allen, this was just one example of how "[f]or more than a decade, past administrations, and the faculty...have allowed and seemingly embraced New College's steady drift away from being Florida's 'honors college' to becoming Florida's 'progressive college.'"[12] (As a former English professor from the University of Ottawa wrote when she learned this fact about New College: "[T]his reality suggests the depth of the rot gender studies has brought to academic departments, a rot that has now spread throughout the arts, humanities, and social sciences, even into many faculties of business, journalism, law, and medical science, as research is corrupted by social and political advocacy."[13])

The content of this article by Robert Allen Jr. was the catalyst for Trustee Reid to charge that the gender studies program was being unfairly targeted.

> *Gender studies has been coming under attack, and I really do think that [the oped] was really reprehensible, and I'm stunned that you sent it out to all of the members of this board, sir.*

She looked directly at me and then continued.

> *[I]f this board is about attacking gender studies, that's what this board is doing. But I believe it is morally reprehensible, and I don't think it is educationally defensible.*

Rufo responded with the quote at the beginning of this chapter, objecting to the framing by Reid of discussions about the nature of the program as "morally reprehensible." Rufo noted that a "deliberative process" should be expected in an academic setting. The frustration was evident in his voice.

[People] can criticize any academic offering.
That is the nature of scholarly discourse.
That is the nature of democratic governance.
That is the nature of the decisions we have to make
as a board...
And I just think that this is a part of a delibera-
tive process.
This is part of democratic governance.
This is part of shaping a scholarly community.
And this kind of defensive orientation toward
this question, I think actually speaks less in favor
rather than more in favor of the program itself.

This was not a new issue to Rufo. In debates on topics such as DEI, CRT, or gender studies, his opponents would often retreat to arguments that it was morally *wrong* for anyone to bring up opposing viewpoints. If someone challenged these opponents on such hot-button ideological issues, that person must be racist or sexist or homophobic—or all three combined.

• • •

The headlines in the press about the move in the days that followed stuck to the familiar storyline that the media had been weaving: "DeSantis's New College Minions Want to Ax Gender Studies: The Latest Battle in the Conservative War on the American Mind";[14] "Florida Fights to Preserve the Future of Gender Studies" with the subtitle "Far-right conservatives ban what they fear most: youth being taught to think critically about bias against women, people of color and LGBTQ+ individuals";[15] and "Florida's Attacks on Academic Freedom Just Got Even Worse."[16]

The *Guardian* ran an opinion column that repeated the charge that DeSantis wanted to make New College ideologically conservative, stating that the board was given "a mandate to make the school conservative, bringing the curriculum in line with the governor's ideological preferences, and reshaping it in the image of Hillsdale College, a private conservative Christian school in Michigan." According to columnist, the "attacks" were "escalated...transforming a board of trustees meeting into an ideologically driven attack on academic freedom—and eliminating the school's gender studies department."

Reid was quoted in the student newspaper, the *Catalyst*, saying that, "I want to emphasize that ideas can't be banned or abolished. Students need to be able to pursue their search for knowledge and truth."[17] She said this despite having participated in the meeting in which the trustees had focused on the fact that gender studies as a discipline was not a part of the traditional liberal arts. Criticisms related to banning ideas were in reference to the fact that *gender studies programs themselves* were the culprit when it came to abolishing free speech.

If reporters had been curious about the part of the discussion in the board meeting related to the allegation that the discipline was ideologically captured, they would have investigated it. They did not.

This was typical as the mainstream media had in large part ignored those in academia who had been sounding the alarm about the lack of free speech around the topic of gender and sex. Gender studies programs, which began to pop up in the 1990's, had generally followed the same playbook as DEI. First, these new departments would utilize common terms, coopting them to sell a product which was much different than the packaging. Second, a recently emerged radical theory based on "social justice" was often embedded within institutions through these programs. Third, if challenged, detractors were typically demeaned along the general lines of being "morally reprehensible".

First, the vocabulary for gender studies utilized the common terms "sex" and "gender" but in a manner different than these terms had been traditionally defined. For example, both of these terms would seem, based on past usage, to refer to biological males or females—or at the very least inclusion of discussion that biological males and females might exist. Judith Butler was one of the influential scholars in this emerging field. In 1990, Butler wrote a book entitled *Gender Trouble* in which she posited a theory that gender is an identity that is "performative", i.e. "what we take to be an internal essence of gender is manufactured through a sustained set of acts, posited through the gendered stylization of the body."[18] As to the word "sex" she wrote that, "If the immutable character of sex is contested, perhaps this construct called 'sex' is as culturally constructed as gender; indeed, perhaps it was always already gender, with the consequence that the distinction between sex and gender turns out to be no distinction at all."[19]

This view of gender and sex and their attendant definitions often began to hold sway in gender studies departments, and dialogue around "biological essentialism", as time went on, was generally not encouraged. In an article from 2020, Butler stated that those who believe sex is biological represent a "fringe movement that is seeking to speak in the name of the mainstream, and that our responsibility is to refuse to let that happen."[20] In a 2021 interview, Butler attacked those who "insist that sex is biological and real" and charged that they seek "to censor gender studies programs."[21]

Butler's assertions that those who think sex is biological should be refused the opportunity to speak "in the name of the mainstream" and are seeking to "censor gender studies programs" illustrate concerns that there is a lack of diversity of thought within these programs, including on the foundational issue of the definition of the terms "gender" and "sex" and whether they could be related to biology. Those within the feminist movement who reject the "concept of gender identity (the feeling of being male or female)" as a substitute for biological sex—often labeled "gender-critical"—can be effectively shunned.[22] A *Vox* writer stated proudly in an article in 2019 that gender-critical feminism is frowned on in the U.S.: "Though [gender-critical feminism] got its start in the US in the '70s, the ideology has largely fallen out of favor as the country's mainstream feminist movement."[23]

Those who attempt to challenge this opinion are often openly denigrated in gender studies programs as well as elsewhere in academia. According to an article in William & Mary's *Journal of Race, Gender, & Social Justice* in May 2023, "[w]hile much of contemporary feminist thought has moved past biological essentialism's outdated embrace of a sex binary to embrace trans-equality, a relatively small but vocal group of self-proclaimed 'gender-critical feminists'...eschew transgender legal rights that they perceive as potentially threatening to the rights of cisgender women."[24] The author warns against such dissenting voices. "Most gender-critical arguments in that regard are fallacious; they are based on myths and false narratives that misconstrue or ignore empirical data from both the natural and social sciences. Worse yet, the gender-critical position not only threatens to undermine equality under law, but also fosters narratives that contribute to the criminal victimization of transgender persons." Basically, those who disagree with the accepted beliefs about "sex" and "gender" in gender studies not only believe "myths and false narratives" but are promoting "criminal victimization" of others.

These new definitions as propounded by Butler and others would typically have followed the course that new ideas traveled in the academy—generating debate amongst scholars in the ivory tower before perhaps eventually moving into larger society. However, like CRT through DEI offices, these definitions of sex and gender, along with other attending ideas, were one reason such ideas were able to escape from this time-intensive and analytical process. The vehicle of gender studies programs in part allowed such ideas to often bypass the normal academic pathways of scholarly discourse. These departments, which generally over time began to eschew debates as to these radical new definitions of "sex" and "gender", formed relationships with other departments through their "interdisciplinary" nature.

Gender studies often became the mothership for discussion on gender and sex for other departments touching on such issues—and DEI programs sometimes began to act as protectors. This could result in a chilling of speech. There was generally little effective pushback when such situations appeared to arise. Academics who felt speech, data, and research were being suppressed sometimes told their stories—but could face negative backlash. Those concerned about the suppression of speech in and around the definitions of gender and sex in the academy aired their concern at conferences, on blogs, in the conservative press, though many themselves personally identified as liberal. However, as to the mainstream media, they were often talking to an empty room.

• • •

In July 2021, Dr. Carole Hooven, the co-director of Harvard's undergraduate program's Department of Human Evolutional Biology, went on Fox News to discuss the suppression of science at medical schools, including in particular using terms such as "male and female". According to Hooven, "[t]he ideology seems to be that biology really isn't as important as how somebody feels about themselves or feels their sex to be." This is simply untrue, Hooven stated. "[I]n fact….there are male and female—and those sexes are designated by the kind of gametes we produce." The reaction from the DEI office was swift.

> In response, the director of my department's Diversity, Inclusion and Belonging task force (a graduate student) accused me on Twitter of transphobia and harming undergraduates, and I responded. The tweets went viral, receiving international news coverage. The public attack by the task force director runs contrary to Harvard's stated academic freedom principles, yet no disciplinary action was taken, nor did any university administrators publicly support my right to express my views in an environment free of harassment…[C]lear talk about the science of sex and gender is increasingly met with hostility on college campuses… [and] administrators are largely failing in their responsibilities to protect scholars and their rights to express their views.[25]

Hooven was shocked by the reaction and lack of support from Harvard. "This was 2021, and I didn't know everything I know now. I had expected that they would (support me), but nobody knew what to do." The facts appeared not to matter, she noted. "There was no evidence provided, and I looked for it… but that was the narrative, that's all you need is just the appearance of something, a narrative."[26]

As a result of the "lack of support from Harvard for the right to express my scientific views in an environment free from harassment," she stepped back from her role.[27] This was mainly covered by Fox News and *The New York Post*, with barely a mention outside of these more conservative outlets.

In his blog in November 2022, Jerry A. Coyne, an Emeritus Professor in the Department of Ecology and Evolution at the University of Chicago wrote in support of Hooven.

> *[W]hat Hooven said is absolutely true: there are just two biological sexes, defined by whether their bodies are set up to produce large, immobile gametes ("females") or small mobile gametes ("males"). There are no intermediate gametes, and thus no third sex. This is not a matter of controversy among sensible biologists…This is the way ideal-ogues chill speech and impede biological research. If the facts don't fit the progressive Left political program, then you just reinterpret (and mischar-acterize) the facts.* [28]

How has the conception of sex as often propounded by fairly new gender studies programs reached into other departments? Less than three weeks after the August board meeting at New College, *Times Higher Education*, a U.K. news outlet, published an interview with Dr. Laura Favaro, a sociology professor in England, who had researched the pushback gender-critical feminists receive. Her research focused for the most part on "academics across many disciplines" who identified as "gender studies academics."[29] This is similar to New College, where the head of the gender studies program was a professor of French. Many gender studies academics are often in other disciplines and only affiliate tangentially with the gender studies programs.

Favaro had interviewed fifty gender studies academics about "whether the warnings about entering [the] domain [of gender studies] were justified, or, as others suggest, spurious claims made by those keen to spark a phony 'culture war.'" Her research revealed the warnings were valid.

> *[I interviewed] gender studies academics across many disciplines, including sociology, psychology, and education, most of whom worked at English universities, to learn about their views and experiences of the dispute. Having approached the topic with an open mind, however, my discussions left me in no doubt that a culture of discrimination, silencing and fear has taken hold across universities in England, and many countries beyond.*

Dr. Favaro discovered that within these programs discussing biological gender differences—which one would assume occurred within the field of "gender studies" given its title—was frowned upon. Instead, the focus was on "genderism," which she defined in the following manner:

> [G]enderism *coheres around the push for gender (identity) to replace sex in most—if not all—contexts. Unlike feminism, its political subject is not female people but rather all those subjected to gender oppression—a concept that is redefined to emphasize lack of choice and affirmation relating to gender identity.*[30]

"Trans-inclusive feminists" hold near-total control in academia, "deciding what was discussed in departments or included in scholarly journals." While occasionally gender-critical feminists in the UK attempted to force their way into the conversation, they were typically persecuted and demeaned for trying to participate. Favaro reported that fourteen of the fifty interviewees described themselves as "gender-critical" feminists, and they reported "fac[ing] negative repercussions for years for expressing their view."[31]

This attempt to silence any respectful discussion on ideas aside from the status quo in the UK—which at least has one small contingent fighting for even a single different viewpoint to be included—was echoed in an article written by two professors in 2021. Judith Suissa and Alice Sullivan wrote an article for the *Journal of Philosophy of Education*. Like Favaro, they were academics in the UK—a sociologist and a philosopher—who had personally found that there was a high price to pay for those who did not strictly follow the orthodoxy of gender ideology.

Suissa and Sullivan described themselves as "fully [in] support" of trans rights; however, they wrote about being shunned by many of their fellow academics because they wrote three articles on how "fellow academics—overwhelmingly women—were being harassed, bullied, verbally abused and threatened for voicing a particular view on sex and gender." As a result, "we have had colleagues refuse to work with us, had complaints about our views directed at our managers, have been subject to calls for students to avoid our classes and have had to report violent threats to the police." One had a flyer with her picture, denouncing her as a "fascist," put up in the building where she worked. The other was not allowed to present at a seminar because she supported "accurate sex-based data collection."

> For gender identity campaigners, simply asserting that sex exists as a meaningful category, distinct from people's self-declared 'gender identity', is deemed transphobic...[P]eople's 'gender identity' trump claims about their biological sex. Gender identity ideology is in this sense, absolutist, demanding that we ignore material evidence of the relevance of sex in any context.... [S]cepticism regarding scientific discoveries and the truth of empirical facts is combined with profound moral certainty. Such demands are fundamentally antithetical to academic freedom.

One of the main attacks the trans-inclusive feminists aim at Suissa, Sullivan, Favaro, and others who speak out about the lack of discourse around the gender-critical viewpoint is that people on the right also think free speech should occur on college campuses. Therefore, gender-critical feminists asking for another viewpoint to be heard are denigrated within the Left—even though many identify with this group on a variety of other issues—because they agree with people on the right who want to allow different viewpoints to be expressed on campuses.

The fact that people from opposite sides of the political spectrum agree on this issue—that it is worth talking about that gender could be linked to biology—is not a negative. That those who disagree on other topics find this one subject straightforward is an argument in its favor. The public should be informed of the crux of the concern—that more than one viewpoint about how "gender" is defined should be included in the study of gender.

The point that Rufo and others made at the New College board meeting in August 2023 was that the discipline of gender studies was ideologically captured in the US. There was an elephant in the room, and that was that critical discussion within "gender studies" as to the definition of gender had in many ways been effectively silenced.

On August 10th, the New College board said nothing that was shocking or unknown to anyone around the gender studies field in the United States. The problem was: they said it out loud where the public might hear it.

Then the New College board did the unthinkable. They did not just debate it. They acted.

• • •

The timing of the New College debate and vote on gender studies came at an interesting moment. This was because on August 3, 2023, seven days before the New College board meeting about abolishing the gender studies program, the American

Academy of Pediatrics had announced that it was going to do a "systematic review of the evidence" behind "gender-affirming" care. In many ways, gender-affirming care operates under similar assumptions held by those who often control gender studies programs—that gender is linked to identity.[32]

Prior to this, the Biden administration had been implementing policies supporting gender-affirming care, a practice which had relatively little research behind it. The gender-affirming approach gained popularity in the United States in the late 2000s when it was introduced by clinicians.[33] The basic philosophy, according to an article in the *New York Times*, was that "minors should be able to live out their gender identities freely, without clinicians or parents imposing unnecessary delays. Their path might involve medications and surgeries, or no medical treatments at all."[34] In this same article, published in 2021, even the *New York Times* reporter noted the lack of data supporting gender-affirming care. "Few studies have followed adolescents receiving puberty blockers or hormones into adulthood," the reporter wrote,[35] though it was known that "some of the drug regimens bring long-term risks, such as fertility loss."[36] The article also noted that "puberty blockers, for example, can impede bone development."[37]

In a Reuters article in October 2022, the reporter noted that "families that go the medical route [with gender-affirming care] venture onto uncertain ground, where science has yet to catch up with practice."[38] In June 2023, *Psychiatric Times*, a US-based publication, published an article by a doctor stating that the evidence around gender-affirming care was "where one might expect [evidence to be] for a field relatively early in its development: evolving."[39]

The lack of research did not seem to concern the Biden administration.

On June 15, 2022, Biden ordered his health agency to "expand access to gender-affirming treatment."[40] It followed Gov. DeSantis's moving to abolish gender-affirming care for minors.[41] The lack of evidence about the efficacy of these practices did not stop Biden's assistant secretary for health in the Department of Health and Human Services, Rachel Levine, from making unfounded assertions such as "there is no argument among medical professionals...about the value and the importance of gender-affirming care."[42] No matter how many times Levine, a transgender woman, made comments such as "[g]ender-affirming care for transgender youth is essential and can be life-saving," it was simply largely unproven by research. (This was in spite of the fact that some research had shown that, without medical interventions, gender dysphoria in children resolves itself during or after puberty in about 80 percent of the cases.[43])

The general silence in gender studies programs as to the gender-critical position paralleled in some ways with the proliferation of gender-affirming medical treatment, with little apparent concern about the amount of supporting research. While the Biden administration's support of medical gender-affirming care seemed questionable given the "evolving" state of the research, it did fall in well with the so-called social justice ideals of the trans-inclusive feminists—the same trans-inclusive feminists who had run amok in academia, often shutting down debate effectively in that arena.

Then came August 3, 2023, when the American Academy of Pediatrics released a report announcing that it had commissioned a systematic review of gender-based medical research on gender-based treatments.[44] The US press generally failed to highlight the importance and significance of *why* they were then asking for the "systematic review." According to the *New York Times*, the review was generally because of "efforts in Europe that found uncertain evidence for their effectiveness in adolescents."

In reality, the reasoning behind the systematic review that became public on August 3rd was actually much more serious than the wording of the AAP announcement—and much of the press's reporting of it—implied. In 2023, the lack of scientific data relating to gender-affirming care in adolescents was becoming evident as a result of the recent release of research in Europe.[45]

In April 2023, *Current Sexual Health Reports* wrote a report entitled "Current Concerns about Gender-Affirming Therapy in Adolescents."[46] It encompassed "[s]ystematic reviews of evidence conducted by public health authorities in Finland, Sweden, and England." The paper asked the question, "Do the benefits of youth gender transitions outweigh the risks of harm?" It concluded that the systematic reviews "failed to show credible improvements in mental health and suggested a pattern of treatment-associated harms." In addition, it mentioned three recent papers that had examined studies that "underpin the practice of youth gender transition and found the research to be deeply flawed." Therefore, it stated the following:

> *Evidence does not support the notion that "affirmative care" of today's adolescents is net beneficial. Questions about how to best care for the rapidly growing numbers of gender-dysphoric youth generated an intensity of divisiveness within and outside of medicine rarely seen with other clinical uncertainties.*

The review of the studies was clear, and the article in the journal bluntly stated: "Because the well-being of young patients and their families is at stake, the *field must stop relying on social justice arguments and return to the time-honored principles of evidence-based medicine.*" (Italics added.)

If this was not devastating enough given the EOs that the Biden administration had put into place months ago, the report then noted that the US was behind the curve on all of this because the "[d]ebate about the efficacy of 'gender-affirming care' in the USA is only recently emerging." Yet the Biden administration had supported through its policies a large system that benefited economically from these treatments.

It was seven days after this that the New College board met on August 10th to discuss abolishing the gender studies program. Inevitably, the board touched on the silence implicit in gender studies programs. It was possible to draw a nexus to what was occurring in the medical world with gender-affirming care and the often effective muzzling in the gender studies world around any topic that questioned whether gender and sex might be impacted by biology.

Since then, even more research has come out which highlights the importance of discussing these issues in academia. In April 2024, a report entitled "Independent Review of Gender Identity Services for Children and Young People" was published. It had been commissioned by the NHS England in 2020 to make recommendations about these services. In the 398-page report, Dr. Hilary Cass wrote that "[t]his is an area of remarkably weak evidence...The reality is that we have no good evidence on the long-term outcomes of interventions to manage gender -related distress." This included research as to puberty blockers as well as social transitioning, in which individuals make only social changes such as changes to their name, pronouns, hair, etc. The report finds that "[g]iven the weakness of the research in this area there remain many unknowns about the impact of social transition…In particular, it is unclear whether it alters the trajectory of gender development, and what short- and longer-term impact this may have on mental health." Like the previous studies reported on in 2023 in Europe, the Cass Report noted that in the medical community the toxicity of the discussion has been an issue in doctors expressing their opinions. "There are few other areas of healthcare where professionals are so afraid to openly discuss their views, where people are vilified on social media and where name-calling echoes the worst bullying behavior. This must stop."

Free speech within academia is not an esoteric question confined to the removed ivory tower of universities. These theoretical debates can eventually affect science, medicine, psychology, and many other fields. Yet open dialogue has been in many ways effectively stifled in gender studies, for similar reasons as to why gender-affirming care has been elevated despite the scarcity of research. In both instances, so-called "social justice" reasoning can be argued to have prevailed over society's interest in vigorous intellectual critiques.

I learned this in the K–12 arena when I was education commissioner in Florida. In academia, there is a saying that the fights are so fierce because the stakes are so low. However, this argument was different. It had high stakes, bursting right into the lives of two Floridian families whose lives were about to be turned upside down.

• • •

I was state commissioner of education when, on March 28, 2022, Gov. DeSantis signed into law the Parental Rights in Education Act, a law that received the misnomer of "Don't Say Gay." While most people know that moniker because of the press's frequent use of it, what they do not know—because it was buried by the press—is that it was parents who led to its passage.

The experiences of these parents are important to hear because they powerfully illustrate the issues around gender-affirming care are not theoretical. On the day the bill was signed, the governor and I were at a school in Pasco County. I also cannot stress this enough: this bill only applied to *curricula* in *kindergarten through 3rd grade*.

DeSantis had props of the types of curricula that had been allowed in K–3rd grade in public schools prior to this bill being signed. There was "the Genderbread person," which looked like the iconic character, except he was no longer a "man." Then there was a picture of a young child sitting on a field of green grass under a blue sky. Its text read, "When I was born, mom and dad said, 'It's a girl!' When I looked in the mirror, I saw a girl. Kind of. But because I'm transgendered, I wanted to be a boy."

On the stage with us was January Littlejohn. Before signing the bill into law, DeSantis paused and motioned toward January.

"I want to thank January for being here today," he said. "When you listen to January tell her story about what they did with her child, without her knowledge or consent, I don't think there's very many parents in the state of Florida that think that's okay. I can tell you I don't think that's okay."

January then walked to the podium and told her story.

• • •

On March 13, 2020, January Littlejohn's daughter came home from Deerlake Middle School in Tallahassee excited to begin her spring break. January and her husband, Jeffrey, were planning to take their daughter on a weeklong vacation. They had rented a condo in Seaside, the pastel-colored town that offered the idyllic scenes for the 1998 film *The Truman Show*, with sweeping views of Florida's iconic beaches on the Gulf of Mexico.

The Littlejohns left for the white-sand beach the next day. They enjoyed the two-hour drive from Tallahassee that concludes on Walton County's famous highway, 30A, which hugs the Panhandle. They basked in the sun and rented bicycles and rode along the coast.

It was a wonderful time in a beautiful place.

"I remember it fondly," January told me, "because it was the last normal thing about my life."

Three days later, the Littlejohns were told, like everyone else in the state of Florida, that schools would be closed for two weeks due to an extraordinary event: a global pandemic.

Schools went online and remote, and education became a virtual experience, as did socializing. The way that American children interacted with each other changed literally overnight. While her grades remained the same, screen time for the Littlejohn's daughter shot way up, and what were once lunchroom giggles became internet slang and group text emojis.

Two months later, the daughter informed her mother that she was experiencing some identity issues and now identified as transgender.

January is a mental health counselor with her own private practice, but she took the news more like a mother. Despite

STORMING THE IVORY TOWER

a combination of hurt, confusion, sadness, and dismay, she walked up to her daughter and gave her a big hug.

"I love you," she said. "And I will always love all that you are, whatever that may be. And I am always your mother, no matter what. We will go through this together."

That night, after her daughter went to bed, January went to work. She began researching everything she could about gender transitioning. Before long, she discovered a stunning new trend of teenage girls across America declaring themselves "trans."

She came across the work of Dr. Lisa Littman, a professor of behavioral and social sciences at Brown University who had extensively researched what she termed "rapid-onset gender dysphoria," which seemed to occur predominantly, if not almost exclusively, in adolescent girls. Littman first became interested in the topic when she noticed that several teenage girls in the same friend group in her small Rhode Island town all started identifying as trans within a short timeframe. As January read Littman's findings, pieces started to click, and the similarities in her own daughter's life jumped off the screen of her laptop.

Littman, who describes herself as "liberal" and "pro-LGBT," surveyed parents whose children suddenly began self-identifying as a different gender. She found several common factors, especially among girls: a significant increase in the use of social media or group texting, having a friend or friends in the peer group who identified as trans, being previously bullied, and being on the autism spectrum.

January was aware that all those factors applied to her own daughter. The pandemic had meant her daughter was on her phone and computer a lot more. Several girls in her circle had recently decided they were trans. She also had been diagnosed with ADHD, was on the autism spectrum, and had experienced several traumatic bullying incidents.

The mental health expert in January couldn't help but think that her daughter was experiencing what Littman had described. So, while being a loving and supportive mother, January had her daughter start seeing a counselor to talk through what she was feeling.

Over the summer of 2020, as waves of COVID cases came and went, the Littlejohns worked to make sure their daughter was as mentally and emotionally supported and healthy as possible. The counselor they had chosen took a faith-based, rational approach, and remained in constant contact with them.

• • •

By August, thanks to our efforts to get schools reopened, January's daughter was able to return to school. Her counseling though was ongoing. The daughter still identified as trans, and now preferred to use a different name. As the situation was already challenging, January decided to reach out to the teachers and staff of Deerlake Middle School—presumably allies to parents—to let them know about the situation.

"This has been an incredibly difficult situation for our family, and her father and I are trying to be as supportive as we can," January's email read. "She is currently identifying as non-binary. She would like to go by [a] new name…and prefers the pronouns they/them. We have not changed her name at home yet, but I told her if she wants to go by the [new] name with her teachers, I won't stop her."

January and Jeffrey did not like the idea of their daughter assuming a new identity, but they decided as a family to allow

STORMING THE IVORY TOWER

their child, still a middle schooler, to use different pronouns and go by a different name at school. What they did not know was that new names and pronouns, seemingly innocent things for kids exploring the world around them, fed directly into robust school designs for fundamentally reengineering the relationship between children and parents.

Based on what school officials claimed was "official district policy," January's email prompted the school to reach out to the daughter to discuss—without parental knowledge or an attempt to get consent—a "Transgender/Gender Nonconforming Student Support Plan." Initiated by the school's designated "safe space coordinator," who is not a mental health professional but merely a teacher, the plan involved asking January's middle school-aged daughter questions about preferred names and pronouns without her parents being aware.

That was just the beginning.

• • •

Like other districts in the state, Leon County Schools was using a guide provided by the Florida School Superintendents Association, which, purportedly, derives its guidance from state supreme court rulings. In reality, the guide has been heavily shaped by the concerted lobbying of LGBTQ activist groups.

Previously, the guide instructed teachers and other school staff to treat students who began questioning their own sexuality or identity as sovereign, independent adults. That meant keeping parents in the dark, sometimes through deception, so they would not be aware that incredibly personal discussions were taking place with their own children. Being risk averse, the lawyers for the superintendents went along with it.

97

Nonetheless, avoiding lawsuits only put kids in danger.

Per Leon County's guide, the safe space coordinator asked the Littlejohns's daughter which bathroom she would prefer to use, boys or girls, and whether she would prefer to room with boys or girls on overnight school trips.

The daughter answered the questions and went back to her third-period math class.

That night, January asked her daughter, as she regularly did, "How was school?"

"It was okay," the daughter replied. "Actually, it was kind of funny. The school called me to a meeting and asked, since I changed my name, what bathroom I wanted to use."

The Littlejohns immediately called the school and demanded to speak with the principal.

"How in the hell are you meeting with my daughter and asking her what bathroom she can use without my presence?!" January demanded.

Deerlake's principal, Steve Mills, was sympathetic to the Littlejohns's concern, but he was also unapologetic.

"We followed district policy," Mills replied. "Because of that policy, I can't tell you anything else about the meeting. By law, your daughter has to be the one to request your presence at the meeting."

"That's insane!" January responded. "My daughter is twelve! She's not even supposed to watch a PG-13 movie! How in the world can you think you can let her make decisions about bathrooms or sleepovers without her parents?"

"I understand," Mills continued. "But your daughter, as young as she is, is protected under a non-discrimination law that does not include parental notification or input."

The Littlejohns pulled their daughter from the school right away. The following week, they filed a lawsuit in federal court against the Leon County School Board and its superintendent, seeking both an injunction against that horrific policy and civil damages for the tremendous toll it had taken.

As a result of the lawsuit, the Littlejohns obtained the paperwork that the school filled out about their daughter involving the Transgender/Gender Nonconforming Student Support Plan.

On page two, under the section "Parent/Guardian Involvement," there are two questions.

"Are guardians of this student supportive of their child's gender transition?"

There are boxes to check either "Yes" or "No." The school checked "No."

The second question: "If not, what considerations must be accounted for in implementing this plan?"

There, the school simply jotted down, "privacy when speaking to parents."

As the Littlejohns continued with their lawsuit, they discovered they were not the only family with a child to have a similar experience that was causing extensive—and potentially irreparable—harm. More and more schools throughout the state, with encouragement from LGBTQ organizations, were interpreting the law in exactly the way that Deerlake had, and they were in turn isolating children at their most vulnerable from their parents.

It is worth noting that Deerlake is located in northeast Tallahassee, the most culturally conservative area in an otherwise liberal municipality. These radical cultural agendas were being implemented in every corner of Florida.

• • •

At the other end of the Panhandle, Fleming Island sits on the western bank of the St. Johns River, with the sprawling city of Jacksonville just upstream. Originally developed as an auxiliary airfield for the US Navy during the Second World War, the community is now a quiet and peaceful suburb well known for its livability.

Its tranquility was shattered for Wendell and Maria Perez on January 5, 2022, by a call from Fleming Island Elementary School. They were told to come to the school immediately. Their twelve-year-old daughter had tried to hang herself from the bathroom stalls.

When Wendell and Maria arrived at the school, they were brought into the school counselor's office. Shocked and confused, but grateful that their daughter's condition was stable, the Perezes were told their child had attempted suicide because of an ongoing issue with her identity.[47]

"What do you mean, her 'identity'?" asked Wendell, himself an educator.

The school explained that their daughter had previously expressed gender-identity issues and had subsequently been meeting privately with school officials for several months. Totally unbeknownst to Wendell and Maria, the school's counselors had gone ahead and validated the "confusion" the daughter was experiencing.

In subsequent testimony, Wendell would tell state officials that "my daughter was living a double life with the school's support and without our knowledge."

Obviously, whatever "counseling" the school provided was ineffective, inadequate, or perhaps inappropriate, as evidenced by the daughter's attempt to take her own life in the bathroom of her elementary school.

Making matters worse, the Perezes were informed that it was their daughter's *second* effort to take her own life. As the school considered this incident more serious, the Baker Act was triggered. This meant that the daughter had to be hospitalized and, per guidance, kept away from Wendell and Maria *for nearly a week.*

Like the Littlejohns, the Perezes filed suit against their child's school district in federal court, alleging violations of their parental rights as guaranteed by both the Constitution of the State of Florida and the Constitution of the United States.

A local TV reporter doing a story about the suit reached out to Clay County School District for comment. As in Leon County, the district responded by touting LGBTQ support guides, which had been issued by gay rights advocacy groups, and it relied upon twisted interpretations of the law to justify meetings with students absent their parents.

The reporter also reached out to gay advocacy groups. A spokeswoman for Equality Florida, the state's leading LGBTQ lobby, conceded that the situation was tragic. However, she added that conversations like the one Fleming Island Elementary School had with the Perezes's daughter are important. "Even children," the spokesperson asserted, "deserve, on some issues, to be treated like adults."

A year after the Littlejohns's suit, the Perezes's finally spurred activity. A bill was filed in the Florida legislature, and the governor signed it, as Florida led the nation—and took the hits by the press—as it was the first to highlight and take decisive action upon this concerning issue.

• • •

Given the activism of Biden's executive orders related to gender, it should have been no surprise to anyone that the Biden administration jumped into the debate on this bill when it came before the Florida legislature. The Littlejohns and the Perezes—families trying to do the best for their children and living out their lives—found out the hard way what the Biden administration and many unelected activists had been quietly implementing through policy capture. The experiences of these families show how the lack of engaging in discourse within academia around the complexity of this new frontier of gender studies is the antithesis of how academia is supposed to work. When it breaks down, so do other important areas of society. The real concern is not just the suppression of free speech, but what happens in society when dialogue around important issues is summarily dismissed.

This may prove difficult as the transinclusive feminists have effectively shut down debate in many places in academia. In November 2023, as part of New College's newly established Socratic Stage series, we sent an email asking a well-known blogger who is supportive of the transinclusive perspective to participate in a forum discussing the issue of whether gender is a social construct. Far from shutting down speech, we were trying to bring different perspectives together to discuss issues.

This apparently was not acceptable.

When Erin Reed received the email, Reed tweeted it out to her over 200,000 followers on November 9, 2023.

I got a speaking engagement request for a debate from the New College of Florida, where DeSantis installed an anti-trans and anti-LGBTQ+ board, including Chris Rufo. No, I will not travel to speak at DeSantis (sic) own college in a place where I will be arrested using the bathroom.

She followed this up with the following.

Like everything about this says "This is a trap."

…It's so transparently a trap it's funny.

Rufo—whom she referenced—had been writing about the need to actively debate these issues, not ignore them. On his blog on April 26, 2023, he had stated that as to controversial issues surrounding the concept of gender that "We have to debate all of these questions." Reed had followed the message of the media, not the actual words of Rufo.

At New College, we are now opening up the ability to talk about these issues as a result of the elimination of DEI and gender studies. We are not concerned about people talking about Butler's ideas about gender or about the CRT concepts in Words that Wound. We advocate including others in dialogue about intellectual issues. We do not accept a one-sided dialogue in a public institution of higher learning.

The mainstream press and the radical liberal left had elevated the New College story originally for a reason. They chose to report it loudly because they believed it would fit their narrative. We were going to shut down free speech! We would not allow dialogue! Instead, we did the opposite.

• • •

On August 17th, seven days after the board's vote, Nicholas Clarkson, the college's only full-time gender studies professor, sent me a letter of resignation. Clarkson asserted in his resignation letter that "Gender Studies offers...practice tolerating the discomfort of the unfamiliar."[48]

In 2017, six years before Clarkson wrote the letter to me, he published an article in the journal *Feminist Teacher*, in which he wrote about his concern that, while gender studies classes can teach that "gender is socially constructed" more needs to be done.[49] "[T]rans material is often used to illustrate how gender is socially constructed," but this was not sufficient. "If no additional trans content is included throughout the semester, this approach reinforces the transphobic idea that trans people's gender identities are artificial and fake while cis identities are real and natural." According to Clarkson, this could lead to the serious problem that "cis students may leave the class thinking that their own gender identities and presentations are biologically-determined." He admitted that gender studies courses have been known to teach that gender is a social construct, but he worried that students needed even more content affirming this. He was concerned that without more content iterating this belief students might fall into the trap of thinking quietly in their own heads that "their own gender identities and presentation are biologically-determined."

Based on his own article, Clarkson himself, as well as much of the field of gender studies, does not tend to "tolerat[e] the discomfort of the unfamiliar." In fact, the discipline of gender studies as it exists today in the US often avoids any ideas that those in control might find uncomfortable.

Hooven pointed out the true cost of hiding from facts in the name of "social justice."

> While some activists insist that asserting the bio-
> logical reality of the sex "binary" is entirely wrong-
> headed and pernicious, the true threat to science,
> and to human dignity is the idea that in order
> to support anyone's rights we must deny or ignore
> reality. While some who are fighting for the rights
> of gender minorities may sincerely believe that sub-
> verting science is necessary to protect an oppressed
> population, department chairs and university
> presidents are tasked with ensuring that the cam-
> pus environment is one in which the fundamen-
> tal ideals of truth-seeking and academic freedom
> are not only defended, but actively promoted. It
> should not be too much to ask that they firmly
> hold the line between ignorance and knowledge,
> between subjective and objective, between our feel-
> ings and the facts.

Likewise, as gender-critical academics in the UK, Suissa and Sullivan expressed their surprise at how easily trans-inclusive proponents—like Clarkson appears to be—assume that the question of "what a woman is" has been decided. Their response drips with British sarcasm.

> The claim that the question of "what a woman
> is" has been settled in favor of the view that wom-
> anhood is determined by identity rather than
> sex is surprising.... If some scholar has made the

argument that "the woman question" was at some point open to discussion, but is now settled, we would be interested to see their case (while regretful that we missed the window for debate). Such a claim implies that a scientific revolution has occurred, over-turning millennia of evolutionary data and a wealth of empirical evidence for the physical and social relevance of biological sex.[50]

They then state that the conversation around gender should be front-and-center in the discussion as to the limits of free speech in higher education. This is because it is so simple. It should not be radical to discuss in an academic setting that gender could be linked to biology. Therefore, it is a powerful example of how serious the suppression of speech is on college campuses.

[We have] focused on the threat to academic freedom in the case of sex and gender, not because it is a hard case, but because it is an easy one, with implications across the disciplines.

If we cannot defend academic freedom in such a case, we cannot defend it at all.[51]

CHAPTER 4

Higher Ed's Response to Hamas Attack: The COVID Moment for Higher Education

One of the peculiar phenomena of our time is the renegade liberal…[T]here is now a widespread tendency to argue that one can defend democracy only by totalitarian methods. If one loves democracy, the argument runs, one must crush its enemies by no matter what means. And who are its enemies? It always appears that [it includes] those who "objectively" endanger it by spreading mistaken doctrines. In other words, defending democracy involves destroying all independence of thought.
—*George Orwell, Introduction to* Animal Farm[1]

At the February 28th New College board meeting, the board voted to abolish the office that implemented its DEI policies.

Forty-nine public speakers addressed the board during the public comment section at the beginning of the meeting, with many drawing a nexus between the New College board and Nazis. According to the speakers, the upcoming vote about eliminating the DEI office was a primary example of how the board was acting in a manner consistent with the Nazism of Hitler's Germany. Hitler was named several times specifically, and the Holocaust was also referenced when a student read the poem "First They Came" about how people looked the other way when the Nazis first began to target Jews.

The last speaker during the public comment section of the meeting introduced himself as a current student at New College who was majoring in economics and finance.

> *Board members, Mr. Corcoran...Folks, I am so far from woke. My grandparents on my dad's side are Holocaust survivors, and my grandfather on my mom's side was born in pre-state Israel and was a tank commander in the Israeli army where he fought for the survival of a Jewish state to fight to have a place where I'd be safe from persecution and if people ever saw Jews as less than human again. Today I fear that other groups of people are being seen as less than human. Today I fear that we may eliminate the office that ensures that the composition of our classrooms resemble that of our great nation. I fear that [this] office that ensures people like me a regular...person gets and thus see the humanity of those different from myself is going to be abolished.*

He then quoted from studies about how it is easier to assume negative characteristics about groups of people if one does not know anyone from that background, concluding as follows:

*Study after study shows that people who know Jews
are less likely to see Jews as less than human. Study
after study shows that people who get to know
other groups of people that are not in the majority
are less likely to see them as less than human. Our
Office of Outreach and Inclusive Excellence is at
its core an office that protects the sanctity of life.*

● ● ●

This student seemed to be unaware that these DEI offices nationwide had become a hotbed of anti-Semitism.

In 2021, researchers at the conservative Heritage Foundation were concerned about reports of anti-Semitism among DEI staff. They decided to put these rumors to an objective test. Focusing their research on large public universities—where they found that the average institution in this cohort had forty-five people working to promote DEI[2]—they looked at 933 DEI staff at sixty-five "Power Five" universities. Using Google searches, they found 741 Twitter accounts that were not protected and, thus, could be searched for specific content. Most of these accounts were personal.

Researchers then searched these Twitter feeds for tweets, retweets, or likes about Israel, and used China as a comparison. They found that these DEI staff "tweeted, retweeted, or liked almost three times as many tweets about Israel as tweets about China."

*Of the tweets about Israel, 96 percent were critical
of the Jewish state, while 62 percent of the tweets
about China were favorable. There were more*

> tweets narrowly referencing "apartheid" in Israel
> than tweets indicating anything favorable about
> Israel whatsoever. The overwhelming pattern is
> that DEI staff at universities pay a disproportion-
> ately high amount of attention to Israel and nearly
> always attack Israel.[3]

DEI staff, whose ostensible job is to promote inclusion, were extremely concerned about a minority group who has experienced extreme persecution and bigotry in the recent past. However, DEI staff were relatively unconcerned about a totalitarian government that was brutally repressing its people. As the authors note, "One who is genuinely interested in human rights around the world had many more reasons to be paying attention to China than to Israel."

> DEI staff have a disproportionate interest in Israel
> relative to China and are far more likely to be
> critical of Israel than they are of China. In to-
> tal, there were 633 tweets regarding Israel com-
> pared to 216 regarding China—three times as
> many—despite the fact that China is 155 times
> as populous as Israel and has 467 times the land
> mass. China has also had many reasons to be in
> the news recently, including being the origin of
> the pandemic, conducting a brutal crackdown
> on pro-democracy forces in Hong Kong, mass im-
> prisonment and mistreatment of China's Muslim
> Uyghur population, increasing confrontation with
> Taiwan and other countries in the Pacific Rim,
> and severe internal repression of political dissent
> and private corporations.

•   •   •

The sudden and brutal attack by Hamas terrorists on October 7, 2023, during a peaceful music festival in Israel "will go down as one of the worst terrorist attacks in history."[4] Some 1,200 people were murdered, including babies and young children, and more than two hundred were taken hostage.[5]

Immediately afterward, Mauricio Karchmer, a computer science professor at MIT, emailed the head of his department, asking her to "issue a statement in support of Israelis and Jews." He did not think this was unusual, as the "university had sent statements before on various issues—such as a message condemning the murder of George Floyd in 2020 and another standing in solidarity with the Asian community amid a wave of hate crimes in 2021."

Instead, the head of the department sent out a message "riddled with equivocations, without mentioning the barbarity of Hamas's attack, stating only that 'we are deeply horrified by the violence against civilians and wish to express our deep concern for all those involved.'" Karchmer was "shocked that my institution—led by people who are meant to see the world rationally—could not simply condemn a brutal terrorist act."

Karchmer was shocked; however, for Karchmer, like the rest of the nation, the shock was only just beginning. Protests broke out on his campus with students chanting, "Free Palestine," and, "From the river to the sea," delivered by these young people "with fury and at times glee, like they were reciting catchy songs instead of slogans demanding the erasure of the Jewish people."

Much worse, though, was when faculty members joined in, including one DEI officer who liked an October 17th Twitter post that stated, "Israel doesn't have a right to exist, it's an illegitimate settler-colony like the US."

When this same DEI officer tweeted that next day that her department was seeking a "diverse pool of candidates" for a teaching position in her department's "inclusive community," Karchmer understood now, like he had not before, "that Jewish academics need not apply."

The last straw for Karchmer was when the faculty newsletter the following month was "almost entirely dedicated to the protests, with several professors parroting anti-Israel propaganda." In the newsletter was an editorial called "Standing Together Against Hate: From the River to the Sea, From Gaza to MIT," in which linguistics professor Michel DeGraff wrote that the protesters calling for intifada "have given me hope for the future."[6] Karchmer noted that, eerily, the "only voices in the newsletter standing up for the Jews were Jewish. But we are too few to fight this battle."

Karchmer's private concerns became concerns of the general public on the day when Sally Kornbluth, the president of MIT, the university he had taught at for years, testified before Congress, along with Harvard president Claudine Gay and the president of the University of Pennsylvania. While Karchmer did not agree with their statements, he saw the problem in a broader context. "I think the problem at MIT—and across American academia—runs much deeper than the figureheads."

> *Students at MIT and other elite colleges have been radicalized by faculty members who have encouraged and even led the student body to become social justice warriors, supporting their highly progressive*

political beliefs. America's brightest minds are being manipulated by a force they don't even understand to adopt a narrow view of the world. That this is happening at a place where they're meant to be exploring a wealth of ideas and have their thinking challenged shocks me. This thinking has led to an illiberalism on MIT's campus.

Karchmer had taught at MIT for years and was only now just realizing this. It had happened so quietly, with professors of one persuasion participating in groupthink and then hiring over and over again like-minded individuals until these ideas proliferated. Then these ideas became quietly institutionalized through DEI bureaucracies. However, with the response of academia to the repulsive acts of Hamas on October 7th, the world was waking up to the fact of the Frankenstein that had been created in higher education.

The response to October 7th was an earthquake to people busy with their lives to gasp and look over at what was happening in higher education, a supposed environment committed to free thought. It was analogous to what had happened with COVID three years earlier in K–12 education. Progressives had taken charge of not just K–12 education but higher education as well and had been happily driving the train right off a cliff. However, America had just woken up. The question was: What could they do about it?

• • •

On February 27, 2023, in a question and answer with a reporter from the local paper, I had addressed this very issue. The reporter had asked if I was in support of the board's effort to end New College's DEI program "and any diversity, equity and inclusion programs." I said yes and then explained why.

> *The nomenclature is wrong. No one is against the actual definitions of what the words mean in and of themselves. However, in actual practice, the result is often the opposite of the words' literal definitions. The current use of DEI programs has propagated homogenous opinions, inequality, and exclusion of all but pre-approved ideas. Students and parents don't sign up for college to have an agenda foisted on them. They want an education that equips people to be critical thinkers.*

There was no follow-up to this by any reporter. This was typical of what was at worst the complicity of the press and at best laziness.

In January and February of 2023, those fighting the New College changes obtained a lot of milage out of calling the board, the governor, and me "Nazis" because of the efforts to shut the DEI office. This was easy in January and February of 2023. Who was going to question it? The media?

It became more difficult after October 7th. The public outcry against the behavior in academia in response to the Hamas attacks grew too loud to be ignored. One prominent example was Bill Ackman. He wrote three letters posted on Twitter on November 4th, December 4th, and January 3rd, excoriating the DEI bureaucracy that he discovered had run amok at his alma mater Harvard, a school to which he had donated millions. The press could snicker with superiority at DeSantis, Rufo, and me when we charged that DEI was an ideological tool because we were conservative Republicans. However, Bill Ackman was a supporter of the Democratic Party who had donated to Barack Obama, Bill Clinton, and Beto O'Rourke, among others.[7] It was becoming harder and harder to find reasons to summarily dismiss the innate problems with DEI and the total control of radical liberals at the top tiers of higher education.

Then, on December 11, 2023, Steven Pinker, a psychology professor at Harvard and a self-described "liberal Democrat,"[8] wrote a piece in the *Boston Globe* that went viral entitled "A Five-Point Plan to Save Harvard from Itself." Number five was "Disempowering DEI."

According to Pinker, getting rid of DEI was key to ensuring free speech was protected in higher education. "Many of the assaults on academic freedom (not to mention common sense) come from a burgeoning bureaucracy that calls itself diversity, equity, and inclusion while enforcing a uniformity of opinion, a hierarchy of victim groups, and the exclusion of free thinkers." Pinker was clear that "these officers stealthily implement policies that were never approved in faculty deliberations or by university leaders willing to take responsibility for them. Universities should stanch the flood of DEI officials, expose their policies to the light of day and repeal the ones that cannot be publicly justified."

However, Pinker had been saying such things for awhile. It was just that no one had wanted to listen. In fact, on September 9, 2023, Pinker tweeted out that "DEI Statements are one of the rituals turning academia into a national laughingstock. They are compelled speech, and either weed out independent thinkers or force them to be liars."[9]

Pinker was one of a small group of academics who had been attempting to alert the public to the increasingly repressive atmosphere within academia, including DEI bureaucracies, for years. The legacy media often acted as if the academics did not exist—as evidenced by the fact that when the debate was occurring at New College, no one would have known from the press coverage that academics like Pinker—not conservatives personally—or others like him such as Lawrence Krauss, largely agreed with the assessment of DEI programs put forth by the board.

Krauss, a theoretical physicist, stated that politics should be more scientific and "[s]cientific data is not Democrat or Republican."[10] On October 20, 2021, he wrote an article in the *Wall Street Journal*—one of the only outlets brave enough to publish such views prior to October 2023—entitled "How Diversity Turned Tyrannical." According to Krauss, DEI offices had been "grow[ing] unchecked" for years.

> *[DEI offices] became huge and expensive offices not subject to faculty oversight and now work to impose "equity" not only by discriminating in favor of female and minority candidates but by demanding and enforcing ideological commitments from new faculty…. This isn't merely pro forma; it's a real barrier to employment. The life-sciences department at the University of California, Berkeley reports that it rejected 76% of applicants in 2018–19 based on their diversity statements without looking at their research records.*

This not only affected hiring but also free speech.

*All this creates a climate of pervasive fear on cam-
pus and shuts down what should be an important
academic discussion. After I wrote an article…
about the intrusion of ideology into science, I
heard from faculty around the country who wrote
under pseudonyms that they were afraid of being
marginalized, disciplined or fired if administrators discovered their emails.*

Beyond the harm to faculty who were often afraid to voice
their intellectual thoughts, he wrote about its effects on students as well.

*Beyond these fearful faculty members, are tal-
ented would-be scientists who will be dissuaded
or excluded from academic research. DEI offices
are working to indoctrinate incoming students.
This year at Princeton, the New York Post reports,
freshmen were required to watch a video promoting "social justice" and describing dissenting debate as "masculine-ized bravado." If such efforts
succeed, a new generation of students won't have
the opportunity to subject their own viewpoints
to challenge—surely one of the benefits of higher
education.*

Krauss believed DEI statements were worse than the loyalty
oaths of the 1950s. While "critics have likened DEI statements
to the loyalty oaths of the Red Scare [in which the] University
of California fired 31 faculty members for refusing to sign a
statement disavowing any party advocating the overthrow of the

U.S. government," this was worse because in that case the statements only "violated their freedom of speech and conscience…a loyalty oath compels assent to authority, a DEI statement demands active ideological engagement. It's less like the excesses of anticommunism than like communism itself."

It was real life imitating fiction.

When *Animal Farm* was first published in 1945, author George Orwell wrote an introduction. This introduction was not published at the time. In fact, it was not until October 1972 that *The New York Times* ran the first known publication of it. Since then, it has rarely appeared in print, including in editions of the book itself, though publishers occasionally insert other introductions by modern academics.

The reason for this effective cancellation of Orwell's introduction likely lies in its topic: why he had difficulty finding a publisher for the book. He lay the blame at the feet of the "literary and scientific intelligentsia, the very people who ought to be the guardians of liberty, who are beginning to despise it, in theory as well as in practice."

Animal Farm was a satire of the Russian Revolution in 1917 and the events that followed. At the time of the book's publication, according to Orwell, the "current orthodoxy" was "[u]ncritical loyalty to the U.S.S.R.," including Stalin, such that "where the supposed interests of the U.S.S.R. are involved" the intelligentsia, including the press, were "willing to tolerate not only censorship but the deliberate falsification of history."

Orwell thought the reasons given for suppression of ideas and facts were specious.

I know that the…intelligentsia have plenty of reason for their timidity and dishonesty; indeed, I know by heart the arguments by which they justify themselves. But at least let us have no more non-sense about defending liberty against fascism. If liberty means anything at all, it means the right to tell people what they do not want to hear. The common people still...subscribe to that doctrine and act on it. In our country...it is the liberals who fear liberty and the intellectuals who want to do dirt on the intellect: it is to draw attention to that fact I have written this preface.

•   •   •

Pinker and Krauss had been sounding a warning prior to the Hamas attacks, but they were generally kept on the sidelines, viewed as Cassandras who were peddling a ridiculous doom and gloom story. That had changed now though. The response by the administrators, faculty, and students at US colleges and universities to the events of October 7, 2023, resulted in a moment for the public that was similar to that of COVID in K–12 education. The testimony of the college presidents before Congress was a particular tipping point. As people listened—first in disbelief and then in consternation—to the words coming out of the mouths of these presidents, the public began to realize that the shouting down of speakers, the safe spaces, the lack of diversity of representation of ideological views among faculty were not aberrations. They were the norm, accepted and even in some cases perpetuated at the highest levels.

In fact, given the Biden executive orders, this was exactly what was supposed to be happening as DEI offices promulgated the definitions of CRT as to "equity" and "oppressed groups."

The point was to undermine the First Amendment and Equal Protection clauses, replacing them with "equity" and its mis-named siblings of "diversity" and "inclusion"—which should be named non-diversity and exclusion. If it seemed undemocratic, unconstitutional, that was because it was in part designed to be.

Ackman wrote that the "issues at Harvard are more expan-sive than antisemitism" but that the anti-Semitism exposed in academia after the Hamas attacks "is the canary in the coal mine." Immediately following Ackman's original letter on November 4th, I wrote an editorial for the *Wall Street Journal* entitled "New College Is a Haven for Harvard Refugees." In it, I referenced Ackman's letter.

> *[Ackman] urged the university to act swiftly, but I wouldn't hold my breath, and neither should its students. Instead, those facing intolerance or physical danger at Harvard should come to New College of Florida, where they can study with free tuition thanks to a newly established scholar-ship program.*

The reality is that Harvard is a private school. While Ackman and others can encourage it to follow time-established principles of higher education, while Congress can excoriate its leaders for terrible leadership, it will be difficult to achieve real change. Even if Ackman and a sizable number of donors with-draw their support, Harvard still has an endowment of over $49 billion.[11]

All is not lost though. Rufo's theory about public insti-tutions and their reliance on the people through the elected legislature proved correct with New College, which abolished the DEI office and the ideologically captured gender studies program in around six months. It will be a cold day in hell before that happens at Harvard no matter how many logical and eloquent letters Ackman and other well-meaning donors write. As I write this book, there is yet to be any institution, public or private, that has eliminated gender studies.

● ● ●

The Jewish student who addressed the New College board on February 28th appeared to believe that DEI offices existed to advocate for Jewish people among others. He was not alone. Prior to the Hamas attacks, Ackman and Karchmer apparently had the same understanding. Who could blame them, given that the Nazis had killed several million Jewish people in an attempted genocide several decades before? In terms of oppression, this would logically appear to qualify for inclusion as an oppressed group. They all soon learned though that the choice of who makes the cut to be "oppressed" under the definition of the DEI bureaucracies is controlled by unseen, unknown, unelected people who reside in large part in and around academia.

On February 28th, those strongly excoriating the New College board charged that some of the people in that room were on the side of the Nazis. They were right.

It just was not those seated at the board table.

CHAPTER 5

New College 2023: A Case Study

After several discouraging conferences, [Nikolai] Tesla had an inspiration.... He said to these men, "Do you know the story of the 'Egg of Columbus'[?]"....
[Columbus] asked some scoffers of his project to balance an egg on its end. They tried it in vain. He then took it and cracking the shell slightly by a gentle blow, made it stand upright...[and thereby] was granted an audience...by the Queen of Spain, and won her support.
—The Electrical Experimenter, *Vol. VI, No. 71, March 1919*

By February 2024, even the staunchest critics of the changes at New College of Florida were admitting that the transformation had worked. On February 1, 2024, Lauren Lassabe Shepherd, an academic who opposed the recent moves at the university,[1] drew a nexus between Harvard and New College. She seemed to believe that the changes at New College had been successful—but that there was little chance of achieving such outcomes at Harvard.

Harvard is an easy target for headlines, but when it comes to a practical application...it's the large state public universities that are most at risk. Those institutions that don't make headlines and can slowly be changed behind the scenes, and it's almost like no one notices.

In red states, legislators have direct control over public education budgets.

This is why New College in Florida was so easy to tear apart.[2]

New College was not "so easy to tear apart" because it was in a red state. New College was a public college in a red state where the governor was willing to take a bold and unprecedented move. DeSantis knew he would be attacked for choosing these particular board members. He selected them anyway.

Membership on a college board is usually a ceremonial role. Those awarded such positions are typically there for the perks, not to make difficult decisions. As a result, no board in the recent history of higher education has accomplished what the New College board did: require a state institution to focus on academic excellence, free from radical liberal projects that are merely attempts to social engineer an entire generation.

Even with the strong support of the governor and board members, it was not a simple proposition to turn New College around. The difficulties inherent in turning around a failing organization have been well documented. It is a complicated task. In addition, this transformation was accomplished under a glaring, hostile spotlight, with every decision, no matter how small, attacked by a press corps acting in essence as the public relations arm of the radical liberal elites in academia.

It required a large amount of mental gymnastics to paint as nefarious decisions such as moving students out of mold-infested dorms or starting sports. Yet the press stuck to a message that each move was sinister, preferably with storylines that the board and administration were racist, sexist, and/or anti-gay.

However, I was not worried because I had been here before. When I was education commissioner, Florida, under the leadership of Gov. DeSantis, was the first state in the nation to fully reopen schools to all students. At the time, the media framed this decision as foolish and potentially deadly, despite the data from other nations showing it was the logical move. Therefore, I already knew the end of the story in which one side of a debate—the one that is supported by the facts—is suppressed and denigrated by the press.

The truth will come out in the end.

• • •

A local reporter interviewed me during my first week as interim president. Here is how he described the scene on campus:

> *Women dressed in red gowns modeled after* The Handmaid's Tale *wander the campus of New College—a colorful statement as Richard Corcoran begins his first week as the New College President. It's one of many symbols of an atmosphere of protest that currently consumes the tiny Sarasota school. But the potential for demonstrations to shift from literary to violent in nature grips the administrator's attention. It's the last day of February and the first day Corcoran will*

offer a report in front of the New College Board of Trustees. He had planned to spend part of this morning in a magazine interview but has to delay the meeting. The announcement the prior evening of an "academic freedom" protest on campus forced Corcoran instead into a hastily scheduled meeting with security. It's the second time in as many days that Corcoran has postponed my interview with him. He originally scheduled the meeting for 24 hours prior but that was Corcoran's first day on campus, and it quickly became clear his daily schedule held no room for conversation. There's definite doubt whether today will prove much better.[3]

I and board members rode to that February board meeting in a golf cart, as police locked arms around us. Protestors yelled at us as we drove by, calling us "fascists" and throwing in curse words here and there. People in the crowd held up their middle fingers as we passed.

Prior to this February 28th board meeting, opinions and conspiracy theories proliferated, both a rally beforehand and in the public comment section prior to the start of the business section of the meeting. I ignored the drama, concentrating on the goal of saving New College. The university, founded as a traditional liberal arts institution, had a powerful mission. For this meeting, I had prepared my first president's report. In it, I would tell the board how we could make New College the best liberal arts college in the nation.

We did not have the luxury of time. The legislature and the BOG would be looking to see if we could show results rapidly.

After all, New College had become known for making promises in the past and then failing to deliver. We needed to show we were different—quickly.

First and foremost, my goal was to increase student recruitment, which—no matter how much the NCF community wanted to ignore this fact—were why I and the new board members were on this campus in the first place. To bring in students, I would concentrate on five things: adding sports, fundraising, improving student life, recruiting additional worldclass faculty, and developing a new and innovative core curriculum.

That was the plan I laid out, and the one I would follow in the months to come to increase enrollment. It worked. At the time, many doubted that we could achieve this goal given the upheaval around the college and the short time to recruit. The local paper noted on April 8th that "the overhaul is causing considerable backlash. There are big questions about how that turmoil could impact enrollment...Recruiting students for a New College in flux could be challenging, and there isn't much time left for Corcoran's team. Most students will make their decisions soon."[4]

Our team delivered even in these challenging circumstances. New College achieved a record enrollment for the school's freshman class in the fall of 2023. The incoming class of 347 students was the largest class in New College history. In fact, the school had failed to enroll even two hundred new students in three out of the last four years.

After years of stagnation, New College would be turned around in just a few short months. Some attributed this solely to the $15 million the governor had given; however, the college had been given approximately $10 million several years prior and dropped precipitously in enrollment. The truth was the school

STORMING THE IVORY TOWER

was finally on the move and poised to become a shining star in the state university system.

Since every situation will be different, the specifics that follow are not directly applicable to other institutions. What is important is the overarching road map—contained in the last chapter—that undergirded these decisions. However, the story itself is a case study in the challenges that can face a higher educational institution trying to break free from the ideological constraints present in the field today.

• • •

Funding

State Funding

On January 6, 2023, when the governor had appointed the new trustees, he had also announced that he was allocating $15 million to the university in the current fiscal year, which ran from July 1, 2022, to June 30, 2023. The college needed more though for the next fiscal year, which was fast approaching, and these allocations would be decided on during the session that ran from March 7th through May 5th. Therefore, as I started my job as interim president on February 27, 2023, I would need to spend a portion of my first few weeks on the job in the state capital, Tallahassee, more than three hundred miles north of Sarasota where the college is located.

During the session, I met with legislative members to explain how New College could meet the goals that the legislature had set out for it—the goals that year after year it had failed to achieve. Many of the legislative members were skeptical of the institution's track record. However, they ultimately were willing to make a one-year bet on the promise of having a successful elite liberal arts college in the Florida system.

The legislative session was successful. When it ended at the beginning of May, the legislature had allocated another approximately $35 million: $15 million in nonrecurring funding, $10 million in recurring operational funding, and $9.4 million to renovate two classroom buildings.[5] This was for the fiscal year running from July 1, 2023, through June 30, 2024.

The 2024 session would begin on January 9, 2024, and the deadline for budget requests was July 14, 2023. Therefore, we had to make a quick turnaround as we only had two months to prepare.

With the July 14th deadline looming, I was criticized by the faculty and student trustees on the board for how quickly I was moving. Their reticence—with little logic behind it—highlighted another reason why New College had in part struggled to get funding from the legislature. In the past, committees upon committees operated to slow down needed moves. This culture had to change. If the board had listened to the pleas to slow down from the student and faculty board representatives, New College would have lost out on millions of dollars in funding for yet another year.

Private Funding—New College Foundation

The foundation was a direct support organization of the university, run by a board which had been created by the college's board and tasked with fundraising. However, while the Foundation board existed only at the pleasure of the NCF board, it was run by its members as if it was a distinct entity without oversight. When I and the college's attorneys began to dig into its numbers, the Foundation's board hired its own attorneys and communications people who worked to contest moves by the NCF board to review its practices. After we began to delve into their history, numbers, and investments, we understood why. As the fundraising arm of one of the state's twelve universities, the NCF Foundation had barely raised $3 million a year in revenues in the last ten years. According to its 990 Forms filed with the federal government, in two of the last three years, its expenses outpaced its incoming contributions. In 2020, its expenses exceeded its contributions by about $1.5 million, and, in 2022 by almost $1 million. The small arts college across the street, Ringling College of Art and Design, raised $17.7 million in 2022, $15.9 million in 2021, and $23.3 million in 2020.[6,7,8] The bottom lines started to make sense as we delved into its books. Within a year, we had replaced every single person there, drastically reduced its bloated costs, and reworked its policies and procedures.

Federal Funding

New College had failed to request certain federal money in Washington, DC, for years. With three historic Ringling mansions on its campus, there were many options to request federal money. In November, I brought on a lobbying firm for this purpose. New College now had people on the ground who could seek federal funding directly, including requests to revitalize the historic estates, to connect walkways from three historic buildings to the rest of the campus, and for flood resiliency projects.

Personnel

There is a famous saying that "people are policy." With my past experience running large, complex organizations, I was a firm believer in this rule. I knew that I needed to quickly hire people who I knew were extremely competent, personable, and would not make mistakes under pressure. If one must micromanage, goals will never be achieved. This was especially true when I could not be physically present much of the time in the initial weeks.

Those who opposed the changes at New College tried to throw up roadblocks to stop the rapid pace of the changes. One of their favorite objections to almost any change we made was that we moved too quickly. This included the speed at which I hired. The NCF Freedom group, formed to fight the changes at New College, complained about the pace of my hires. The organization posted an article to its website about how quickly I was making hiring decisions, noting with disapproval that "hiring at a public entity is usually a slow process."[9] Trustee Amy Reid, the faculty representative on the board, told reporters she was "concerned about how personnel decisions are being made under Corcoran." Reid said she was "very concerned about the process for hiring and firing on campus" because hires had happened "without any official notice much less a hiring committee."

Almost every decision we made over the next months seemed to be criticized based upon arguments that we were violating process and/or moving too quickly. It would have been comical unless one was living it. In addition, those who were complaining about actions to save the college not only were in active disagreement with steps taken to extricate it based on "speed and process" they also failed to bring ideas themselves to the table.

I made sure I was following processes—but as rapidly as possible. In my past roles, I had fought to make systemic changes, and these moves would frequently invite legal challenges. For this reason, I had a mantra I would say to those working with me: in law, there are white areas where the law is clear, gray areas where it is vague, and black areas where the law is clearly violated: we will always stay firmly in the white areas. After numerous lawsuits, I had always won in the end when people sued me—and I had been sued quite often as House Speaker and education commissioner.

On the day I was chosen president, Bill Galvano was chosen by the board to serve as outside counsel. One of the things discussed when I was considering being interim president at New College was that I would want Galvano in this position. Galvano, a local Sarasota attorney who had a large private practice, had been Senate president designate when I was House Speaker. We had worked closely together, and he understood the importance of holding the moral high ground legally and ethically, as well as how to be aggressive when needed. In mid-May, I also hired David Brickhouse to be an in-house attorney. I knew David from my legal work in the private sector. He had practiced corporate law for years and had experience working with a large law firm as well as serving as inside counsel for a corporation. Wherever I have gone, my first hire has always been my legal counsel because if one wants to be bold and make a difference, there will likely be litigation as a result. I immediately checked that box with the hirings of Galvano and then Brickhouse.

Increasing enrollment for the upcoming school year was my primary goal. Therefore, within a week of starting the job, I hired Kevin Hoeft as the college's new vice president of enrollment management to be over student admission. Kevin had worked with me at the Florida Department of Education when I was commissioner and at the Florida House when I was Speaker. I knew his work ethic and his ability to get along well with people even in stressful circumstances. In addition, on March 23rd, I hired Sydney Gruters as the new executive director of the New College Foundation. I had known Sydney for years and knew she was dynamic, organized, and well-connected in the state and locally. In July, I hired David Rancourt as dean of students. David was a former "mega-lobbyist" who had left lobbying to pursue a PhD.[10] Having been a founding partner of one of the biggest lobbying firms in Tallahassee, David's charisma, people skills, and perfectionism would be a huge asset in this role.

While I knew Bill, Kevin, Sydney, and David from the past, I brought on three administrative hires to the core team who were relatively new to me. I made sure I interviewed each personally. In this situation, it was a gamble which—if they had not worked out—I would have replaced quickly because of the nature of the situation. Thankfully, though, they ended up being strong additions to the team.

First was Almeda Jacks, whose resume came from an employment agency after we indicated we were looking for a director of housing. Jacks was the former director of student affairs at Clemson, who had retired a few years prior but now wanted to take on a short-term project. She was a perfect fit and having her steady, practiced hand overseeing the complex operation of moving students to hotels was key. Nathan Allen, a graduate of New College in the 1990s, had been writing about the need for an education such as New College used to provide for years. He had been vocal in these articles about the need to create a brand out of New College's unique program, as well as the liberal arts in general.[11] In April, I hired him as vice president of strategy and special projects. Finally, I promoted a current member of staff, Christie Fitz-Patrick, from legislative affairs director to chief of staff. After working with her for two weeks, I realized she was an outsize talent. She also knew the budget inside and out, and how to work with different constituencies.

I firmly believe that who is not kept on in a restructuring can be as important as who is brought onto the team. On March 3rd, I fired the dean of diversity, equity, and inclusion, Yoleidy Rosario-Hernandez.

On March 10th, the *Washington Post* ran an interview with zir (Rosario-Hernandez's preferred pronoun) about the termination. (A complaint was made in a report following the termination that Rosario-Hernandez was offended that Rufo mis-gendered zir.) The reporter asked if ze felt "targeted" because ze was transgender and "BIPOC" (black, indigenous, people of color). Rosario-Hernandez, "who identities as trans fluid, which is an identity under the transgender umbrella, and uses the pronouns ze/zir/zirs," said ze "definitely 100 percent think that I have been mistreated because of my identity."

"I believe that's the reason I got fired was because of my gender identity," Rosario-Hernandez said. Ze then expounded on zir feelings about DEI, which the board had directed to be abolished. "DEI is really under attack at the moment. When I think about what has been happening, particularly at New College, it's sad to see that…Professionally, I am in mourning because I see that DEI is being attacked."

Ze also charged that Rufo had "one idea, and that is white supremacy." When contacted by the *Washington Post*'s reporter about this accusation, Rufo replied that Rosario-Hernandez's "false and inflammatory comments are further confirmation that President Corcoran made the right decision" in terminating zir employment.

Enrollment

I had high expectations for Kevin, and, as he would update me, it became increasingly clear that there was a lack of urgency in the staff he had inherited. Despite the low enrollment, applications moved through the admissions department at a snail's pace. Only about fifty applicants had been enrolled by the end of March—which was about twelve more than when I had started on February 27th.

As my number one goal as interim president was recruitment, their lack of energy needed to be addressed. It was a department that was undermining Kevin and fighting his instructions to work with urgency. Therefore, on March 31st, I met with this staff to set the bar for the level of performance that would be expected of employees in this office going forward.

I told them to give me a printout of every single application. I then took them home and went through them and offered the most outstanding ones a newly minted presidential scholarship.

I also had everyone introduce themselves and tell me their title. After they were done, I told them I told them, "My name is Richard Corcoran, and my title is recruitment officer—just like yours. Now, if I do my job really, really well, I also get to be called president. That is the same for you. Your first title is student recruitment officer, and, if you do your job really, really well you also get to have your other title. I've personally recruited five students to come here next year. How many have each of you recruited? This is an amazing school with a powerful vision. If you believe that, you should be telling everyone you meet about it."

I then told them that this was a battle to save the school. In a conflict, the elite team on the front lines is often called the Seal Team. In this instance, the recruitment team would be most crucial to our success. Therefore, I told them, they were our "Seal Team Six." I also gave them a sales pitch to present about the changes happening on campus, including that the dorms would be completely renovated by the fall when the new students arrived. To give them a vision, I told them that the renovations would make the dorms comparable to those at the Sarasota branch of the University of South Florida, located right next door to the campus.

Rather than get right to work and improve their performance, they went and complained to the press that the title of "Seal Team Six" was a violent term because this unit had once killed Osama bin Laden and that I "encouraged them to misrepresent the facilities available." I was beginning to see another facet of why New College was having problems with recruitment. While many of the current staff seemed intent on complaining and continuing their slow pace, I ended up authorizing Kevin to hire additional people to move applications through, including two newly recruited baseball players to help prospective student-athletes with their applications. At this point I had also reached out President David Armstrong at St. Thomas University in Miami, a well-respected and accomplished leader in higher education. After numerous phone calls with President

Armstrong, he helped me hone the bulk of the admissions strategy, including which sports we should start first. This was crucial in driving enrollment, and he was an amazing asset in this recovery period.

We were facing strong headwinds. Even some of the new trustees told me not to have high expectations for enrollment. They indicated they would not be surprised if there was a decline in enrollment numbers and that this could even be expected as a result of the tumultuous changes taking place. Additional obstacles were presented by the fact that most athletes and students made their decisions before March 1st, and we were late in the game for recruiting faculty as most had already signed contracts for the next year. However, I believed that if we added sports and could secure additional money from the legislature—along with making the campus more attractive to students and adding to the faculty and curriculum—increased enrollment was achievable even this early in the transformation process and with our significant obstacles. However, to be successful in this objective, we had to achieve the goals of adding sports and securing money quickly.

As April progressed, the applications began moving more quickly through the admissions office. On April 17th, the board's Academic, Student and External Affairs Standing Committee met, and I updated them on enrollment, telling them that—while year-over-year, enrollment for the freshman class was slightly lower—based on my recent work with the staff in admissions, I felt positive about where we would end up. Since I had met with the staff over two weeks prior, the pace of enrolling students had vastly improved.

"If you look at our tracking, we're a little bit down from last year, but it's picked up considerably," I said. We had doubled the number of enrolled students in the two weeks since I had met with admissions staff and now had one hundred students enrolled. In addition, we were rapidly increasing the number of applications received, as well as decreasing the amount of time required for an application to move through the process to receive approval for admission or denial. While admitted students did not count as fully enrolled yet, this metric was vitally important to complete in the path toward enrollment.

I updated the board committee on these metrics as well, stating that we had recently received "another one hundred and fifty applications, which is very strong, and we've gotten one hundred and fifty kids that we've admitted just in the last few weeks. Not applications, actually admitted through our process." I also noted that the increased number of applications was due to the fact that we were broadening our advertising reach and improving our marketing strategy.

I again highlighted that we were going to meet the legislature's mandate to fix enrollment. "If you look at New College's admissions record, it's quite abysmal," I said. "Probably we average somewhere—if you looked over the last twenty years—somewhere between one hundred and twenty students as a freshman class to a record, I think last year, of two hundred and forty-nine. Even the record is abysmal. We need to be up at (three hundred), four hundred admits in a year."

Since students typically make their decisions by the end of May, I told the committee I should have a final estimate by then. "We're very confident," I said. "I think we're on pace."[12]

At the next board meeting on June 1st, I was able to predict that a record freshman enrollment in the fall is almost "a certainty," as we were currently at 230 students and counting.[13]

On July 27th, the local paper reported that "[a]dmissions data from New College of Florida shows that new leadership installed as part of Gov. Ron DeSantis's conservative makeover of the institution has succeeded in drawing a record number of incoming students this fall." While the reporter kept repeating despite all the evidence to the contrary that it was a "conservative makeover," he was right about one thing: we had "succeeded in drawing a record number of incoming students" for the fall.[14]

In August, the final numbers for enrollment after the first week of school were 347 incoming students, 150 of which were athletes. Even without the athletes, given that New College often did not break two hundred for an incoming class, it was still on the high end. Add the athletes, and the legislature now had definitive proof we could make a plan and do what they asked.

Athletics

On March 31st, thirty minutes after the meeting with the enrollment staff to challenge them to perform at a higher level, we announced that we were creating an athletic department.

Adding athletics had been in the college's strategic plan since 2016, but like many projects at New College, it languished from lack of leadership, mired in the tiny squabbles that seemed to take up much of the college's time previously. Having become somewhat acquainted with how the college had been run, it was likely that the "speed and process" of adding athletics had been debated widely despite its never launching. However, I knew that this had to be accomplished—and as soon as possible.

My goal was for New College to join the National Association of Intercollegiate Athletics (NAIA).[15] Begun in

1937, the NAIA currently has approximately 250 members and has added twenty-one new member institutions in the last three years. It was soon to be twenty-two when New College was approved to compete in the 2023-2024 season and fully approved for the 2024-2025 season.

If a small college wanted to increase enrollment and retention, it was basically a no-brainer to try to join the NAIA. David Ridpath, a professor of sports business at Ohio University, stated in an article in the summer of 2023 that there is a trend for small colleges to join the NAIA because it "has been a rare reliable lifeline for higher ed institutions in an age of increasing precarity."

The real question was why had this not been done before?

I hired Mariano Jimenez to take on this large project. I was introduced to Jimenez—who had been the director of athletics at Inspiration Academy, a local school that focused on sports—by former New College Trustee Eddie Speir. Speir's recommendation of Jimenez was excellent. Jiminez was young, energetic, and a natural leader who had many inroads with the local, state, and national sports community. Jimenez was able to attract excellent coaches quickly, to recruit from his deep inroads in the world of high school sports, and to bring in talented transfers.

We also had the benefit of being located ten minutes away from IMG Academy's six hundred-acre, world-class sports organization. This gave us access to fields and other facilities that we could leverage in starting a program quickly.

At the beginning of May, we announced our goal to have six sports for the fall: baseball, softball, men's and women's basketball, and men's and women's soccer. Jimenez began working with representatives of the NAIA and officially turned in our application. In a May interview, he told a reporter that twenty athletes had already committed and that he could "hardly keep up with the calls" from athletes interested in playing at New College.[16]

At the June 1st board meeting, the board approved the athletic budget. I updated the board on the application to the NAIA, telling trustees that for the 2023–2024 school year, New College had provisional membership. For the fall season, we would play most games on the road since the athletic department had to schedule games with colleges on its own. Our teams also would travel off-campus to practice at IMG Academy or other nearby complexes. Both David Armstrong from St. Thomas, along with David Hoag from Warner College, had been of assistance during this process to join the NAIA. Armstrong was chairman of the admissions committee, and they both helped in the achievement of joining the organization.

On October 2, just six months after starting its athletic program, New College was accepted into the NAIA.[17] The NAIA vote to approve our application was unanimous, and we would have full membership in the Sun Conference of the group beginning on July 1, 2024. Often schools applying to the NAIA receive associate membership prior to getting full membership. However, thanks to Jimenez and the team he had assembled, as well as the support of Armstrong and Hoag, New College went straight to full membership.

"They were not expecting us to be as prepared as we were…I really think it speaks to the amazing people that are on campus, that are here, the people that we brought in and added on," Jimenez told a reporter. "They were blown away by our vision for athletics here and our vision for being the number one liberal arts college in the country."

As athletics became a reality, I knew we needed a mascot, which was necessary to compete but also would add to the student life and experience. In 1997, the campus community attempted to adopt a formal mascot but could not agree on one, choosing to have a stand-in be a set of empty brackets, which they termed the "null set." It was originally to be a placeholder, but it stuck. However, for branding and competition purposes, it did not make sense. First, I tried to get the campus community involved, but many of the current students were against bringing in sports and were intent on keeping the null set. When I sent out a survey to have the students be involved in choosing a mascot, it fell flat.

Then, a freshman student, Anna Lazzara, approached Jimenez with a drawing of a banyan tree, of which there are many beautiful examples on the campus. In Lazzara's concept, the banyan tree became a person with its branches extended like arms, flexing powerful muscles. It seemed to catch the spirit of the college, which I did not want to lose—smart, quirky, creative, and with a love for the nature with which the campus was surrounded. I asked Lazzara to present her idea to the board. At the June board meeting, she explained how she came up with the idea of the banyan tree for a mascot. She was sitting on the campus one day, looking at the banyan trees scattered throughout, and they reminded her of the spirit of the institution.

It was also important to Lazzara to be respectful of the null set, a part of the college's history, and she incorporated it in the banyan tree's eyebrows.[18] The board loved the idea and adopted the banyan tree as the school's mascot. The student and faculty representative voted no. They wanted to have more time and more process to discuss the choices.

Facilities

Dorms

One of my first priorities was to renovate the dilapidated dorms. However, this plan immediately hit a roadblock when, on my first day on the job, I received emails from students about mold in the dorms. These messages included pictures of visible mold in many places around the rooms and other living spaces.

After touring the dorms, I commissioned a Targeted Mold and Moisture Assessment Report with an engineering company. On March 20th through the 22nd, the engineers were on campus to study the issue. On May 22nd, they presented their report. It found three of the dorm buildings "should not be occupied in their current condition." It stated that we would need to undertake repairs including replacing the HVAC systems and mold remediation. These three buildings had been built in the 1960s by renowned architect I. M. Pei and were well-known locally because of this.

Some of the Pei rooms were deemed too difficult to remediate in the short amount of time. We immediately shut those down. However, the report indicated remediation was possible for some of the Pei rooms. With the start of summer, we brought in crews that worked day and night to renovate all the dorms. Dorms that did not have mold issues were repainted, retrofitted with new cabinets, kitchens, flooring, and furniture. The roadway on the side of campus where the dorms were located was repaved. To ensure we kept to the tight schedule, Itza Frisco, the vice president of facilities, and I were in daily contact with the engineers and contractors who were doing the work, often around-the-clock. Some days Itza and I were on the phone about this hourly.

At the end of July, the cleaning was done on the Pei rooms that were deemed eligible. However, before putting a single student in them I wanted to see a report by an expert that they were completely safe for students. Therefore, I commissioned another Targeted Mold and Moisture Assessment Report. The engineers were on-site July 31st and August 1st, with the report delivered to me on August 16th, two days before students were expected back on campus. The report indicated that even with the cleaning, many problems remained that were related to the structure of the buildings themselves. The cost to fix the issues was cost-prohibitive. We decided to shut down all the Pei dorms. Rancourt and Jacks went right to work and immediately negotiated a contract with excellent hotels almost adjacent to our campus.

A college policy requires that freshmen and sophomores be offered campus housing before juniors and seniors. For this reason, as most of the athletes were freshmen, they got the new housing that had been renovated on campus. Once all freshmen and sophomores were given on-campus rooms as required by pre-existing college policy, the two hundred students housed off-campus ended up being primarily juniors and seniors. About eighty of these found out about their move from dorms to hotels about a week before they moved in, as they had been originally assigned to rooms in the Pei dorms. It was frustrating to have this issue, but we had inherited it and refused to put students in a potentially harmful situation. The previous administrations had not done enough to address concerns about the mold.

We were committed to ensuring that we made the changes as minimally disruptive to the students' lives as possible. The

Hilton Garden Inn, Hyatt Place, and Home2 Suites were all accommodations located close to the campus and exceeded the quality of dorms at most colleges. Meal plans and shuttles were provided. Medical requirements, grade level, and access to transportation were factors in considering which students would be housed in the hotels. There were some stressful conversations with parents, but Almeda Jacks had previously handled moving students to hotels during her tenure at Clemson. Her expertise coupled with her kind and caring demeanor, and Rancourt's similar talents, helped ease the stress during this time for parents, students, and staff.

Reimagining Pei Contest

A complete renovation of the Pei dorms would be cost-prohibitive if not impossible. Built in 1968 by the renowned architect I. M. Pei, however, we felt it was important to somehow preserve a part of them because of their historical significance to the campus and the local community. Therefore, we partnered with Architecture Sarasota to put on the Reimagining Pei competition. Together, we ran an international competition where the goal was to design a comprehensive campus on the corner where the Peis currently existed that would incorporate some parts of the structures themselves.

Like everything else we were doing, we were on a tight timeline to show the legislature that there were plans in the pipeline so we could ask for funding. The international competition drew forty entries from around the world. In September, Architecture Sarasota pared them down to three.

On November 15, representatives from the three finalists presented their submissions to more than two hundred New

College students, faculty, staff, and local community members. I also now had a proposal for which I could seek private and public funding. Again, there were those who wanted to slow down this project, but they were unsuccessful.

Car Museum

While the past administrations had complained about lack of funding, the university had rented a prime piece of property to a tenant for years at a rate well below the market value. Currently, it could have been rented at around $30,000 or more a month, but the college was renting it for $10,000 a month—having just increased it from $7,500 approximately a year earlier. This was a loss of approximately $240,000 a year in revenues the college could have been making. This tenant, a car museum, was on a month-to-month lease. In May, I had the college's lawyers issue the tenant a notice to terminate the lease on June 30th. We would be using these to replace the dilapidated office buildings on campus that were approved for demolition, as well as for athletic offices.

The Mansions

New College has three historic Ringling mansions on its property. These date from the early 1900s and were built when the Ringling family, which made its money from traveling circuses, would spend winters in Sarasota. All three mansions were in various stages of disrepair. The historical nature of these buildings meant they were eligible for federal and state funds as well as grants. We began leveraging all avenues available to restore them. Sydney Gruters was contacted by a group of designers in the community who had been asking for years to work on one of the mansions that was most in need of renovation, free of charge. These local designers had formed a group that had a vision to save historical buildings in the Sarasota area. They had been frustrated for over a decade because of the nonresponsiveness of the past administrations at New College to their offers to volunteer to help. Gruters welcomed them to begin work on the Caples mansion so that it could be opened to the public for tours. On February 4, 2024, the college hosted a ribbon cutting to kick off several weeks of public tours of the newly refurbished mansion. The proceeds from these tours helped raise funds for further renovation.

Land

Manatee County Land Donation

On October 9, 2023, the Manatee County Board of County Commissioners voted unanimously to donate nine acres of waterfront property contiguous to the New College campus to the university at no cost. It was to be used for purposes such as housing or educational buildings. The county had contacted me several weeks earlier because, while the commission had tried since 2020 to donate land to a satellite campus of the University of South Florida (USF Sarasota-Manatee), which was located next to New College, after three years of questions from the USF Sarasota-Manatee board, they were tired of the delays to merely donate a piece of waterfront property.

The lag time in simply accepting a piece of beautiful property on the water at no cost had frustrated the commissioners. Commissioner Mike Rahn, whose district the land is located in, told the paper that negotiations around the use agreement came to a standstill with USF, which led the county down a different path—to my office and our quick acceptance of the parcel contiguous to our own that could be used for needed dorms and classroom space as we grew. As usual, the student and faculty board representatives had questions about process and speed in relation to accepting for free a donation of 9 acres of land worth almost $20 million.

Purchase of Airport Property

On October 13, 2023, news broke that New College was working to finalize a land deal with the airport that was located next to the land on which the dorms and several administrative buildings of the college were located. According to the airport's CEO, Rick Piccolo, this would "avert a financial nightmare for New College of Florida that awaits at the end of a 100-year land lease agreement with the Sarasota-Bradenton International Airport…. If the lease is allowed to expire in 2056, the airport-owned land and all of the New College buildings on it revert to airport ownership."

New College was renting the land for "a very low rent…a little over $108,000 per year in rent for roughly 32 acres," Piccolo told the paper. However, there was a vast complication quickly approaching. "Fast forward to 2056…They'll have to buy buildings back from us that they built. So let's say, for the sake of argument, that is for a quarter of a billion dollars by that time. Well, they are going to have to walk in front of the state Legislature and say, 'By the way, our rent went from $100,000 to $20 million, or we need to buy all of this land, and we need a quarter of a billion dollars.' That ain't gonna happen."

Piccolo had been telling NCF presidents this for years. Previous New College presidents had an opportunity to address the situation, but "I couldn't get anyone to listen…I have tried for many years to warn the college about what was on the horizon if this issue wasn't addressed," Piccolo told the NCF trustees at a board meeting.

When I started, Piccolo contacted me, and we immediately started working together to get a win-win-win for the school, the airport, and the community. On December 12, 2023, the board approved the purchase agreement of $11.5 million that would result in the college owning 30.9 of the acres it was leasing from the airport. Approximately four additional acres would be kept by the airport. While the agreement still had several hurdles before it received final approval, it was finally moving forward. As usual, the student and faculty board representatives had questions about process and speed in relation to accepting for free a donation of 9 acres of land worth almost $20 million.

Maintenance

In early February, I drove down to Sarasota from my current home in Tampa to see New College for the first time. As I turned left into the campus, the sun was setting, and my headlights illuminated the "New College of Florida" sign. It had weeds growing over it, and the paint was faded. The edges of the beds underneath the sign were not trimmed. The entrance looked apocalyptic, as if the university was shuttered and in foreclosure.

My first week on campus I realized it was not just the external grounds that were an issue. I was horrified—as the father of three college students myself—to find out the extent of the malfeasance. The campus was simply unsafe. Of thirty-six emergency phones on campus, only ten were operational. Cameras near a side of the campus where the local airport's land abutted the campus and homeless were known to congregate were not working.

Curriculum

Techne/Logos

The main reason I wanted to be interim president at New College was not because of real estate deals, staff restructuring, legal compliance, or even student life. While competent execution of those areas is absolutely necessary to have a successful higher educational institution, my true passion was to offer an excellent education to students. This would rest in large part on the curriculum.

New College had an excellent program but little structure in its course progression. We wanted to have a core curriculum for the first two years that met the goals of a liberal arts education, combining learning about the wisdom of the past with an exploration of skills needed for the future. Our goal was to create a program that was based on the liberal arts but contained components that were relevant to today. Steven Jobs had articulated this well in his discussions over the years regarding the power that is present at the "intersection of the liberal arts and technology." In the spring and summer of 2023, we worked to create two first-year courses—one in Logos to be based on a study of Homer's *The Odyssey* and one in Techne, which would be an intro to AI through the field of data science that would introduce students to be the emerging field of AI and how it would affect any industry. These foundational courses would introduce students to the Logos/Techne curriculum which would be further added to over the next few years.

New Master's Programs

We also began working on creating additional master's programs. Currently, the school had one master's program in data science that was very successful, and we wanted to build upon this. To obtain approval for a master's program is a complex process. Therefore, we immediately began working to develop three more, and in February 2024, the board approved the first one, a new master's degree program in marine mammal science.

Online Program

On January 11, 2024, New College launched an online liberal arts degree in collaboration with one of America's great entrepreneurs, Joe Ricketts. Of the twelve colleges in the Florida system, New College was one of the only ones that did not have an online option for students. It was a revenue source as well as an avenue for driving on-campus enrollment. New College should have built such a program long ago. Ricketts had been working on an online program based on the Great Books for several years. Through the governor and Rufo, we were put in touch. There was a natural synergy, and Ricketts's hard work allowed us to get a unique and dynamic online program up and running quickly.

Safety

It became readily apparent in my first week that students were not required to comply with the law or the Student Code of Conduct. The campus police were generally told not to patrol on-campus parties or the dorm side of the campus, despite two student deaths from drug overdoses in 2015 and an ongoing lawsuit from 2017 for sexual assault during a scheduled on-campus event. In addition, the student conduct officer felt she would endanger her job if she enforced the Student Conduct Code.

To put it into perspective, when Trustee Rufo had a student spit at him in mid-May, I instructed my general counsel to begin the process of student discipline. I wanted the process to be started quickly because—if the student ultimately were to leave school—I wanted the student to have plenty of opportunity to apply somewhere else. The attorney came back and told me that there was good news and bad news. The good news was that there was a clear process under the law, the first step of which was to convene the student conduct board. The bad news was that a student conduct board had apparently never been constructed at New College. We moved swiftly to start one. The student ultimately chose to withdraw with a five-year trespass.

Such failure to observe basic laws and rules was dangerous to both persons and property. I asked Brickhouse as the in-house counsel and Rancourt as the student affairs leader to make sure both the law and the Student Code of Conduct were enforced, just as they were at any other university in the Florida system. Their primary goal was "just to follow the existing rules," Rancourt said. The Student Code of Conduct was "reasonably written" but "completely unenforced."

Rancourt and Brickhouse spent time communicating to the students that the expectations were changing. They held events in which, for example, they taught students how to put on an on-campus event, including how to communicate with student affairs and how to check IDs. Rancourt quoted Almeda Jacks—the new student housing coordinator who had worked for many years in student life at Clemson—who would shake her head frequently during this time and say "never in my life…," letting the phrase trail off meaningfully.

Despite the changes, Rancourt felt that in the end the students responded positively to the new culture. While there was some pushback from students initially, they slowly came around because "the students understood there were safety issues. Anarchy is not a great way to live."

ADA Accessibility

Many of the speakers at the public portion of the first board meeting at which the new trustees were present in January complained that the college was in violation of the ADA. I discovered the first week I was there that this was true. Along with many elevators not working, a large portion of the automatic door buttons required for ADA compliance were also inoperable. The college is separated by a major highway. At the large intersection between the classroom side of campus and the dorm side, the necessary legal requirements for crossing the road for those with visual impairments had never been installed as required by law. Finally, the college's website was out of compliance with the legal requirements for the visually impaired. We immediately set to work to fix these issues.

Once Brickhouse had addressed the emergency needs for ADA compliance, we formed an accessibility committee on August 14th to ensure there were adequate processes and structure going forward on these and similar issues. However, we still had to deal with continuing fallout from the previous administration's lack of legal compliance. In the first week of September, the federal Department of Education notified us that there was a compliance issue with the website under the ADA. The DOE attorney came to campus and met with Brickhouse and others, who walked her through where the college was in the process of ensuring ADA compliance and how we had already been working for months to bring the college into compliance. On September 28th, we announced that we had entered into an agreement with the US Department of Education to take immediate action to fix the compliance issues from "years of inattentiveness to maintaining online compliance standards and effective guidelines for digital communications."[19]

Title IX

This section only pertains to Title IX as it existed in 2023 when I was installed as interim president at New College. In 2024, the Biden administration has attempted to expand it. The below discussion does not deal with those expansions, with which no university in Florida is currently planning to comply.

When I first arrived, I heard from several students who were concerned about the past administration's legal compliance with Title IX. I immediately hired an outside consulting firm to perform an assessment of current practices. On May 5, 2023, the outside consultant provided their recommendations. After examining several cases, reviewing policies and other documents, and conducting "extensive interviews…with faculty, students and staff involved with Title IX," the consultant reported that the college's current policy was "inconsistent with current Title IX regulations and case law" and therefore had "significant issues."

According to comments she heard about practices of the previous administration, "Title IX is a mess and has been for years." She said that there had been "multiple staff turnovers and multiple and varying supervisors and supervisory structures over the past decade, leaving the status of the office confusing for the NCF community and resulting in a lack of trust or confidence in the Title IX operation."

Galvano and Brickhouse restructured the office based on the outside consultant's recommendations. As a result, at the February 2024 board meeting, I asked Brickhouse to give a report about the office. In the 2022–2023 school year, there were forty-three total Title IX reports and three formal complaints. Thus far in the 2023–2024 school year, with the changes Galvano and Brickhouse and the outside consultant implemented as well as the enforcement of law and the Code of Conduct on campus, there were thirteen total reports and zero formal complaints.

Safety App

In the fall, we rolled out a safety app called the Mighty Banyan Safety App. It allowed students to ask for police escorts if they were on campus, particularly at night. Students were also able to receive emergency notifications so that administration could immediately contact all students in case of an issue. Maps and other resources were available on the app for navigating the campus as well.

STORMING THE IVORY TOWER

Student Life

Food

We immediately renegotiated the contract with the food vendor at the cafeteria to provide a higher quality of food options for the fall of 2023. In addition, we worked to provide food on the classroom side of campus immediately, which had not had food options for four years. The dorm cafeteria is located on the dorm side of the campus, on the other side of a large highway. A student-run café on the classroom side of campus had been effectively closed since the beginning of 2019. To get students food on that side of the campus would be a challenge, but it was one of our highest priorities. While the school would likely have been shuttered without DeSantis's intervention, from the perspective of many of the students, it was not what they had signed up for. Food was a way to communicate that we cared about them.

Our first attempt, achieved soon after we started, was to have shuttles running frequently during the school day to the restaurants located in the downtown, which was about ten minutes away. This proved too inconvenient, and students were not utilizing it. We then tried food trucks. This also did not work on a consistent basis. We had been calling around to local restaurants trying to see if they would come to provide food, as we had a building with a kitchen. However, no local restaurants could get in during the spring, though several indicated they were interested for the fall.

On April 25th, two months after coming to campus, we finally found a way to provide food on the classroom side of the campus. The local paper reported the following:

*The Four Winds Café on New College of Florida's
campus buzzed with students Thursday afternoon
as many studied for their end-of-semester class-
work—coffee in hand. The building, which has
long held a student-run café but is now used as
a study space, had new life as an outside vendor
served free coffee to students as part of a pop-up
business for the end of the semester.*[20]

The vendor—a friend who owned two bakeries in Tampa,
which was located about an hour north—had agreed to help
out for a few weeks until the end of the school year. He was
only contracted from April 25th through May 18th, but it was
a symbolic victory for our team to try to provide food for the
students who had been vocal about their lack of food on that
side of the campus.

In the fall, we contracted with a local restaurant, which
proved to be too high a price point, and then quickly pivoted to
another local restaurant that has worked out well.

Activities

Over the summer, along with the dorms, we worked to upgrade
other student spaces. We renovated the pool and added new
pool furniture. We overhauled the landscaping and repainted
many areas of the campus. We also fixed up the sports fields
on the dorm side of campus so the dorms could have better
recreational facilities. In addition, throughout the fall of 2023,
we added a landscaped park near the water on the classroom
side of the campus. We installed lights in the trees, as well as a
fire pit, Adirondack chairs, and a small stage for a band. Soccer

games in the fall, basketball games in the winter, and softball and baseball games in the spring provided events for students to attend, which was important for a campus that was lacking in extracurricular activities.

Campus

As I told the admissions staff in my first meeting with them in March, my job title first and foremost is "Student Recruiter." One of the first things I tell prospective students about, after the academic program, is the incredible beauty of the campus. It has acres of frontage on Sarasota Bay, along with three historic mansions. As we began to clean up the grounds and perform basic maintenance, its beauty became even more striking. When we added the park near the water, pulled the weeds, painted the buildings, planted sod, installed turf where grass could not grow, and offered food during the day near the classrooms, students wanted to be on the campus more. Every day as I head to work now, I cannot wait to get to campus to see what other improvements have been accomplished. One of my favorite places to drive by is a building near the front of campus where we installed turf because the grass would not grow. It now is frequently filled with students lying in the sun on the new groundcover—talking, studying, eating—enjoying the warm weather and their time at this amazing institution.

Free Speech

Orientation Leaders

Orientation for the 2023–2024 school year started on August 20th. During it, we had presentations that highlighted the importance of free speech and civil discourse. However, on the first day, we had to address an issue with our seventeen paid orientation leaders, most of whom were sophomores and older and thus had entered the college under the former administration. Many were wearing political pins on their uniform shirts as they worked during the college's mandatory introductory program for new students. As paid employees of the university working with incoming freshmen, they were instructed to remove these. As I noted on X (formerly Twitter) the next day, these were employees working with freshmen students, many of whom were away from home for the first time. We wanted to project a welcoming environment, free of indoctrination from any side of the spectrum.

Some of the orientation leaders then moved the pins from their shirts to their pants and back packs, which we also asked them to remove. Several of the students then went to the press. In the ensuing article, one student said that he found it "infuriating...I will not censor myself for someone else's comfort."[21] I posted on X that while "all of our students, including ambassadors, are free on their own time to wear any kind of button they want," when they are paid orientation leaders, "ambassadors can't wear buttons of any kind (NRA, BLM, etc.)."

Freedom Institute

At the July 6th board meeting, the board also agreed to ask state lawmakers for $2 million to establish a "Freedom Institute." The proposed institute will promote "tolerance of opposing views" and "engage such views in civil discourse."

The Socratic Stage

To model free speech and civil discourse, we created a series of dialogues on campus between people of differing viewpoints on important issues. For a template, we looked at the Munk Debates that are held in Canada. On November 30th, we held our first Socratic Stage event with Jason Greenblatt, a former White House special envoy to the Middle East, and Ghaith al-Omari, a senior fellow at the Washington Institute for Near East Policy. While often on different sides of issues, Greenblatt and al-Omari know and respect each other from working together over the years on the Israeli-Palestinian relationship. That night, they discussed the Israel-Hamas war, the Israel-Palestinian conflict, and the future of the Middle East. It was refreshing to hear two people talk over a complex problem and over their perspectives—which on their disgust for Hamas aligned many times during the discussion. Since that first successful event, we have continued to host other events as we rapidly expand this important program.

Faculty

The first week I met with faculty. I had the same message then that I had at every subsequent meeting with them: we have three goals—grow students, grow money, grow prestige. I encouraged them to schedule one-on-one meetings with me if they had ideas or questions. I also gave out my cell phone number and told them they could call me directly. Immediately, several took me up on the invitation for a meeting. This group was positive about the changes and brought me many excellent ideas both then and later.

I followed this up with a letter on March 9th stating that "I know many of you have questions about what the future will be, and I understand that with change comes uncertainty, and uncertainty can be unsettling. But I want to assure you that we will be thoughtful in considering potential changes and there will be opportunities for the voices of students, faculty, and staff to be heard."

I also emphasized the board's vision: "I want New College to serve as a beacon of free speech, free inquiry, and free debate in Florida and beyond." I then attached a question-and-answer article from the local paper. I had asked for this because I wanted the public—and now the New College faculty—to hear my vision "in my own words and without editorial context or framing." I knew that while New College had current faculty and students that did not want this type of vision, it had many that just wanted to study and teach free from harassment. It was to these that I was speaking.

Processes

At its April meeting, the board considered granting early tenure to five who had requested it. This year had seen a record seven faculty applying for early tenure. The student trustee argued in favor, noting that about one-third of those who had applied for tenure in the past had done so through the early tenure route.[22] I found this concerning. Early tenure is typically an unusual distinction reserved for exceptional candidates or unusual circumstances. Given other practices of the past administrations that we had uncovered—including lack of compliance with the ADA, Title IX, and state law in student discipline—I needed time to review the early tenure process. I did not want to simply recommend awarding early tenure, thereby setting a precedent, when I did not have sufficient information.

Originally, seven professors had applied for early tenure. I met personally with them as a group and asked them to withdraw their applications and apply for regular tenure the next year. By then, I would have had time to do the necessary review of the tenure process. Two agreed to withdraw. The other five wanted to proceed with the early tenure requests. Therefore, on April 20th, I sent a memo to board members in preparation for the meeting, explaining my reasoning for my request to delay offering early tenure. I stated that the reason for the delay was because of the "extraordinary circumstances" and "current uncertainty of the needs of the divisions/units and College." At the August 26th board meeting, the board agreed with my request to delay.

The media framed this as an attack on tenure, and the public comment section of the meeting was dominated by those who were enraged at my request, as it was viewed as an attack on tenure in general. More than fifty speakers addressed the board, many expressing the view that this move was hostile to the idea of tenure.[23] This was a complete misunderstanding of the situation but a natural response given the headlines and coverage by the press. One parent commented that "your disruptive agenda is clearly not in the best interests of the students. Tenure and academic freedom go hand in hand." There was a rally beforehand with speeches, and people carried signs such as "Defy. The Political Pawns Strike Back." An overpass connects the classroom side of campus with the dorm side of campus. Banners were hung from this that read "Protect Professors" and "Resist Fascism."[24]

When the board voted, the crowd at the meeting chanted "shame on you." The local newspaper ran a picture with people standing up in the audience during the meeting with their backs to the board wearing T-shirts reading "Ban the fascists. Save the books," holding signs reading "Protect academic freedom."[25]

New Faculty

As with the dire predictions in the press that the turmoil would mean we could not attract students, rhetoric that we would not attract impressive faculty proved empty as well. From the spring of 2023 on, we have been inundated with CVs from professors from all over the nation wanting to work at a college committed to academic freedom and free speech. For the 2023–2024 year, even with the relatively short recruiting season since the new board took over in January, we hired twenty new faculty members. I also created the Presidential Scholars in Residence (PSR) program to provide an avenue for New College to attract highly distinguished individuals to impact the entire college community, teaching, offering engaging panel discussions and public lectures, advising on the development of new programs, and elevating the profile of New College. For the fall of 2023, we hired three professors to participate in the PSR program.

The bitter fact was, to the press, we were attracting impressive faculty. This was confounding to reporters. On November 15, 2023, the *Chronicle of Higher Education* wrote an article trying to understand why eminent and respected scholar Stanley Fish would come to teach at New College. The article was entitled, fittingly from the press's perspective, "Why Is Stanley Fish Teaching at Florida's New College?" According to reporter Len Gutkin, "Stanley Fish is in the last phase of his storied career as a Renaissance scholar, law professor, and college administrator.... I wanted to know how Fish, who has written a series of important books about the law and theory of academic freedom, felt about New College's new direction."

Gutkin got right to the point asking Fish why he would get involved with a "political project." Fish, who had spent time talking with me before taking the job, pushed back on the reporter's smug assumptions. "I wouldn't want to get engaged in a classroom experience if I felt that that classroom was being monitored for political or ideological reasons," Fish said. "But I've had no hint of any such monitoring in my discussions."

Frustrated, Gutkin pivoted, trying a different tack since Fish clearly was not going to agree with him, asking why Fish was attracted to teach at New College since a "lot of academics feel that the new New College is more of a threat than a way forward." Fish answered simply.

> *I'm going to go in, I'm going to teach my classes,*
> *I'm going to interact with the faculty—because*

I'm a company man, always have been. I like to go to all the lectures and the discussion groups and have lunches with faculty members and so forth.

And if there are times in which these hot button issues are discussed, I hope that I would be asked to participate in it. And I would participate in it, and not tailor my views, which I couldn't possibly do anyway because they've been in print for many years, on issues like academic freedom or critical race theory or the other hot button matters that come up.

This did not comport with the storyline Gutkin's publication had been propounding. Rather than follow up with objective curiosity, Gutkin doubled down on his incorrect assumptions that had been encouraged by opinions flung about by other reporters like him. He stated that on the governor's web page, the governor mentioned the changes at New College, including that the governor wanted to replace "far-left faculty with new professors that aligned with the university's mission." Gutkin asked, "How do you feel about this posture toward higher ed?"

This was a mistake because Gutkin was not talking to one of his newsroom colleagues. Fish was a scholar who understood that the governor's quote could easily be interpreted to mean, based on everything else DeSantis and those around the New College changes had said, that there would be no more tolerance for intolerant left-wing faculty. If left-wing faculty agreed with the free speech mission, they were welcome.

Fish demonstrated in his answer how objective, thoughtful reporters should be thinking about any issue, not merely New

College. Fish indicated that he would need to know more. Were Gutkin's assumptions of the quote's meaning based in objective facts or merely a subjective interpretation of the quote? Fish then returned to his original point, that he supported freedom of speech as a scholar.

If the idea is to replace ideological left-leaning academics with ideological right-leaning academics, then I'm not your boy. It's been my mission, notably unsuccessful, for many years to make people understand that academic work, including in your writing and in your classes, is one thing and political work is another, and that the two should not be confused nor should they be intermingled. You can have any number of political issues brought into the classroom so long as they are brought into the classroom as objects of analysis or description and not as agendas either to be embraced or rejected. That's what I've been arguing, one might even say preaching, for a long time. I too—like I assume DeSantis and others associated with him—I don't want my classroom, or any classroom in a college or university that I'm teaching in, to be thought of as the vehicle of some program or agenda.

Gutkin continued the interview asking questions based on his false assumptions, and Fish continued patiently answering him, trying to steer him toward sanity and away from histrionics. I knew how Fish felt.

Messaging

I messaged constantly, though with little expectation that it would reach the public. While the mainstream press reported on New College frequently, and I would talk to them, it was mainly an attempt to correct them, though they would not typically report much of what I said.

I was accustomed to this treatment. As both Speaker and education commissioner, I had to be creative to get my message out, and I brought in my experience in those roles to this position. I tweeted. I released videos that focused on the vision. I wrote columns in national publications, though only those on the more conservative side such as the *Wall Street Journal* and the *Federalist* were interested. I wrote my own columns in local publications when possible.[26] I did interviews with television stations. Other people also assisted, when possible, particularly the governor and Casey, his wife, through visits to the campus as well as on their social media accounts. Friendly alumni and board members did their own columns in publications explaining the changes. For example, on June 22nd, Bob Allen, a New College alum, wrote a column about how no one had ever said New College should be like Hillsdale because it should become a Christian college. The comparison was to Hillsdale's strong success as a liberal arts school.

> *Critics of change at Sarasota's New College of Florida have read too much into statements by Gov. Ron DeSantis' chief of staff and others that they would like to see New College become more like Hillsdale College.*

> *Hillsdale is a private Christian college in Michigan, which unlike virtually every other college or university in America, accepts no government funding. Suggesting that the governor wants to turn New College into Hillsdale is misinformed. As a unit of the state of Florida, it is constitutionally prohibited from advancing Christianity or any other religion. Gov. DeSantis, the trustees, interim President Richard Corcoran and their teams of course understand that completely. What Hillsdale's admirers are referring to is its "classical liberal arts" curriculum, which Hillsdale describes as "a journey through literature, philosophy, theology, history, the fine arts and the natural sciences," with the goal of allowing students "to see the world as a cohesive whole."*

I assume the reporters at the paper do not read that editorial section, because after June 22nd, the paper continued to report such claims in news articles.[27]

On September 15, 2023, I was the featured speaker at a meeting of the Tampa Tiger Bay Club. The club is nonpartisan and aims to foster conversation on important issues. One way Tiger Bay tries to ensure audience members represent different viewpoints is by requiring that any audience member who asks a question has a paid membership. However, this attempt at moderation is often overridden when a guest who the radical Left does not like is featured. Membership is one hundred dollars, and—as happened when I was announced as the speaker a few weeks in advance—opponents purchased memberships to attend and be able to ask a question. When one of the club's leaders had called to invite me, she mentioned that this sometimes was a problem and that it was becoming more difficult to find any Republican to speak because the audience was often uncivil. However, she said, "I told them, 'Don't worry, I'll call Richard. He doesn't care about that.'"

Groups on social media had been busy getting the word out that I would be speaking at the group—and attacking Tiger Bay for inviting me. "I think this is disgusting. By having this jerk speak, Tiger Bay is condoning and criminalizing criminal behavior," Susan Smith, the former president of the Democratic Progressive Caucus of Florida, wrote on Facebook earlier in the week.

For this event, several of the people who strongly disagreed with the change in leadership bought memberships and ensured that they were placed at the two tables right in the front of the stage so that they could ask questions. While about two hundred people were present, a number of the questions came from these tables during the question-and-answer portion of the event. One of the questions came from a local liberal activist who asked the following question:

> *Your speech about the value of a liberal arts education as well as your anecdote about kindness flies in the face of the reality on the ground of what is happening at New College. Faculty, students, people of color, LGBTQ people do not feel welcomed; they are leaving the school in droves...Are you capable of seeing the contradiction in what you're saying here?...Are you capable of seeing the contradiction in what you're sitting up here saying and what the reality at your school is?*

This question was asked at around the forty-three-minute mark in the video that is posted on the Tiger Bay website. I had just said at the 27:30 mark to another questioner that enrollment as to people of color had increased drastically—Black enrollment was up by around 300 percent, and Hispanic enrollment had increased by around 100 percent.

The fact that this questioner did not even acknowledge that I had already given data on this in answer to a previous question—that directly contradicted his own question—was a poor use of the audience's time. I responded that while "I appreciate the line of questioning…I'll just say as nicely as possible, one hundred percent of what you said is not based in fact." Those opposing me in the audience started laughing. I was glad to have the opportunity to speak the truth, unfiltered, to them.

> *It's just simple. Can you give me one fact? How many people of color have left the campus? I could do that with all your points, and you're going to say the same thing. Can I get a real question please? [inaudible] what part? What part? Tell me the exact question you want me to answer. Have people of color left the campus? No. They've come to this campus by a three hundred percent increase. It was just a bunch of opinions that aren't based in fact.*

I did have data and facts. However, facts do not really matter when I am relying on the press to report what I say. Of this exchange, one reporter wrote, "Corcoran said emphatically that people of color hadn't left New College, but in fact were now coming to the school. *Corcoran didn't provide specific numbers.*"[28]

(Italics added.) In my answer that the reporter referenced, I had just said that there was a 300 percent increase in people of color. In addition, I had already given this information at approximately the 27:30 mark of the video on the website with more detail: the percentage of Black students had increased 300 percent and the percentage of Hispanic students had increased approximately 100 percent.

Following this question, a mother who felt her child had to leave the school because she did not agree with the new direction told me that my numbers about the increased enrollment were not correct. I explained to her that these numbers were submitted to the state, and if they were not correct, it was a fraudulent offense. She might feel that they were not correct, but that was not verified data, that was an opinion.[29]

After the event, I was surrounded by reporters who wanted to take issue with much of what I said. One wrote of my discussion with them that "Corcoran said he was sorry if people didn't believe what he said. 'Facts are facts,' he said. 'Water's wet. Fire's hot. That's a fact, and what our enrollment is, what teachers left prior to any changes happening. All of those are facts, and all they're verifiable. Nothing I said was untrue.'"

Alt New College

On September 28, 2023, we sent a cease and desist letter to a new organization called Alt New College. It had just been started by a group that included some disgruntled faculty and alumni. The demand was sent on the basis of trademark infringement as to the New College name. Alt New College did not fight this and immediately changed the name to Alt Liberal Arts. We also demanded they issue a public apology, pay our attorneys' fees and costs, and turn over intellectual property that they had taken.

Hamas Attacks

The Hamas attacks revealed to the world the true nature of DEI, as well as the repression of speech and academic freedom that was occurring on college campuses around the nation. I wanted to highlight that New College was fighting successfully against such oppression. On October 11th, I tweeted about our support for the Jewish nation during this difficult time. On November 8th, I published an editorial in the *Wall Street Journal* offering Harvard students who had experienced anti-Semitism at the school a scholarship to New College. I also went on Fox to tout the program.

Graduation

The graduation was a key moment for messaging. Dr. Atlas was a natural choice. He was an academic who spanned a variety of viewpoints—he was a Democrat, he had worked for Trump, he sometimes criticized Trump. He was not easily pigeonholed. His primary message was that he was passionate about free speech and civil discourse because these were bedrocks of self-government. He also it turned out contrasted nicely with the speaker chosen for the "alternative graduation" the night before by those who opposed the governor's changes. Maya Wiley, the speaker at that "alternative" event, turned out to be a political activist known for her far-left stances. In terms of free speech, Wiley—with her overt political activism—starkly illustrated the view of free expression embraced by the "old New College" group.

It was a narrow tent. Dr. Atlas with his varied background and proven ability to stand up for science and data against rabid opposition was a strong counterpoint. While the governor, the new board members, and I did have political allegiances that others used to obfuscate our message about free speech and civil discourse, Dr. Atlas was another person who could explain the vision, one that I hoped the public would hear despite the press's attempts to muffle it.

• • •

Those are a few of the specifics as to how we achieved transformation quickly at New College. New College was and is an institution with many positives, particularly its strong commitment to the liberal arts, its unique individualized program, and its stunning location. However, it needed leadership. Once that happened, we were poised to reach the goal: becoming the best liberal arts college in the country.

CHAPTER 6

Barking Dogs

You will never reach your destination if you stop
and throw stones at every dog that barks.
—Winston Churchill

As I mentioned earlier, on May 12th, New College attorneys wrote a letter to a business that had been renting part of the university's property. The letter notified the tenant, a car museum, that the lease would be terminated effective June 30th. While the car museum had leased the property for around $20,000 a month below market value, the main reason we were ending the lease was because the college was now growing and needed the space.

On June 12th, the local paper ran an article entitled "'Logistical Nightmare': Sarasota Classic Car Museum Faces Hasty Eviction by New College." The article told the story from the tenant's point of view, painting the college as if it were a real-life Mr. Potter trying to evict a George Bailey-like character in the movie *It's a Wonderful Life*. According to the paper, the "lease termination took [Martin] Godbey [the car museum's owner] by surprise...If the college were looking to move the museum off the property, he said he would've hoped for more notice and time to vacate." Godbey told the paper it might take "one to two years" to find another place.

> *Facing a deadline barely three weeks away, the museum has to find a new location and move more than 3,000 pieces to a new location. While cars move fast, museums do not. Facilitating a move can take years and cost millions of dollars, Godbey said. "You're looking at one to two years to identify, renovate and move into a suitable structure[.]"*

The article does not mention that the car museum's lease was month-to-month or that the past administration had rented the building out for far below market value—at the same time the college was complaining to the legislature that it was underfunded. It also does not mention that lawyers from the college had been in contact with Godbey and were working toward a solution for both parties. We realized that the termination of the lease was likely a challenge for Godbey; however, New College was not a charity, and we were working toward resolving the issue while ensuring that the college was operating in a manner in compliance with its fiduciary responsibilities. Godbey indicated that he had told the paper this, but the reporter had not been interested. In general, significant facts were left out of the story that would have been helpful to the average reader seeking to understand the situation.

After this article, I had our lawyer again contact Godbey and iterate that we were terminating the lease. Godbey asked to meet with me personally. I went and walked the property with him, and we worked out the museum could have a few more weeks in the building if the school could use about one-quarter of the building for staff for those weeks and the museum agreed to pay $20,000 a month, along with putting $50,000 in an account and signing a writ of possession. This did not affect our timeline in terms of planning.

As we walked the property, Godbey was thankful for the resolution and commented that my current offer might result in less vitriol from the press. I told him, "I don't give a f***." I was not angry. It had been a cordial meeting with a positive resolution.

The deal made sense for the college and for him. As to the press: I. Did. Not. Give. A. F***. If what I was fighting for was the right thing to do morally, ethically, and legally, I could not lose. The press could twist facts to fit a false narrative. In the end, the premises these fictions were based upon would be exposed as faulty.

As a result of this perspective, my opponents call me "pugnacious." What I try to be is a long-term thinker who makes decisions based on facts and does not capitulate to bullying. The goal is to get the best results for the people who are served, and that is done by looking at outcomes.

I relate that story to provide context as to why I have included this chapter. I did not intend originally to go through the details that follow because I consider them "barking dogs." By "barking dogs," I am referring to distractions that are not relevant to the goal; therefore, in some sense, they are not pertinent to the story.

However, one of the most important functions of an executive leader is to be able to tell a true problem from a manufactured crisis. In this case, there were many "barking dogs": the skewed press coverage, the lawsuits not based on legal support, the baseless faculty grievances, the unsuccessful complaints to our accreditation agency, the unfounded allegations to the US Department of Education. I tried to give as little of my personal attention to these as possible. In fact, to have done so would have hindered our ability to achieve success.

Sadly, though, many times the "barking dogs" win. They are loud, and they are annoying. As a result, they can often be effective. However, they only have power if they shift focus from the goal. If one does not give time and energy to the sideshow, the best "barking dogs" can do is to catch the bumper—while the driver speeds toward the finish line.

• • •

I split the "barking dogs" at New College into three categories: chihuahuas, poodles, and wolves in sheep's clothing.

Chihuahuas yip loudly to draw attention because they do not like the goal. They can be well-meaning—confused but not necessarily ill-intentioned.

The second group is the poodles. While they also do not like the goal, they mainly are seeking attention. They love the spotlight and may even need it to fund an endeavor.

Finally, there are the wolves in sheep's clothing. This refers to those who present themselves as objective but, in reality, have a strong viewpoint. This includes the mainstream press as well as other organizations that operate in and around the higher educational ecosystem.

Chihuahuas

Lawsuits

On August 3rd, in state court, a New College professor along with faculty unions filed a lawsuit against the BOG and the New College board alleging that SB 266, which had passed during the 2023 legislative session in the spring, violated collective-bargaining rights and impaired a union contract. While there are many higher education institutions in the state, only New College was included. There was a simple reason for this: New College was the only one currently complying with SB 266. The New College professor, who was a plaintiff in the suit, had been one of those denied early tenure at the April board meeting. New College had an internal process that allowed the professor to ask for review of this decision under the union contract. This process allowed for two levels of internal review. The professor worked through the first level prior to SB 266's effective date of July 1st. However, the second level of review occurred after July 1st. Therefore, after Galvano, Brickhouse, and I conferred, we decided that the mandates of SB 266 would apply and—when the professor lost the second round of the internal review under the union contract—he had no arbitration right to appeal the decision outside the university. If SB 266 was not applied, he would have been able to appeal.

On August 14th, a similar lawsuit was brought. Once again, only New College—of all the universities in the Florida system—had applied SB 266. Therefore, only the BOG and New College were sued in federal court. New College in essence prevailed when, in mid-February 2024, the plaintiffs filed a motion to voluntarily dismiss the lawsuit because thus far they had been losing on issues. The local paper published the story about the case's dismissal with a headline and beginning paragraph that stated that the group was "pausing" the lawsuit. I tweeted the following:

> *In one headline, the* Sarasota Herald-Tribune *demonstrates how it does journalism. This case ended in a dismissal. There is no such thing as "pausing" in the law. Try sticking to the facts.*

The paper quietly then changed the headline to read "New College Activist Group Drops Federal Academic Freedom Lawsuit over State Law."

Complaints to Accreditation Agency

On September 7, September 25, and October 2, 2023, New College received letters from its accreditation agency, the Southern Association of Colleges and Schools Commission on Colleges (SACSCOC), that SACSCOC had received "unsolicited information" that New College was not in compliance with its *Principles of Accreditation*. Our lawyers responded, and on December 14th, SACSCOC notified New College that it had reviewed the information presented and that the complaints "did not support" the allegations that New College had violated SACSCOC's *Principles*.

Complaints with US Dept. of Education, Office of Civil Rights

On August 22nd, students, faculty, and staff filed a "Civil Rights Complaint" against the board and administration with the US Department of Education. It replayed many of the greatest hits they had so successfully sold to the press, including that the board's "goal" was to "remak[e] New College into 'a little Hillsdale,' a private Christian school."[1] They also claimed Chris Rufo had "misgendered" the former head of the OOIE office.

Dramatic Exits

On April 8th, Aaron Hillegass, the department chair of the data science department at New College, posted a letter on Twitter stating that he was quitting. At the end, he included the line, "if I were more patriotic, I would burn the college's buildings to the ground."[2] According to the *HuffPost*, the newsworthy angle of this letter was "Director at Florida Liberal Arts College Likens Ron DeSantis' Takeover to 'Fascism.'" When people on Twitter and elsewhere in the press expressed shock at his language, Hillegass went on Twitter again on April 10th and stated, "The line about burning buildings is pretty mild."[3] He also told the *Sarasota Herald-Tribune* that the line was a "poetic flourish."

On April 26th, at the end of the three-hour board meeting, faculty representative Matthew Lepinski—an associate professor of computer science—stated, "I am very concerned about the way this board is going, and the destabilization of the academic program. And so I wish you the best of luck, but this is my last board meeting. I'm leaving the college." He then pushed his chair back from the board table, gathered his things, and walked out to loud cheers from the audience. Board of Trustee Chair Debra Jenks then adjourned the meeting. Matthew Lepinski's action was in response to the board's vote immediately before this when the board—on my recommendation—denied early tenure to five professors.

Lepinski told a reporter with the *Chronicle of Higher Education* that he had not planned on leaving prior to the meeting. "But by the end of the meeting, Lepinski said, he couldn't point to a single thing that indicated the board valued the students and 'what they were going through.'" Students had testified during the public comment that they liked these professors and thought they should get early tenure. "Lepinski said he had hoped the board members were paying attention to the stories and would be moved by them, but the trustees denied all five cases. At one point, Lepinski wondered what he would tell those students, the ones working with the denied professors, the next day."

I would have suggested he told them the truth—that the college was in danger of being closed because of mismanagement, and the board was tasked with fixing all aspects of it. This entailed looking into its processes, which included reviewing the record amount of requests for early tenure.

Faculty Resolutions

On May 23, 80 percent of the faculty present at a faculty meeting- which many do not attend- voted to censure the board of trustees and sent a letter signed by Faculty Chair Amy Reid to me as interim president.[4] The letter charged that the board was "failing in their fiduciary duties of first: caring for the institution's reputation and for student, faculty, and staff well-being; and second: endangering the College's ability to fulfill its mission." In the article, the reporter stated that "trustees have echoed the governor's desires to turn the school into the 'Hillsdale, College of the South.' Hillsdale College is a small, Christian private liberal arts school in Michigan." No current trustee ever said this. In fact, Spalding had stated the opposite.[5]

In a statement from a university spokesperson, the college responded that the items outlined in the censure were false and that the vote was taken "out of fear of the unknown." In the statement, I said that "I think their concerns will subside once the faculty see how all of the changes we are making at New College are moving us in a direction of improvement and future stability for our campus."

On January 17, 2024, certain faculty passed a resolution against the addition of the online school. The "symbolic resolution" was approved by a group of faculty members who voted 25–1 against the plan. According to one faculty member, the resolution was taken because of "process," as they felt they wanted more input on the program. Again, the desire to slow down the pace of change at a university—mired in malaise for years—highlighted the very issues that had caused the downward trajectory in the first place.[6]

FIRE Letter

In June, the Foundation for Individual Rights in Education (FIRE) wrote me a letter asking me to take "swift action" because Rufo had tweeted his personal opinion about the fact that the one-year contract of a visiting professor was being allowed to expire. FIRE is an organization that describes itself on its website as a group that "defends and promotes the value of free speech for all Americans in our courtrooms, on our campuses, and in our culture."

Rufo had tweeted: "New College of Florida has let the contract for visiting professor Erik Wallenberg expire. He will not be returning to the campus. I wish Professor Wallenberg well and hope his work on 'radical theatre and environmental movements' finds a more suitable home."[7]

Not renewing a visiting professor's one-year contract is not an uncommon practice in academia. FIRE is an organization that had worked to increase free speech on campus. Yet it was writing to protest Rufo's free speech.

I replied in part as follows:

> *It is interesting that you have taken the time to write a five-page letter but cannot sum up in a few words what the "swift action" is that you want the university to take. The reason is clear: your letter asks New College to take "swift action" against a private citizen making comments on his own personal Twitter account. In fact, you directly state in* the letter *that Mr. Rufo is protected in this instance by the First Amendment…Therefore, I can understand the difficulty in making a direct ask to New College which would violate FIRE's core mission… To presume otherwise would be to act against not only New College's mission but your own.*

FIRE's original letter was reported on by the press. My response was not.

Poodles

California Gov. Gavin Newsom

Gov. Gavin Newsom made a surprise visit to campus on April 5th. "I want you to know you're not alone, you matter, we care," Newsom told New College students.[8] According to Newsom,

DeSantis "has one thing that is common with everything he's doing—bullying and intimidating vulnerable communities… You're not only on the right side of history, you have something he'll never have—moral authority." Newsom would appear on CNN in September to apologize for his response to COVID. At that time, he did not mention that DeSantis had been shown to be on the "right side of history" in his approach to COVID in Florida—though I took the opportunity to tweet that I "can't wait for [Newsom's] next mea culpa," which I predicted would relate to his April visit to New College.

MSNBC "Documentary"

On August 29, 2023, MSNBC ran a "documentary" on the changes at New College that was entitled *The War on Woke*. The press had recently learned that New College had achieved record enrollment. The segment claimed that New College was in essence recruiting athletes under false pretenses. For one thing, it reported, the baseball team "doesn't have a baseball field for them to play on." MSNBC also claimed that New College was no longer offering courses in marine biology, as well as designating the student who had spit at Rufo and been disciplined by the school as a "free speech martyr."

When contacted, MSNBC agreed to correct the record on the final two pieces of misinformation; however, it refused a request by Rufo to clarify that the school did indeed have baseball facilities. The team did have a field, and Athletic Director Jimenez had expressly told the MSNBC crew that there was an agreement in place to use IMG's college-level baseball facility. This was not mentioned in the story, as Rufo noted in an article online after the segment aired.

An email from MSNBC senior producer Tina Cone to Rufo's chief of staff stated that "[w]e have carefully reviewed the points raised in your note and have concluded that no changes are warranted. The statement that the college does not have a baseball field to play on is accurate, as it's undisputed there are no baseball fields on campus." Others jumped to New College's defense, including *Spectator*'s editor-at-large Ben Domenech. He posted on Twitter that "[t]his is an absurd refusal to correct. Colleges at this level often have agreements with local facilities rather than paying for upkeep or using up land on campus."

New York Times *Opinion Writer*

New York Times columnist Michelle Goldberg wrote three opinion pieces in 2023 on the changes at New College. On January 9th, she wrote one entitled "DeSantis Allies Plot the Hostile Takeover of a Liberal College." In it, she predicted that this change would "set the stage for an even broader assault on the academic freedom of every instructor whose worldview is at odds with the Republican Party." On April 29th, she expounded on her conspiracy theory with "This Is What the Right-Wing Takeover of a Progressive College Looks Like." She repeated the incorrect assertion that, as the board had agreed not to allow early tenure in 2023, it was an attack on tenure in general. She asserted that the move was "widely seen as a referendum not just on the individual candidates but on faculty independence," and it had "overridde[n] the typical tenure process."

On August 14th, she wrote an opinion piece about how adding sports was sexist entitled "At College Targeted by DeSantis, Gender Studies Is Out, Jocks Are In." According to Goldberg, "Rather than reviving some traditional model of academic excellence, then, it looks as though New College leaders are simply trying to replace a culture they find politically hostile with one meant to be more congenial. The end of gender studies and the…incoming athletes have the effect of masculinizing a place that had been heavily feminist, artsy and queer."

I tweeted the following in response:

> *Interesting how the author in this recent opinion piece in the NYT thinks bringing in sports is "masculinizing a place." As a father of three daughters who play sports, that's offensive. FYI NYT, women play sports too.*

I then noted the obvious—basically all liberal arts colleges have sports.

> *Also—almost all liberal arts colleges have sports programs. Currently waiting for the follow-up piece from the NYT on how Amherst College and Swarthmore have been "masculinizing" their educations through having sports….[9]*

Of the twenty-one colleges who joined the NAIA in the past three years, only New College has been accused of being sexist for doing so. While athletics did boost male enrollment by bringing the college more in line with national averages, that was because the ratios had previously been so wildly out of proportion—with almost 70 percent of the college being female. Goldberg failed to mention that bringing in athletics also boosted minority enrollment. It would have spoiled the fascist plotline.

Maya Wiley

On May 22, 2023, students held an "alternative graduation" with a far-left speaker named Maya Wiley. Wiley had recently run for mayor of New York, and the *New York Times* stated at that time that she "sparked enthusiasm that she could become the standard-bearer for New York's progressive left."[10] She was a lawyer for Mayor Bill de Blasio and an analyst for liberal mouthpiece MSNBC. As part of her platform for mayor, she wanted to cut $1 billion from the budget of the police and eliminate 2,250 officers.

She spent most of her speech to the New College graduates praising them for standing up to "fascism." "You have had to be strong in the face of a few who would tell you that you can't read what you want to read, that you can't speak what you want to speak, that you should get in line with an ideology that is not yours and call that…freedom," she said.

While no one had told these students what they could not read or that they could not say what they wanted, they were happy to play along. They steadfastly ignored that the point was the exact opposite: everyone, including them, would be welcome on campus.

Opinion Articles in Local Paper

On June 18th, Robin Williams, the president of the Democratic Public Education Caucus of Manasota and a retired educator, wrote in an opinion piece in the local paper that the new banyan tree mascot was a "tree that has been anthropomorphized to closely resemble an angry, threatening brown individual." She expounded on this.

It is an image that is also reminiscent of the historically offensive imagery perpetuated by the "Tarzan" books, which featured a main character who lived in an African jungle and boasted of being a "killer of beasts and many black men." Though generations have passed, there is no getting around the reality that the "Tarzan" literary series remains one full of vile racial stereotyping, with Black men portrayed as "primitive natives" and "savages." "The Mighty Banyan" mascot also appears to bear similarities to race-oriented memorabilia that was especially popular during the Jim Crow era in the United States and, unfortunately, served to ingrain racial stereotypes in the American psyche.[11]

As Rufo tweeted after the article's publication, "Advice for white libs: if you see a tree and immediately think 'looks like a scary minority to me,' you might be the racist."[12]

An opinion writer for the *Sarasota Herald-Tribune* wrote two articles about how adding sports was an absurd move. On February 11, 2023, Chris Anderson penned a column entitled "If New College Turns to Sports the School Will Be Thrown for a Loss." In the first line, he confidently asserted that "just wait, sports will be next at New College, as certain as the plan will fail."[13] On June 16th, he doubled down on this opinion. In a column entitled "Sports at New College Sounds Good, but Will Have Little Impact," he stated that "I am a big fan of NAIA sports. In fact, my daughter will likely play NAIA soccer at a small school in the Midwest. But sports programs work at those schools because they are supported by small towns where the school is the primary focus and source of jobs. Would our community support college sports at NCF? Not likely. The area's too big, too transient and there are too many other options."[14] No data was cited, just his feelings about the matter. Two months later, the largest class in New College's history was on campus. Around 150 of them were athletes.

Wolves in Sheep's Clothing

When I was education commissioner, I said during a State Board of Education meeting that I would encourage people "never to read" the coverage on the pandemic in the *Washington Post* or the *New York Times*. It was September 23, 2020. We had just opened schools, and the reporting in those papers was confounding. "You're going to see reports from time to time…the reporting on this [the pandemic] is just all off," I told the board, as a member questioned me about the decision to open schools.

> *You know, you'll read of someone who was a teacher's aide has died—had nothing to do with the school system. [He or she] contracted the virus from a brother, who was a first responder, way before the school opened—and had nothing to do with the school system. As tragic as it is, it's important for people to know it wasn't a school issue. But the headlines will say 'teacher's aid…dies,' tragically—but it did not have to do with schools.*[15]

I was speaking of the common refusal by the press to give context to a factual situation, in essence performing a sleight of hand that leaves the reader with an incorrect understanding of the totality of the circumstances. Such behavior continued with much of the media's coverage of New College.

The press often chose to frame our decisions for the reader, rather than allowing the facts to stand for themselves. In doing so, reporters failed to report crucial information behind the decisions. The question should be: Would the average person, after reading the article, understand what New College's position was and what the opponents' position was? If the answer was that the average reader would only understand the opponents' framing, that is a problem.

Mainstream Media

The members of the media had a fixed idea formed by their conformist groupthink that went something like this: Republicans are scary fascists who want to take over the pristine higher educational landscape of today and suppress free speech, burn books, take away women's rights, and persecute LGBTQ people. In addition, according to the press, since they viewed us as opposing open and intellectual discussion, we were sure to fail on academic measures.

The stories to fit this narrative were already written in a sense. All that was required was to take any move we made and twist it to conform with this messaging.

National Rankings

In September 2023, *US News & World Report* released its ranking for liberal arts schools. New College dropped twenty-four spots to a tie for one hundredth. This led to quite a few articles along the lines of this one in *Politico*, which wrote as follows:

> *[T[here was bad news for New College of Florida, which dipped 24 spots to a tie for 100 in the standings for liberal arts schools amid an overhaul triggered by DeSantis appointing conservative trustees to the struggling campus, Florida's smallest state university.*[16]

The local paper, the *Sarasota Herald-Tribune*, ran an article with the headline "New College of Florida Plummets in National Rankings amid DeSantis Conservative Overhaul."[17]

To put this in context, readers would need to know that this ranking was normal for New College. While it had ranked seventy-sixth in 2023, it ranked eighty-second in 2022, eighty-fourth in 2021, 102nd in 2020, ninetieth in 2019, and 101st in 2018.

It was merely fluctuating in its normal pattern as it had for years. In addition, readers would have benefited from the understanding that this ranking was based in large part on data from previous years, not what had happened since January 2023.[18]

Early Tenure

On April 7, 2023, the *Tampa Bay Times* ran a story entitled "New College Urges 7 Faculty Members to Stop Seeking Tenure as Changes Build." The subtitle was "The move by conservative leader Richard Corcoran is a clear signal of the Florida school's new direction." The article does not mention early tenure. On April 26, 2023, AP News and Yahoo News both ran a story entitled "DeSantis-Backed New College Board Scraps 5 Professors [*sic*] Tenure." While there is one brief mention in one of my quotes about early tenure, nowhere else in the fifteen-paragraph story, which focuses on attacks on regular tenure, is this explained. It ends on a quote by Gov. Newsom from his visit three weeks before: "I can't believe what you're dealing with. It's just an unbelievable assault." On April 27, 2023, *Inside Higher Ed* ran a story with the headline "New College Board Denies Tenure for Five Professors." The story itself primarily discusses attacks on general tenure. On April 30, 2023, the *Bradenton Times*, a local paper, ran a story with the headline "New College Board Denies Tenure for Five Professors." Nowhere in the story does it mention or explain early tenure or my reasoning provided at the meeting and in the board memo.

Many other outlets ran similar stories. For the average reader, there was little way to discern that the issue related to the process.

Conservative-Only Institution

On January 7, 2023, the *Washington Post* ran an article with the headline "DeSantis Moves to Turn a Progressive Florida College into a Conservative One."[19] On February 14, 2023, the *New York Times* ran a story about the changes at New College with the blurb under the headline reading "Gov. Ron DeSantis's plan to transform New College of Florida into a beacon of conservatism has left students and faculty members at the tight-knit progressive school reeling."[20]

While I was used to such impressive ability by the media to ignore that the sky is blue, this instance was particularly egregious. It just went on and on—no matter how many times I, the governor, board members, even outsiders such as Stanley Fish, told reporters that the point was to stop the suppression of speech that was currently occurring in higher education. On September 23, 2023—after eight months of this—the *New York Times* was still running with this angle with another story about the changes, which included a blurb directly under the headline that stated, "An influx of athletes is among many changes since Gov. DeSantis of Florida vowed to transform New College, a public institution into a bastion of conservatism."[21] The local paper parroted this too. On August 18th, an article stated DeSantis wanted the transform the school "into a more conservative, classical liberal arts college in the mold of the Christian Hillsdale College in Michigan."[22]

Dorms

On September 22, 2023, the New York Times wrote a story entitled "Sports Are In, Gender Studies Out at College Targeted by DeSantis."[23] At the beginning of the article it stated that "more than 200 students have been moved from on-campus dorms to off-campus hotels to make room for the recruited athletes and other new students." The article does not mention that one of the main reasons for this was New College regulation 6-3002 which required that "students shall live on campus for the first two years." Most of the athletes and new students fell into this category—and most of the older returning students did not.

Misrepresentation of Sports

Once the press saw how successful the college was in its sports programs, the attacks began. Rather than merely reporting the facts, the media often framed the narrative to charge that New College was underhanded because it recruited athletes before full acceptance to the NAIA and when it did not have athletic facilities on campus. For context, it would have been helpful to readers to be informed as well that almost all colleges seeking acceptance do so under these circumstances. That is simply how a program is built. The press often did not report this important detail.[24]

Weird and Wacky

The Alum Who "Found" $29 Million in Donations on a Tally Sheet

One alumnus, Charlene Lenger, a former member of the New College Foundation for over thirty-five years whose term had recently ended, reached out to the local paper with an interesting angle for a story. The article, published on March 10, 2023, was entitled "DeSantis' Takeover of New College of Florida Puts $29 million in Donations at Risk." While the foundation languished for at least the last several years under her watch, she was suddenly now able to pinpoint "$29 million in donations."[25]

According to the article, Lenger had "spoken to a number of major donors about their giving plans since Gov. Ron DeSantis began transforming the school." Lenger had been on the foundation board for thirty-five years. Twenty-nine million was more than half of what it currently had in the bank.

If anyone wanted evidence, Lenger had the sheet of paper on which she kept the tally of the anonymous people she spoke with. The newspaper noted though that it actually could be more because "Lenger's informal tally doesn't include many lost donations." The reporter noted that the donors Lenger spoke to did not want to be identified. However, to corroborate Lenger's "informal tally," "an anonymous statement" was "sent the Herald-Tribune...through an intermediary." This anonymous statement was from "a donor who canceled a planned gift of $1.5 million." No other details from this interesting use of a source were given.

The reporter noted seriously, and it was picked up by other outlets that: "Lenger's tally indicates that whatever boost New College gets in state funding could be partially offset by a big loss in private donations." She lamented, "It is painful to watch the goodwill the Foundation Team created over decades dissipate over the last 2 months."

I called up the reporter and asked if he would use the same metrics and write a similar story from the university's perspective, i.e. that I had called up anonymous people who gave me numbers that they would now give to the college as a result of the change. The reporter did not agree to use these metrics from the university's standpoint. While I entitled this Weird and Wacky, this may be the most idiotic thing either written or said about the changes at New College—and that is a very, very high bar.

Given that the facts were readily available on public 990 forms, rather than rely on such flimsy information, perhaps the reporter should have looked up those public documents and run a story on those numbers instead.

Food

At the end of April, I was finally able to get a food vendor for the last four weeks of school on the classroom side of campus—a bakery with two locations in the Tampa area. The owner agreed to have an employee drive food from his distributor in Tampa the hour to Sarasota every day, as well as provide an employee. He would also offer free coffee. Then the paper uncovered a major news story. It turned out the plastic cups, which were brought down from the bakeries in Tampa, had a very small Bible verse reference—"Philippians 4:13"—printed on them. (While it was only the reference on the cups, the actual verse is "I can do all things through Christ who strengthens me.")

This was concerning to certain students who were interviewed by the paper about this important and riveting topic. However, despite "the cups with Bible verse references," a student the reporter spoke with said he "was happy to take free coffee. '[I]t's kind of like we're already getting demolished,' Locke said. 'I'm going to take the free coffee, even if it has a Bible verse on it.'" The conspiracy theory the paper and students seemed to be propounding was that someone at the college and/or the vendor had the time, money, and inclination to have special cups printed with Bible verses in order to proselytize. Why? Unsure. However, after the Lenger story, I supposed nothing was too far-fetched to be believed.

"Fascism"

While there are many bizarre paragraphs of "serious" news coverage relating to the changes at New College, this is a particularly interesting one. It is from PBS—yes, this paragraph was subsidized by taxpayers.

> *Professors at the New College of Florida are using personal email because they're afraid of being subpoenaed. Students are concerned, too. Some fear for their physical safety. Many worry their teachers will be fired en masse and their courses and books will be policed.... The effect at New College has been chilling and disruptive...It feels even more jarring because the school is for many students a haven of open-mindedness and acceptance.... One of the new trustees is Christopher Rufo...[an] architect of the right-wing outrage against critical race theory, a legal term that has come to represent teaching about the effects of slavery.*[26]

No explanation is given for why professors and students are in "fear for their physical safety" or if there is any factual basis for "worry" that "books will be policed." The final sentence is an egregious and unethical misrepresentation. Rufo has written extensively about CRT, and nowhere does he conflate it with "teaching about the effects of slavery." The entire article sounds vaguely like the beginning of a bad made-for-TV movie, and it is just as much a fiction.

The above are just a few examples of the absurdity of the press coverage of New College during this time. The fact was that the press was going to soldier on with the narrative of racist, sexist, anti-gay despite the evidence to the contrary. If evidence needed to be twisted, manufactured, or contrived, these reporters and editors were all in.

However, just like with all the other "barking dogs," I would not spend time and energy on such absurdities. My focus would be on the goal. The barking dogs only win if you let them.

CHAPTER 7

With the Press, It's Always Groundhog Day: COVID and New College

Well, it's Groundhog Day...again....
—Bill Murray, Groundhog Day

In the 1993 movie Groundhog Day, Bill Murray plays a character who must relive one day, Groundhog Day, over and over. Every morning, he wakes up—and it is still Groundhog Day. One day, the alarm goes off, he opens his eyes, looks at the ceiling, and says in a resigned monotone: "It's Groundhog Day.....again."

That describes what the press's coverage of New College felt like to me.

In COVID, the framing of the media was that it was dangerous to open schools. The governor and I pushed back with the data attempting to get out the scientific facts. The press often ignored or misrepresented our efforts to inform the public.

At New College, the messaging after DeSantis made the new board appointments was that free speech would be stifled, and LGBTQ people would be in danger if New College was restructured. The governor and I pushed back with the data attempting to get out the facts. The press often ignored or misrepresented our efforts to inform the public.

This is not surprising. Just like in academia, the vast majority of journalists identify as liberal. In 2020, the *Washington Post* published an article by three professors about their research into the personal political persuasions of reporters. Their research found that 80 percent of those who "identified with a political party...were liberal/Democrats."[1] In addition, in 2018, researchers questioned 462 financial journalists from around the country. They were surprised to find the percentage of these journalists that skewed Left also, as financial journalists were presumed to be less liberal than their political counterparts. Of those interviewed, 58 percent identified as politically Left, 37 percent identified as moderate, 3 percent said they were "somewhat conservative," and 0.046 percent identified as "very conservative."[2]

As they do with this exact same issue in academia, the liberal intelligentsia dismiss this as a problem. In the 2020 article in the *Washington Post* about the number of reporters who identify as "liberal/Democrat," the focus was not to raise a concern but to ensure the public that this was nothing to worry about. Entitled "Journalists May Be Liberal, but This Doesn't Affect Which Candidates They Chose to Cover," the article stated, "despite being overwhelmingly liberal themselves, journalists show a great deal of impartiality in the types of candidates that they choose to write about when a potential story is presented to them." This was because researchers had found that if they emailed a journalist, that journalist was just as willing to do a story on a state legislative candidate who was a Republican as they were to do a story on one who was a Democrat. In addition, researchers also examined the journalists' Twitter accounts and found that they followed Democratic candidates as well as Republicans.

These researchers miss the forest for the trees. The concern is not that the press does not cover candidates from both parties. The issue is that when they cover both parties, they do so in a skewed manner. For example, reporters clearly covered New College—ad nauseum. In addition, many of the reporters who have covered me as House Speaker, education commissioner, as a potential candidate for governor, and/or as president of New College, follow me on Twitter. Whether or not a journalist covered me or followed me on social media had absolutely nothing to do with if they could report a story from a neutral viewpoint.

In April 2024, Uri Berliner, a senior editor at NPR for more than twenty years, wrote an article for The Free Press, about how his newsroom had made critical miscalculations on three important stories: the Hunter Biden laptop, Trump's purported collusion with Russia, and whether COVID originated in a lab in China. He felt that reporters' and editors' personal opinions, which skewed liberal, had affected the coverage. Prior to the publication of this article, he said that he tried repeatedly to voice his concerns internally.

"I love NPR and feel it's a national trust," he said in an interview several days after The Free Press article was published. "We have great journalists here. If they shed their opinions and did the great journalism they're capable of, this would be a much more interesting and fulfilling organization for our listeners."

However, Berliner did not see that happening. Instead, as he wrote in The Free Press, listeners to NPR hear "the distilled worldview of a very small segment of the U.S. population." He then explained the narrow representation of the public in the NPR newsroom was an issue in these three stories.

Berliner, as of this writing, still works for NPR though perhaps not for long. The CEO of NPR responded with a letter the next day to staff stating that "[q]uestioning whether our people are serving our mission with integrity, based on little more than the recognition of their identity, is profoundly disrespectful, hurtful, and demeaning." A letter to Berliner stated that he was to have asked for permission before publishing elsewhere. He was briefly suspended and told that the suspension was a "final warning." If Berliner does leave, he will follow the path of others before him who have tried to survive in a field that rewards those who follow its biases.

In February 2024, Adam Rubenstein wrote an article for the Atlantic about his experience working at the *New York Times*.

In one of my first days at The New York Times, *I went to an orientation with more than a dozen other new hires. We had to do an icebreaker: Pick a Starburst out of a jar and then answer a question. My Starburst was pink, I believe, and so I had to answer the pink prompt, which had me respond with my favorite sandwich...I blurted out, "The spicy chicken sandwich from Chick-fil-A," and considered the ice broken. The HR representative leading the orientation chided me: "We don't do that here. They hate gay people." People started snapping their fingers in acclamation. I hadn't been thinking about the fact that Chick-fil-A was transgressive in liberal circles for its chairman's opposition to gay marriage. "Not the politics, the chicken," I quickly said, but it was too late. I sat down, ashamed.*

This was just the first of many examples he gave in the article that led to him quitting his job. He started in 2019. He had quit by December 2020.

> *Being a conservative—or at least being considered one—at the* Times *was a strange experience. [If I asked certain questions,] I'd revealed that I wasn't on the same team as my colleagues, that I didn't accept as an article of faith [a] liberal premise… [T]ake the Hunter Biden laptop story: Was it truly "unsubstantiated," as the paper kept saying? At the time, it had been substantiated, however unusually, by Rudy Giuliani. Many of my colleagues were clearly worried that lending credence to the laptop story could hurt the electoral prospects of Joe Biden and the Democrats. But starting from a place of party politics and assessing how a particular story could affect an election isn't journalism.*

Rubenstein did not just feel marginalized as an employee, he was also concerned about the silencing of non-favored viewpoints in the paper itself.

> *There was a sense that publishing the occasional conservative voice made the paper look centrist. But I soon realized that the conservative voices we published tended to be ones agreeing with the liberal line. It was also clear that right-of-center submissions were treated differently. They faced a higher bar for entry, more layers of editing, and greater involvement of higher-ups.*

Rubenstein was merely the next in line. Bari Weiss, a center-right writer and editor for *The New York Times* opinion department, had already made similar points in her resignation letter in July 2020 after working three years at the publication.

I was hired with the goal of bringing in voices that would not otherwise appear in your pages: first-time writers, centrists, conservatives, and other who would not naturally think of The Times *as their home…But the lessons that ought to have followed the [2016] election—lessons about the importance of understanding other Americans, the necessity of resisting tribalism, and the centrality of the free exchange of ideas to a democratic society—have not been learned. Instead, a new consensus has emerged in the press, but perhaps especially at this paper: that truth isn't a process of collective discovery, but an orthodoxy already known to an enlightened few whose job is to inform everyone else.*

Weiss, Rubenstein, Berliner. The drumbeat continues, but the mainstream press does not stop the bus to check why the light might be flashing.

Particularly egregious is the gaslighting by the mainstream media about its coverage during COVID. On the night of the New College graduation in May 2023, Dr. Atlas reflected on his experience to get the truth out during COVID. He pointed out that we must not just forget how the facts around why draconian lockdowns were allowed to happen.

*Many call for simply "forgiving and forgetting"
the unconscionable decisions to close schools and
implement reckless lockdowns.*

*No. That must not be allowed—
Because Truth matters in an ethical society—
the public needs to know the truth, after all they
have been through.*

Even Gov. Newsom has been willing—likely with much coaxing from political consultants—to fess up to his failures during the pandemic. In his apology for his COVID response in September 2023, Newsom stated that "hindsight" gives perspective. He is correct. One side was proven to have made the right decisions. The other was wrong and is apologizing.

The facts were hard for the public to ascertain because of the media's narrative, as Dr. Atlas noted. The reality was that the mainstream press often seemed to choose a side during the pandemic and actively demeaned those who disagreed with the storyline they were weaving. This did not help the public. Dr. Atlas noted this as well.

*[So] many people desperately wanted to hear the
facts, spoken logically, to clarify the truth—I received
hundreds of emails per day, thousands of
emotional emails from everyday working people,
seniors, doctors and scientists, teachers, priests
praying for me, fathers and mothers, whose husbands
and daughters had committed suicide from
the isolation and lockdowns—who implored me,
literally begged me, to keep it up because they were
afraid to speak up. I could never let them down.*

> The press never understood the motivation—
> my responsibility to my fellow Americans com-
> pletely dwarfed the media's slurs and criticisms.

Gavin Newsom, Randi Weingarten, and Andrew Cuomo were often praised by the press, while DeSantis, Atlas, and many others, myself included, were often vilified.[3]

• • •

NEWSOM

On Sunday, September 10, 2023, in a pre-taped interview on NBC's *Meet the Press*, California governor Gavin Newsom said his approach to the pandemic was wrong.

"I think we would've done everything differently," Newsom said.

In response to criticism of his responses to COVID, Newsom stated that "[a]ll of it's legitimate in terms of reflection…I think all of us in terms of our collective wisdom, we've evolved. We didn't know what we didn't know. We're experts in hindsight. We're all geniuses now."[4]

Newsom looked like a hostage in a video asking for ransom. Host Chuck Todd pressed the California Democrat on specifics. Newsom squirmed. "I think there's a lot of humility. And we didn't know what we didn't know," he said vaguely.

After taking responsibility, he then deflected it. "And it was hardly I; it was we, collectively." Who is "we" in Newsom's quotes? It was not Florida. "We" were not confused. I remember very well Newsom's hypocrisy and flawed reasoning, even if he has selective amnesia.

I remember it because I was the education commissioner in the state Newsom continually criticized for its opposite approach to the pandemic. I remember when California parents sued Newsom in August 2020 to reopen schools.[5] I remember in October 2020 when Newsom's own children returned to private school, and he kept the public schools shuttered.[6] I remember in February 2021 when, despite the science, Newsom did not require schools to reopen.[7]

He knew what we were doing in Florida—the first state in the nation to fully reopen schools—and he chose to do the opposite, becoming one of the last governors in the nation to fully reopen schools.

In response to Newsom's interview where he tried to obfuscate the facts regarding his poor leadership during the pandemic, I tweeted out the following on September 12, 2023.

> *As Gov. Desantis' ed commissioner during COVID, schools reopened because we knew data—the same data @GavinNewsom ignored.*
>
> *Newsom today: "We didn't know what we didn't know."*
>
> *He now wants to "save" NCF from DeSantis. Can't wait for the next mea culpa.*

I had to push back in some manner from the popular mainstream media narrative. While some outlets highlighted the apology, much of the ecosphere of the national press appeared to downplay it. NBC reported on it with the headline "Newsom:

I'm not convinced we've learned the lessons from COVID."[8] In RealClearPolitics, the headline was that "Gov. Gavin Newsom on Covid Response Mistakes: 'It was hardly I, It was we, collectively.' "[9] An article in *The Hill* about the interview was entitled "Newsom worries about 'fetishness for 'autocracy' in the U.S."[10]

Consider for a moment how such an interview with DeSantis would have been received if the facts were flipped.

WEINGARTEN

Newsom had many reasons for his poor decisions, one of which was that he seemed to allow the teachers' unions to dictate his policies. Randi Weingarten, the American Federation of Teachers president, took a page out of Newsom's playbook and issued a similar statement accepting blame while at the same time deflecting it. She was also free with her use of the term "we." In April 2023, she appeared before the House of Representatives to provide testimony that was, according to the *Wall Street Journal*, "unbelievable."

Weingarten told the House, in testimony that echoed Newsom's dubious recollections of COVID history that "we spent every day from February on trying to get schools open. We knew that remote education was not a substitute for opening schools."

The *Wall Street Journal* refuted this.

> *Alas, [Weingarten] omitted a few things. Such as her description in July 2020 of the Trump Administration's push to reopen schools for in-person learning that autumn as "this reckless, this*

callous, this cruel." That summer she also endorsed teacher "safety strikes" if unions deemed local reopening protocols to be inadequate. Hundreds of private and charter schools did open that fall without the surge of illness that Ms. Weingarten claimed to fear.

I remember what Weingarten said during the pandemic very well because she was a critic of Florida's approach. I was one of the education commissioners fighting her local union affiliates, which sued me, the governor, and others, when the order to reopen schools in Florida was issued in July 2020.

In that July, immediately after the order to reopen schools was issued, I remember when the local teachers' union responded as follows:

"The Governor and Commissioner are pushing a political and economic agenda over the safety and well-being of students, teachers and school employees," the Orange County Classroom Teachers Association (CTA) said in a statement that week. "CTA will not support a reopening plan that could expose students, teachers or their families to illness, hospitalization or death."

When she tweeted on December 5, 2023, about her odd recollection of events, I responded on December 6th: "An ironic rewrite of history. What actually happened—you publicly backed the FEA in a lawsuit against Gov. DeSantis and me in July 2020 seeking to stop Florida's schools from reopening."

Again, Weingarten, like Newsom, seemed to get a pass for these critical errors, which it would be hard to conceive DeSantis getting if the situation was reversed. In fact, on April 28, 2023, *The New York Times Magazine* ran a feature about Weingarten in which it noted she was a "lightning rod of criticism." Entitled

" 'The Most Dangerous Person in the World' "—a term Mike Pompeo had applied to her—the article seemed to insinuate that Republicans were slightly unhinged to be holding her up for such intense criticism, including about school closures. On April 26, 2023, when Republicans questioned her about why she—someone with no medical background—suggested language to the CDC on closing schools, ABC News ran a story entitled "Republicans grill teachers' union head on COVID classroom closures." The focus was on Republicans' behavior at the moment—not her behavior during the pandemic which was the focus of the criticism—and the anger of many Americans whose children had suffered and were still suffering as a result. Again, consider how the framing would likely have differed if the facts had been switched on who made the right calls.

• • •

CUOMO

In October of 2020, while the pandemic continued to paralyze New York state, *CBS Sunday Morning* sent correspondent Tracy Smith to profile its governor, who had been spending the COVID era quarantining with his daughters Michaela, Mariah, and Cara Kennedy-Cuomo. The TV segment began with the governor and his daughters eating at the dinner table and talking about Grandma's recipe for spaghetti sauce.

Andrew Cuomo's daily briefings were mentioned, and how, for 111 days straight, "He said he tried to present just the facts, but the facts were often grim. On one day alone, April 8, New York lost 799 lives to the virus. 'That is so shocking and painful and breathtaking,' he told the state, 'I don't even have the words for it.'"[11]

He did, however, have words about leadership, which he helpfully wrote down in a book, which coincidentally would be released the following week. According to CBS, because of the incredible success the state had in dealing with COVID, numerous requests came in from all over the country.

"'How,' people wanted to know, 'did you do it?'" Tracy Smith asked.

His daughter Cara had the ready answer. "Right from the first day, we were all saying, 'You have to write this down. You have to communicate this somehow.'"[12]

Thus, viewers were told, *American Crisis: Leadership Lessons from the COVID-19 Pandemic* was born. Andrew Cuomo apparently read all of his own clippings and took them to heart. He had a lot of clippings. Cuomo's press conferences were nationally televised in the effort to portray him as a sane, sober foil to Trump's erratic leadership on the issue.

The sense of brand-name familiarity, along with the carefully choreographed COVID press briefings delivered with a New York-centric attitude, made Cuomo a star. That is actually an understatement. Cuomo was a "pandemic superstar," in the words of a *Washington Post* columnist.[13]

Celebrities such as Ben Stiller, Cher, Robert De Niro, Rosie Perez, and Sarah Silverman lionized him. Comedienne Chelsea Handler penned a March 31, 2020, letter in *Vogue* magazine titled, "Dear Andrew Cuomo, I Want to Be Your First Lady." "Thank you for reminding us that there are men who can lead and be clear and tell the truth—even when the news is bad," Handler gushed to the married New York governor, adding an

"I love you" and expressing a desire to vote for him for president one day. "But, most of all, thank you for your competence."[14]

In April 2020, comedian Trevor Noah would claim he was a "Cuomo-sexual."

"Yeah. People online are falling in love with him," the quarantined *Daily Show* host told his viewers from his home. "And I'm not gonna lie. Those people include me. My Tinder profile now lists me as Cuomo-sexual."[15]

The same month, Ellen DeGeneres also expressed her loving support for Cuomo on her once-popular daytime TV talk show. In a since-deleted tweet, *The Ellen Show* posted a fawning picture with the message, "Andrew Cuomo has emerged as a leader many people are looking to for strength. I'm so happy he's on my show this Thursday."[16]

"Can I say that I am a Cuomosexual?" she asked during their interview. "We know that that's going around, that people are saying they're Cuomosexuals."[17]

"Yeah, I think that's a good thing," Cuomo responded, grinning. "I don't think it's a bad thing."[18]

The International Academy of Television Arts & Sciences even gave him an Emmy award for his "masterful" pandemic briefings. "The Governor's 111 daily briefings worked so well because he effectively created television shows, with characters, plot lines, and stories of success and failure," said the academy's president and CEO, Bruce Paisner, when announcing the award decision, according to NPR.[19]

Cuomo also did not think it was a bad thing to cash in from his pandemic fame. He even sold a poster called "New York Tough," which he designed himself.

"I love history. I love poster art," Cuomo declared. "We went up the mountain, we curved the mountain, we came down the other side and these are little telltale signs that, to me, represent what was going on."[20]

For $14.50 (plus shipping and handling), the cartoon poster was supposed to tell the story of the early pandemic months.[21] It featured a crude-looking mountain shape with the words, "Wake up America! Forget the politics, get smart!" at the top, along with "Love wins!" The poster also showed an airplane with "Europeans" and "COVID-19" on it, suggesting the virus came from Europe instead of China.[22]

Cuomo also nabbed $5.1 million for his book, which became an instant *New York Times* bestseller.

While DeSantis was being accused of imperiling the lives of children because we opened up schools, the *Washington Post*, in its review of Cuomo's book, raved that it was "an impressive road map to dealing with a crisis as serious as any we have faced."[23]

The book's Amazon page proclaimed this sales pitch: "Governor Andrew Cuomo tells the riveting story of how he took charge in the fight against COVID-19 as New York became the epicenter of the pandemic, offering hard-won lessons in leadership and his vision for the path forward."[24]

The path forward would have a few twists in it that neither Governor Cuomo nor his celebrity and media fans saw coming. Cuomo had insisted that New York nursing homes admit recovering coronavirus patients, and the New York State Health Department issued an order mandating the policy. "Despite protests from administrators and the families of residents, as late as April 25 [2020]—several weeks into the crisis—Cuomo was still publicly insisting that the order be enforced. It would not be until six weeks after it was first issued that Cuomo rescinded the rule," *Newsweek* later reported.[25]

As the howls of grief and demands for justice grew, Cuomo denied responsibility. Then, the play was to minimize his manmade casualties—only five thousand deaths by June 2020. He and his defenders used the "blame President Trump" card ad nauseam, and then they claimed the nursing home debacle was born from unknown factors and a humanitarian desire to make sure the elderly had a place to stay.

Cuomo effectively chose not to utilize the 2,500 emergency beds at the Jacob Javits Convention Center in New York City or the US Navy hospital ship *Comfort*, which President Trump had rapidly dispatched to New York Harbor.[26] They were options in which appearance mattered more than their use. Sharing any credit with Donald Trump wasn't in the script.

Emails later surfaced showing a top navy admiral practically begging Cuomo to use the emergency pandemic resources for stricken New Yorkers.

"We could use some help from your office," Vice Admiral Mike Dumont wrote to Melissa DeRosa, Cuomo's top aide, on April 7, 2020. "The Governor asked us to permit use of USNS COMFORT to treat patients without regard to their COVID status and we have done so. Right now we only have 37 patients aboard the ship. Further, we are treating only 83 patients at the Javits Events Center.

"We have been trying for days to get the Health Evacuation Coordination Center (HECC) to transfer more patients to us but with little success. We are told by NYC officials the HECC falls under the State's Department of Health," the email continued, referring to the Cuomo administration agency that issued the nursing home mandate.

"Our greatest concern is two-fold: helping take the strain off local hospitals, and not wasting highend capabilities the US military has brought to NYC. We appreciate the help."[27]

By February 2021, the Associated Press had figured out that Cuomo's nursing home deaths were much higher than previously admitted. More than nine thousand recovering COVID patients were sent to hundreds of New York nursing homes, which was 40 percent higher than the New York State Health Department had claimed.[28]

The Cuomo administration had been exposed, and it was forced to acknowledge that it was underreporting coronavirus deaths at long-term care facilities. "It is now nearly 15,000, up from the 8,500 previously disclosed," the AP reported.[29]

In May 2021, the progressive hero was facing a criminal trial for allegedly groping a female aide at the governor's mansion, and he was ordered by the New York Joint Commission on Public Ethics, by a vote of 12–1, to forfeit all book proceeds.[30]

The board had already determined that Cuomo's COVID memoir agreement had occurred under "false pretenses," and the book's publisher had cancelled all paperback promotions after the *New York Times* reported in March 2021 that Cuomo's "most senior aides had rewritten a state Health Department report on nursing home fatalities to hide the number of actual [COVID] deaths."[31]

In June 2021, the New York State Bar Association's Task Force on Nursing Homes and Long-Term Care issued a 242-page report accusing Cuomo of keeping the "unreasonable" nursing home mandate in place after it should have been rescinded.[32] The report noted that the directive "drew almost immediate criticism, caused the Governor to lash out at nursing homes, spurred a congressional inquiry, and, ultimately, an investigation of the Governor himself."[33]

By August 2021, Cuomo was gone. The three-term hero governor resigned amid multiple scandals and ahead of a near-certain impeachment.[34] During his resignation speech, the so-called pandemic superstar still failed to take responsibility but could no longer rely on media propaganda to bail him out. He blamed politics for his demise.

As a final humiliation, the International Academy of Television Arts & Sciences revoked his Emmy on the day Cuomo was replaced by Kathy Hochul. Andrew Cuomo's deadly nursing home decisions occurred during the early period of his draconian lockdowns and media-celebrated national press conferences. He was responsible for the deaths of thousands while he was simultaneously being praised for his leadership excellence.

• • •

Meanwhile, back in Florida, DeSantis and I were derided for opening schools.

While there are many examples of the way the press ignored the facts during COVID, one that sticks with me was my interview on Jake Tapper soon after schools were reopened.

On August 21, 2020, shortly after schools reopened in Florida, I went on Jake Tapper's show on CNN. As the interview progressed, it became painfully obvious that with every data-driven, factual answer I gave, Tapper had a look of complete ignorance and shock—as if he had never heard of any of it, despite it being in the information stream for months.

I was there to give an update on how things were going in Florida and to try and alleviate concerns for parents around the state whose schools had not opened yet. While I was speaking to and for Florida, I also wanted to encourage the rest of the country. Tapper opened my segment by framing the opening of schools in Florida in this manner: "So, let me just put it this way: Florida has more than ten thousand COVID deaths," he began.

I knew right then that he was probably going to follow a typical media narrative of conflating cases with outcomes. We knew from the data that one did not equal the other. As he continued his introduction, it became clear that this was going to be the case.

"Today marks the third straight day of more than four thousand cases being reported in your state. Of the twenty-eight Florida school districts that have opened, four districts already are reporting COVID cases, and the number of COVID cases in Florida in children has more than doubled in the last month. All the data suggests that while children may suffer less than older Americans from this disease, reopening in-person education will cause the virus to spread more. Why are you mandating that all schools have to reopen in-person classes?"

Tapper was cherry-picking information to try to frame a narrative that supported the actions of people like New York governor Andrew Cuomo, who happened to be the brother of one of Tapper's network colleagues.

However, this was in August 2020, and the governor and I were the ones being accused of putting lives at risk.

I explained to Tapper that the data that the risk to children was extremely small—less than the seasonal flu. In addition, there were dangers that were real. "We have to recognize that

STORMING THE IVORY TOWER

the consequences of not allowing those kids back in school is so much more grave than the risk of COVID," I said.

Tapper conceded that there are issues that will arise from not allowing in-person school. However, he followed up with a specious claim.

"I'm not discounting the consequences of not allowing in-person school. I get it. I really do. *But I also know that reopening schools as we've seen in other countries has set the table for a greater spread that has affected other people,*" Tapper said.

I italicize this because he was the host, and he said it with such certainty. I immediately started shaking my head. The way he was framing it—that cases conflated with outcomes and other countries had had this happen—was simply 100 percent untrue.

He did not allow me to answer though, jumping straight to introducing a pre-prepared clip. "I want you to take a listen to this Florida student talking to his school board."

The clip showed a young man testifying before a school board. "There is one thing that I value even more than in-person education," the teen boy's voice began. "And that is human life. Therefore, I pose this question to you. 'How much is one human life worth?'"

Tapper asked: "Will you feel any responsibility if this decision to reopen schools during a pandemic—when people are still dying, while this disease is still spreading out of control all over the country—will you feel any responsibility if any lives are lost as a result?"

I commiserated with him—who apparently thought I was blithely sending children to their deaths given the framing of the question—and then told him the research that I had spent weeks poring over.

"Listen, I'm a father first and foremost, as you are," I said. "Of course we care about our children's lives, and we also recognize that there's nothing that's one hundred percent certain in any aspect of our children's lives. Giving them an aspirin, there could be consequences. *What we have to do is look at the science*, and to your point, Jake, if you talk to the experts, I don't care what country you choose there has been nothing that has shown that children-to-children spreading is real. It's either de minimis or none at all. Every single country, I don't care which one you choose—Germany, England, Denmark, Iceland, Greece, it doesn't matter. There isn't a spread [from children to children]."

I then explained to him the risk to children in context. "We didn't shut down schools last year, and we had over twenty deaths because of the seasonal flu. We're not even close to that. We're two hundred percent below that with COVID. But what we do know is suicide deaths are up. We do know drug overdoses last month hit sixty thousand—we've never seen that kind of number. Those are the real consequences of not giving that safe haven for those children."

Those were the facts then, and those are the facts now. Newsom, Weingarten, and Cuomo could have studied them, and the press could have too, if they wanted to leave their echo chamber.

● ● ●

The data was the important thing. We did have children's lives in our hands, and it was something I thought about every day. In February 2020, as we began to realize the impact this disease could have in Florida by seeing what it was doing around the world, the governor held a meeting with Shane Strum, his chief of staff, and other key executive branch leaders.

We knew something was coming, and we needed to understand what it would mean for us. At the Florida Department of Education, I told my chief of staff, Alex Kelly, to take two top staffers to get every report, study, statistic locally, nationally, and internationally. We needed daily briefings. We also immediately allocated millions to upgrade the state's virtual school infrastructure in case of a doomsday scenario that would force children to be stuck at home for extended periods of time. We had seen Japan send their kids home for months. We did not want to do that, but we wanted to be prepared.

By early March, we saw the numbers of positive cases rising, but we were still prepared to keep schools open based on what we could see from the data presented in our daily briefings. We were learning that schools did not have much of an impact in terms of negative health outcomes. Specifically, it was not impacting children. For that reason, even in the early days, there was no reason to close schools.

As cases started to increase in the US, we put a plan into motion to buy a little extra time—just to breathe and prepare. Florida schools all take spring break at different times. We had each district take an extra week either on the front or the back end of their planned break so they all would have two weeks to prepare. In the early stage of the pandemic, each day's data report was like a patient chart in the hospital ER. We would look at it and see what it told us about our relative health, then decide what we needed to do, if anything. There was no playbook.

Florida is made up of sixty-seven counties, and each of them has a school superintendent who runs the local school system. The superintendents were on board with our plan and were grateful for the guidance. Other states might be closing down their schools, but DeSantis was comfortable with this position. He'd seen the studies too, and he knew them better than anyone. Then I got a phone call.

Florida universities are run by a separate governing entity called the Board of Governors (BOG). On March 12, 2020, a representative from the BOG called to tell me they had decided to make all state universities virtual for the rest of the semester, which only lasted another six weeks for them.

I knew this extremely poor decision was driven by the liberal leaders who dominated college campuses and had little to do with student safety. They had used every tool in their arsenal to force this very poor decision. (Interestingly, most of them are no longer presidents today, in what I believe was an indirect result of such stances.) However, the idiocy of this choice was not to be realized until later.

At the moment, however, I knew this was a colossal overreaction by the BOG. We were still analyzing the data for patterns, and what we had gleaned did not merit this type of call. The whole point of extending spring break was to prepare, plan, and buy time to figure out what was happening with the virus and make a measured, surgical plan based on data. Our approach was very different from the nuclear reaction the BOG was forcing down college students' throats by shutting down universities. I was livid.

I told the BOG representative that the BOG was not acting in a vacuum. How could they shut down a college or university in any city because it was not "safe" for those students to attend class—and then corner the Department of Education into telling panicking parents in those cities, probably with siblings in elementary, middle, or high school, that everything was fine and to continue to send their kindergartner or twelfth grader to school?

In a sense, the BOG, with its power over universities that mainly served eighteen- to twenty-two-year-olds, was logically linked in people's minds with the Department of Education, which mainly served five- to eighteen-year-olds. The superintendents were being put in an untenable position with their districts because their local parents would be more confused and scared than ever. It would have been impossible to convince parents that it was completely safe to keep their younger children in school but not their older children. My ensuing anger was driven by the fact that I knew this decision was dictated much less by actual health concerns and much more by the political and cultural influences of the large percentage of liberal leaders on the college campuses. However, the BOG was not asking for my opinion. They had decided on their own to shutter the state's major higher educational institutions.

As soon as the major universities shut down, some of the superintendents of the sixty-seven school districts were ringing our team off the hook wanting to close K–12 schools. They were extremely frustrated and realized that this was going to cause chaos and panic in their local areas. After talking to many of these superintendents who felt the pressure, we decided that we would have to shut down for a moment and regroup so we could effectively show parents that their K–12 students were not in danger. There was no way in the short term that we could keep K–12 schools open if universities were going to be doing remote learning.

Reluctantly, we announced that all of Florida's schools would go virtual—for a time. I refused to say the rest of the school year because at that point, I was buying time to look at all the options. However, I knew that we had to keep the pre-schools open because the parents always made the decision as to whether they wanted to drop their kids off that day. Since the data showed that preschoolers were not vulnerable, and parental discretion was allowed for attendance, we were able to keep these schools open despite immense pressure to shut down this lifeline to working parents. The Left fought us on this, but I knew it was the lifeline for the working poor. The state agreed to subsidize these preschools, even though at one point they were only at 38 percent capacity. That 38 percent represented the working poor and essential workers. We could not let them down. Quickly, it began to rise to where it was 80 percent again as it became clear that it was safe to have children in centers.

Then Governor DeSantis and I set out to find a way to get Florida's K–12 kids—the ones who wanted to, anyway—back in a classroom as soon as possible. That meant studying the data. Everyone on my team was on it, but none of us were as well read as our governor. Sometimes, I'd get a phone call from him first thing in the morning. "Richard," he'd say with urgency in his voice, "have you seen the latest study out of South Korea on COVID among children?"

"No, Governor, I haven't seen that one yet. But I'll take a look at it," I would say.

"Yeah, you should," he'd respond. "It posted at four thirty this morning on a medical site." This happened all the time.

After the initial three weeks of diving further into the data, the governor wanted the students back in class ASAP. The problem was that the students had been out of school for two to three weeks. That meant we only had less than six weeks left in the school year. It made no sense at this point to put students back in school because most of what students did in the last six weeks were field trips, end-of-year events, and testing. (This was why two years later, we overhauled our entire testing system, revamping the assessments to be less time-intensive, thereby focusing time more on instruction.)

In addition, while the governor and I knew that the data showed students were at more risk from seasonal flu than coronavirus, FDOE could use this time to message directly to parents and teachers as much as possible (over the hysterical shrieks of the teachers' unions and the liberal press) the facts about the data and to get superintendents on board with the plan. Therefore, the rest of April and May could be used to build an iron-clad strategy to get students back to school for summer school in June—and to work with the superintendents as well.

I proposed using the final weeks of the school year to start putting together a plan to get students back in school for summer school in June and the next school year. It also gave us time to keep compiling the data that was revealing more and more with each consecutive week that passed that COVID was not seriously affecting school-age children. The time spent getting districts on board with the plan proved crucial to the eventual successful opening of schools. By the time we opened, only a small minority were up in arms.

While ten districts (unsuccessfully) sued me in my capacity as education commissioner to remain closed, the rest were not only onboard but partners in ensuring as smooth an opening as possible. When we announced the executive order that schools would be open in the fall, we had mountains of data on the impact COVID was having in schools and, specifically, the impact it had on children in those schools from around the world. Trust me, we looked at all of them. While the press might view DeSantis and me as uncaring, we both understood the responsibility on our shoulders and took it extremely seriously. That was why we pored over the data morning, noon, and night. We also talked to as many experts as we could. People from our staff consulted with medical and academic experts from around the world. When Israel's schools reopened, and we saw an instance at one school that looked like a super-spreader event, Governor DeSantis had us immediately research it. I also had a phone call with Swedish epidemiologists, whose country had taken a far different approach than anyone else in Europe by not closing schools.

In every place, regardless of culture, language, or geographic region, the data we saw was clear: COVID didn't impact kids the same way it impacted adults, and children-to-children spread was not like adults. That's why we were so confident that opening schools was the right move for Florida. Which made the reaction from the teachers' unions—and, ultimately, the media—so baffling.

• • •

After the announcement to order Florida's brick-and-mortar schools to open for the new school year, two things happened: parents cheered, and teachers' unions went into panic mode. Despite the fact that, based on our communication, the vast majority of teachers wanted to return to the classrooms, their unions chose to incite fear rather than illuminate a path forward. Suddenly, instead of celebrating the fact that—by looking at the data and trusting the science—we would be able to return Florida's schools to some semblance of normalcy, the governor and I, as commissioner, seemed to replace COVID as public enemy number one in the media.

On July 8, 2020, two days after it was announced schools would reopen, my chief of staff, Alex Kelly, told me, "I had to walk past coffins, tombstones, and a guy in a grim reaper costume to get in to work today." Alex worked at the Florida Department of Education building, not a cemetery. But in the summer of 2020, as "two weeks to stop the spread" turned into too many months of fear and loss, we knew there was a better way forward.

Around the state, local school board meetings, which typically were poorly attended, drew huge crowds and loud voices. Parents, teachers, administrators, and students were passionate on all sides of the issue. We had been living with the virus for months at that point. There were a lot of data points for public health. The overwhelming, definitive data on the positive effects of having kids in school—from learning to mental stability—made the choice an easier one.

However, four months of media manipulation and pandemic-induced fear had made it increasingly difficult to have a dispassionate, honest conversation on the topic. Our actual reopening order was hardly cause for hysteria. It simply read that all "brick-and-mortar schools" must open for "at least five days a week for all students" in the fall. If parents were not comfortable with their kids being back in person, we also required schools to offer virtual learning for any children who would be staying home.

That was always important to Governor DeSantis. "We have to give the parents the choice," he would say on our calls with his staff. "They have parents. We aren't them." Parents who wanted to keep their kids at home already had that option. We'd made sure of it when we first made the decision to conduct the rest of the 2020 school year in a virtual learning environment.

Our announcement at 11:00 a.m. on July 6th that schools would fully reopen in Florida came four hours before President Trump tweeted, "SCHOOLS MUST OPEN IN THE FALL!!!" I retweeted it later in the day, and many in the media assumed there had been some collaboration with the White House. The fact was, though, that Florida's plan to reopen had been a months-long effort rolled out with comprehensive guidance from the state level and a strategy to require compliance of all sixty-seven districts.

Despite the evidence of extensive planning, can you believe that the White House tweet didn't exactly help our cause with the media? A fair headline could have read "Florida to Offer Both In-Person and Virtual Learning This August." Or, "Florida Empowers Parents to Decide Their Children's Schooling Option." Or just any focus in any article on the research, data, and strategy that clearly had gone into the effort.

From the articles in the media, it appeared that we were "ordering" schools to reopen and just jumping into opening schools on a whim with no evidence. In reality, it was the complete opposite. We were paying attention to the data—the media didn't. But they had control of the narrative and had no intention of letting the facts get in their way. Instead, CNN went with "Florida Will Require Schools to Reopen in August Despite a Surge in Coronavirus Cases." One statewide news service decried, "Amid Record COVID-19 Cases, Florida Schools Are Ordered to Reopen This Fall." Two weeks later, CNBC warned, "Infectious Disease Experts Warn against Reopening Schools in Florida, Texas."

The governor and I fought back against this mountain of misinformation the best we could with actual data and facts, which we disseminated through social media, press conferences, and a 143-page reopening plan that we made available to media as well as all schools and superintendents. But it was an uphill battle with the other side intent on telling a narrative that did not comport with science. By the time August rolled around, some schools around Florida opened up with no problems. Others opened with some COVID cases, but they had few, if any, serious health issues. That always was the key for us: cases of infection didn't equal sickness, and sickness didn't equal hospitalization. But, again, few in the media were interested in that distinction.

Two weeks later, schools in Florida were still open, and life was returning to normal. Or at least the pandemic-era version of life. Not only were kids in the classroom without incident, but they were doing things that helped give their lives meaning. That meant, among other things, high school football on Friday nights.

The governor, his family, and I were invited to attend one of those games. As a show of gratitude for his role in helping to make Friday night football a thing again, Governor DeSantis was asked to give a pregame speech in the locker room of the home team. Looking around that room, I saw in each player's face how important being back on the field was to each of them. Pregame meetings in a football locker room are always energized. But that night—after having their lives basically put on pause for the better part of six months and having so much anxiety and uncertainty about what the future would look like— these kids were especially fired up. When their governor walked in, it was like a rock star had jumped on the stage. Everyone let us know how appreciative they were to be able to have the opportunity to play ball and simply live their lives again. For his part, Ron DeSantis let them know not to take it for granted because it wasn't the case everywhere. "If you all lived in California, do you know where you'd be tonight?" DeSantis yelled. "On your couch! But not in Florida. Now go out there and play your tail off!" The kids and coaches went wild. Florida was back. Our people were free. And our students were learning. Our kids didn't just get a Friday night football game that kids on the couch in California or New York didn't get—they got an education.

Tragically, that wasn't the case in other parts of the country. Two years after schools opened in Florida, more data emerged about the impact of the pandemic on schoolchildren. But these statistics weren't about COVID infections. The California Department of Education had hidden the results of statewide student testing assessments long after they should have been published—only to reveal in October 2022 that only 47 percent of their students were on grade level for English language arts (which includes reading), and just one-third were on grade level in math. Only 16 percent of African American students tested as proficient in math.

Dr. Jay Bhattacharya, an esteemed professor of medicine at Stanford University—and one of the people we consulted as we were preparing to reopen schools in Florida—ripped into California governor Gavin Newsom on Twitter. "Gov. @GavinNewsom kept my kids out of their public schools for nearly a year and a half with no good scientific or epidemiological justification. His record on education is the worst in the country."

Years of academic progress in California were wiped out. Because of the loss of learning that the state's lockdown policies have wrought, California's students will now face a much bleaker future. Florida's kids, on the other hand, face a brighter tomorrow.

A May 2022 Harvard report called "Road to COVID Recovery" singled out Florida for protecting students against widening racial and economic achievement gaps that had occurred in hardcore school-closure states like New York and California. "Interestingly, gaps in math achievement by race and school poverty did not widen in school districts in states such as Texas and Florida and elsewhere that remained largely in-person," said Thomas Kane, professor Harvard Graduate School of Education. Using testing data from 2.1 million students in ten thousand high schools in forty-nine states and the District of Columbia, study researchers found that remote learning during the pandemic was the primary driver for racial and economic achievement gaps, particularly in high-poverty schools.

The most recent National Assessment of Educational Progress, often called the Nation's Report Card, showed similar results. Two decades of learning gains were erased in states that mandated lockdowns and kept kids out of schools. The greatest decline in results was in minority students in low-income families who had less access to technology or safe and quiet spaces to learn during the pandemic.

As a result, the states whose liberal leaders claim to want to do the most to help the historically disenfranchised, often through misguided policies like teaching Critical Race Theory, actually ended up causing those groups the most harm. Those weren't the only kids being harmed in schools. Because of the pandemic and the threat it placed on schools being open, parents started paying a lot more attention to school board meetings and started engaging much more with the people in charge of their children's education. Exactly what was happening in schools became a matter of much greater scrutiny than it had ever been before. While we had worked to empower parents to make their own choices about what was in the best interests of their children and whether their kids should attend school in person, parents had been losing power over what was happening inside the classrooms in alarming and threatening ways. We did not realize how bad the problem was. But we were about to find out—just the like the public would in higher education after October 7, 2023.

• • •

In 2005, the writer David Foster Wallace gave a commencement speech at Kenyon College in which he told a story that demonstrated that "the most obvious important realities are often the ones that are hardest to see." The story is about two young fish who are swimming along.

> *[T]hey happen to meet an older fish swimming the other way, who nods at them and says, "Morning, boys. How's the water?" And the two young fish swim on for a bit, and then eventually one of them looks over at the other and goes, "What the hell is water?"*

I would compare the press to these two young fish. They do not see the water. As in Wallace's illustration, awareness is difficult because in the world in which most reporters operate, everyone thinks just like they do. It is simply the water they swim in. They do not even recognize it is water because it is such a part of the landscape that they have become blind to it.

However, there is the evidence. The vast majority of the press are liberal Democrats. They miss or elevate repeatedly stories that are in accordance with their own view of the world. At some point, they might consider that if something looks like water and acts like water, it just might be water.

After Wallace told this story in his speech, he immediately told the audience that "if you're worried I plan to present myself here as the wise, older fish explaining what water is to you younger fish, please don't be. I am not the wise older fish." I would add this as well. I do not think I am better than reporters because I recognize the bias. However, I do not swim in that water. As a conservative, I have to confront everyday viewpoints that are radically different from my own because so many major parts of this society have been co-opted by radical liberals. It forces me in a way that elite liberals rarely encounter to consider my stances and personally assess and critique my understanding. I know their arguments by heart because I am frequently presented with them. I do not think the same can be said for the radical left. They have actively manipulated the world to be one in which they rarely confront anyone who does not think just like they do.

J. S. Mill in his classic *On Liberty* states that the suppression of free speech takes something important away from those who no longer have to interact with opinions they do not agree with. According to Mill, this is because "[i]f the opinion is right, they are deprived of the opportunity of exchanging error for truth," and "if wrong, they lose, what is almost as great a benefit, the clearer perception and livelier impression of truth, produced by its collision with error."

• • •

On a sunny March morning in 2024, I welcomed a group of principals from high schools in Sarasota County to the New College campus. We were highlighting for them the reasons the university would be a great option for their graduates.

To start the presentation, I opened by thanking them for attending and then gave them a layout of what they could expect during their time on the campus.

> *I want to welcome you today and invite you following the program to the baptisms that will be held in the Bay at lunchtime. Also, we will be having a mandatory prayer service at 10 a.m. in between presentations.*

The crowd immediately got the joke and started laughing loudly. There was only one reason the joke worked—because that was the storyline they had been reading and hearing in news outlets about New College. While facts did not exist to support this narrative, it had somehow become a dominant thread in the stories because of specious opinions that had been elevated.

The press coverage had become the punchline.

It is Groundhog Day…again.

CHAPTER 8

Florida Is Florida for a Reason

You can't get from A to Z by passing up B.
—Nick Saban

In higher education, as with COVID and many other policy issues, Florida has become a national symbol of bold and transformative leadership. There is no question that DeSantis has led the state with foresight and courage.

While less visible, the Florida legislature has stood strongly behind him. This fact supercharged DeSantis's efforts to enact visionary public policy. Though Republicans in other states control both the executive and legislative branches, Florida has been uniquely successful—as evidenced by the ferocious attacks directed on it by the Left.

The fact that the Florida legislature was a dynamic force when the governor called on it to make quick responses in a crisis was not surprising to anyone who had been watching its evolution over the past two decades. While it may appear as if Florida became an overnight sensation, the legislature operating under the DeSantis administration was forged by a series of changes that made it the unique and effective organization that it has been when the governor has asked it for quick action.

The main flashpoints that helped create it as it exists today were found in events that happened in 1992, 1996, 2000, 2010, and 2016. In 1992, the voters passed term limits. In 1996, the Republicans took over the legislature for the first time in over one hundred years, and, in 2000, the first full class elected under term limits came to power. Then, in 2010, the Tea Party revolt swept into office a large class whose new members typically would have lost to better-funded, establishment candidates. Finally, in 2016, new ethics and budget transparency rules were passed because of this class of Tea Party rebels. All of these elements—term limits, Republican control, dominance of idealistic conservatives beginning in 2010, and ethics and budgetary reform—formed the building blocks for making the legislature, particularly the House, a dynamic force for visionary change.

I was incredibly blessed to have a front row seat as these changes occurred. In different capacities, I was working in or around the institution during these moments. Science has shown that humans think in stories. As someone who was there, I could tell you the black and white facts in the paragraph above, a bird's-eye view of what was happening in Florida before the nation started to notice that something was just different in this state, that Florida was able to achieve bold policy while others were only talking about it. Here is my story, though—a peek from the inside—of how it felt and looked from in the hallways of Tallahassee as these changes occurred.

• • •

On November 3, 1992, the voters passed term limits for all elected officials with 77 percent of the electorate voting in favor of the proposal,[1] which after a Florida Supreme Court ruling only applied to state officials. This was the beginning of the transformation of the state of Florida from a swampy, good-old-boy government to leading the way nationally on policy.

I arrived in Tallahassee shortly before this historic vote. In late 1991, I began my first job with the legislature as an aide for a representative. It was quite a different time in Florida politics. Today, Republicans have controlled the executive as well as the legislative branches for over twenty-five years. In late 1991, Republicans were nonentities. Democrats had been in control for over one hundred years, and, in the House, only thirty-nine of the 120 members were Republicans.[2] In addition, term limits were not yet a reality. With no term limits, the Democrats who had been in charge for so long wielded their power with a singular disregard for the voters who had sent them there. They also gave no thought to listening to a Republican idea at all. Ever. Republicans had been so beaten down for so long, they accepted this type of behavior meekly, desperate for any crumb they might be tossed by their masters.

While all this was about to change with term limits and a Republican takeover, no one seemed to see these upheavals coming when I started my job as a legislative aide for state Rep. Paul Hawkes, even though in one year term limits would be passed. Paul was an attorney in private practice who lived on the West Coast of Florida, two counties directly north of where I had grown up in Pasco County. I had met him just out of college a few months earlier when I was working for the Republican Party to help candidates who were running for office.

I immediately recognized in Paul a kindred spirit. He was young, ambitious, and had a clear desire to try to make a difference. In 2024, a Republican trying to make a difference in the state legislature is expected. In 1991, it was absurd.

Paul was joined by three other younger Republicans who were elected in his class and who also wanted to be more than seat fillers: Tom Feeney, Chris Corr, and Buddy Johnson. Working with them and their staffs, we started on a journey to navigate bureaucratic processes trying to find any way to make an impact. In the spring of 1992, the country was in the midst of a recession. The poor economic conditions eventually would cost then president George H. W. Bush his reelection. However, the Democratic governor wanted to raise taxes by $1.3 billion. Being so dramatically outnumbered in the House, Republicans did not seem motivated to try to fight back.

None of the four freshmen in our group—Hawkes, Feeney, Corr, and Johnson—were important enough to be on the appropriations committee. However, they were up to trying a Hail Mary pass when Paul and I presented the idea of creating a "Priority Budget," an answer by the House Republicans to the Democratic budget.[3] After all, our members had been elected too, and even if they were not on the committee, we still felt that offering a different solution was something we should try. Though the Democrats controlled the House, we were able to get our budget printed, which made our ideas concrete. To create the Priority Budget, Paul and I pored over each item that hardworking Floridians were being asked to pay for through taxes. This exercise became the basis of how I was first introduced to the intricacies of the Florida budget, knowledge that was to serve me well over the coming years.

Thirty-six of the forty-six Republican members agreed to put their names on it.[4] By the time we had finished, we had a 194-page-long proposal that raised no taxes. This was our first shot at doing anything like this, and we had no idea what the response would be. We thought it a very real possibility that it would be met with a collective yawn—no publicity, no acknowledgement. On March 23, 1992, the four members held a press conference to release the Priority Budget. To our surprise, reporters actually turned up. There were stories about it in the statewide papers.[5] Then, in an even bigger surprise, the Democrats produced a "Special Summary of the Republican Priority Budget." This was more attention than we had ever dreamed we would get.[6]

When we went to print a new version with amendments, the House Printing Office refused to print it. We did not care: articles had been written, and the Democrats had responded. For a brief moment, we were at the table. The Democrats might have treated us like we were at the kids' table, but at least we had been invited to the meal, and our ideas were being discussed. We were ecstatic. In the end, with the House resistance and a stronger percentage of Republican representation in the state Senate, the governor signed a budget that was leaner, and a proposed $1.3 billion tax increase was reduced to an increase of $374 million, an almost a $1 billion savings for hard-working taxpayers.[7]

• • •

In 1993, I left Paul's office to go to law school—and when I returned from law school in 1996, it was to a completely different world. The Republicans were just taking over the House majority for the first time in more than one hundred years. I contracted to consult during this period with Florida House Speaker Dan Webster—the first Republican Speaker in over one hundred years—who later would become a member of the US House of Representatives. Republicans had never been in power before. There was giddiness, and there was trepidation. No one had any idea what to do. This resulted in a palpable fear among leadership who did not want to fail at this task. My primary feeling though was one of urgency to enact policy. This led to a lack of alignment in vision, a tension that continued during much of the two years I was in this role.

For example, from my perspective, the first thing I thought that should be done was to fire the budget director. I knew him from my experience when I had worked on the Priority Budget, and I knew he did not share our vision in any manner. However, others were worried that they needed his expertise. They asked me if I could find someone to fill his shoes. I had a candidate in mind, but when she was unable to take the position, they settled for the status quo and kept the original budget director, who would then become a darling of the Republican leadership for the next two decades. I strongly disagreed with him being kept on. That would be a pattern for me: I would make a recommendation, often one that seemed to go a bit too far and too fast for those newly in control, and, as a result, I would get pushback. Eventually, I got frustrated at the slow pace of change, and I decided to run myself.

I returned to Citrus County where I had been based when I worked with Paul Hawkes as a legislative staffer to practice law with my wife, who had just graduated from Florida State law school. At the time I ran, the Republican representing Citrus

County, Nancy Argenziano, had become known as one of the most moderate Republicans in the House. In fact, she later tried to run as a Democrat. I decided to throw my hat into the ring. I got 29 percent of the vote. Argenziano had good relationships and favorable coverage from the local paper, which seemingly ran a different front-page article defending her every week. The local Republican Party came out against me for calling into question her moderate voting record in a primary. I then spent the next six years practicing law; although my cases were mainly related to non-political representation, I continued to represent the party on certain legal issues, including redistricting.

• • •

While term limits passed in 1992, and the eight-year time limit began ticking then, it was not until 2000 that the first wave of new members came into the House, and with them a young man named Marco Rubio. When he considered running for Speaker shortly after he was elected, he reached out to me to see if I would be interested in running his Speaker's race, as I was one of the few people who had run Speaker races since the Republicans had taken over.

Legislators in the Florida House can serve up to four two-year terms, so the legislature is divided up by freshmen, sophomores, juniors, and seniors—the latter who have been there for the full four terms. Every two years, all incoming freshmen legislators elect the person who will become Speaker of the House when they are seniors. This meant that Marco would be running for Speaker in 2001 but could not officially be the Speaker until the 2006 to 2008 term. (Not only does Florida have term limits for state offices, the House and Senate in their rules limit executive leadership to one two-year term.)

We met in a Chili's in Ocala. I was enjoying practicing law, but I saw in Marco something similar to what I had seen in Paul. He was talented, articulate, and was drawn to conservative ideas. We hit it off, and I agreed to work on his Speaker's race. When he won, I ended up moving back to Tallahassee to work as his chief of staff at the party when he was Speaker designate—the traditional role for the Speaker-to-be—and then as his chief of staff when he started his term as Speaker.

During the time running up to his speakership, we worked on *100 Innovative Ideas for Florida's Future*. I had been in the process when Republicans were in the minority, and I knew now was the time for change with this new class and new leader. It could not happen when he became Speaker. It needed to have a carefully crafted plan for legislation. The one hundred ideas contained in the book reflected the thoughts of many public meetings we held to listen to people about their desires from government for themselves and their families. Marco is a good friend, as he remains to this day. The vision presented in the book laid the road map for a very successful speakership.

In many ways, I felt like I was relitigating the same fights as I had the past two times I was in Tallahassee, in 1992 and 1997. The same budget director was still in place, but this time in an even more powerful position: chief of staff to the Senate president. At one point, Marco was negotiating the budget with the minority leader, Dan Gelber. Gelber asked him to stop bringing me to the negotiations. "I can deal with you, but I can't deal with Richard," he said. "He's like out of the Jet Li movie, where he has just been released from a cage and wants to fight everybody." This was in the middle of a very busy legislative season.

It was an exciting time, but with the amount of work, I rarely had time to sit back and consider the bigger picture of what I wanted to do with my life. That changed though one day when, as I often did, I met for lunch with Mat Bahl, a good friend in the process and one of the best political advisors I have ever met. We were discussing legislative strategy and, at one point in our conversation he looked me and said something that I will never forget. He cut right to the point: "Richard, do you want to be the man or be the man behind the man?" His words kept returning to my mind quite frequently in the weeks that followed. Then, a special election for a state Senate seat opened in Citrus County. I decided to resign my position in Tallahassee and run in the 2007 special election, though I ended up dropping out when a candidate with much more name ID—who had originally told me he was not going to run—decided to jump into the race at the last minute.

For two more years, I returned to my law practice and a business development firm I had started. During this time, I consulted with a medical company run by Rick Scott, who shortly thereafter would run for governor. He was in the private sector at this point, and I only learned later that he had political aspirations. He and his wife are wonderful people, and I had the chance to get to know them when neither of us was particularly involved in politics.

Then, in 2009, I was contacted by two good friends and my brother, Michael, who lived in my old home county. Located one county away from Citrus County, Pasco County was an area I knew well, as I had grown up there and attended elementary, middle, and high school in the area. When I was a boy there, it was a sleepy rural area slowly growing through the migration of retirees from the North. Now it was one of the fastest-growing areas of the state as a result of its proximity to the Tampa Bay area. Sheriff Bob White and state senator Mike Fasano were popular officeholders in Pasco County, and my brother Michael was involved in governmental consulting. I had run Bob's first race for sheriff back in 1994, and I had met Fasano when I got involved in Republican politics in 1984.

They knew I was at a crossroads in my life and had a business that I could run from anywhere in the state but was unsure where to move my growing family. They also knew there was a House seat coming open within two years. They encouraged me to move to Pasco and run for the office with their support. I decided to go for it. I prevailed in a brutal primary against a moderate Republican and another Republican who was also running in the conservative lane. The "conservative" candidate turned out to have recently jumped on the Tea Party bandwagon, and he was only in the race for the promise of elective office rather than the policy ideals he was supporting in the race. In fact, during the election, my campaign discovered that just two years previously, he had given money to a liberal, pro-immigration group called La Raza. Unfortunately, this type of behavior—candidates spouting commitment to causes they personally do not believe in just to gain elective office—happens much too frequently. My campaign worked tirelessly to get our message out. On election night in August 2010, I won the primary election with just over 40 percent of the vote. As the district was overwhelmingly Republican, I then won the general election with no opposition in November.

• • •

While the legislative classes were stronger and more talented than those prior to term limits, the 2010 class broke the mold. The Tea Party wave turned conventional campaign wisdom on its head—much as Donald Trump's campaign would do six years later in the presidential race. In it were now US representative Matt Gaetz, US representative Greg Steube, ambassador Carlos Trujillo, and a number of other stellar members. Many of those who won that year—including myself—would have typically lost in a normal year in which establishment candidates who had more funding would have won out.

Many of the members swept in were idealists and wanted to fight—even their own party if necessary—to pass the policy that energized them. The reality was, we would have to fight our own party to stand for the ideals its members were running on. This was unheard of, but our class was different.

While I was chosen to be Speaker of this class, in any other year, my path would not have been successful. However, this was no ordinary group. They shared my frustrations with the process. As one reporter wrote in a profile of my speakership, "Years before Donald Trump crashed the scene with his anti-establishment rhetoric, [Corcoran and his class] promised to overhaul a system fixated on personal advancement…[Corcoran] is outraged by the system that shaped him and now wants to tear it down."

Like my class's path to the legislature, I did not win the speakership because I was the establishment favorite or the best-funded candidate. Our class was elected in November 2010. The speakership race takes place quietly behind the scenes in the months that follow. In the weeks in between my primary win in August 2010 and when I won the Speaker's race in January 2011, I doubted frequently whether I would be chosen by the class to be Speaker.

I had had a competitive primary, which meant I was not able to work members for votes during the primary season as my opponents had. Therefore, once I was elected, I was starting far behind my competitors. Most importantly, though, they were well-funded. The interest groups had worked with me when I was chief of staff to Rubio several years before, and they were generally not fans of mine. Such support brought one of the most coveted benefits of a speakership run: the ability to deliver large checks to members desperately trying to fund their ongoing campaigns. However, I had another challenge: it was expensive traveling the state trying to garner votes. It required staying in hotels for nights on end and the ability to take members to lunches and dinners.

My competitors were traveling the state on PAC dimes, staying in nice hotels, and wining and dining potential members as they tried to win their votes for the speakership. By contrast, I was a self-employed lawyer in private practice with my wife, and my campaign for office had severely curtailed the time I could spend on working for and billing clients. With five small children ages one to nine, and because my tough primary campaign stretched out over more than a year, money had become tight. After the primary, rather than spending time in my law office, I was using these weeks to drive the state, meet with new members, and try to convince them to vote for me for Speaker. Hotels and fancy meals were not in the family budget. I decided to improvise. I still traveled the state, but I would stay in cheap hotels or sleep in my car and meet people at coffee shops rather than expensive restaurants.

It all felt rather bleak. I had met almost none of these members. I had delivered exactly zero dollars to each of them. In a typical political year, I would have had no chance.

In fact, several weeks into my push for the speakership, at the beginning of 2011, I was within a hair's breadth of quitting. I had driven down one Sunday afternoon in early January to Miami to meet with a new member to try to convince them to sign on with me. On the drive down, I had taken a phone call from someone in the process who told me that two members had signed on with a competitor.

Before the meeting, I checked into my hotel, and I went to my room to unload my bag. I went and stood at the window, looking out at the miles of concrete and the Palmetto expressway in the late afternoon winter sunlight. I made a call to my wife. When she answered, I could hear the kids in the background. I told her about the two members that had signed on with my opponent. There was a long pause. I took a deep breath and said that I thought I should fold in and take a high-ranking leadership post in return. For me, it was one of those moments in life where time seems to stand still. I found out much later, when we spoke about that split second in time, that it was the same for her. Anne was at our house in Pasco County with five small children. She had been almost single-handedly running our law office, including much of my caseload, for weeks. She was making dinner, and she remembers where she was standing in the kitchen, how our toddler who had just started walking, was holding onto her legs. The other kids ran in an out of the kitchen from the backyard. She told me absolutely not. This was not the time to fold. I agreed, half-heartedly, and left for the dinner. Slowly, things began to turn in my favor, thanks in large part to the Miami delegation.

The fact was that the freshman legislative class of 2010 was different, refusing to view my competitors' prior investments in relationships and money as favors they should return in the form of votes for Speaker. Most were motivated by something other than the typical quid pro quo relationships that many politicians pursue. Rather, they tended to be willing to sit down, get to know me, and listen to my vision. They heard me out on my plan to reform the process, and they were more than interested in the legislation I wanted to pass. My hope was we would create an agenda that would be more than just moving the furniture: it would affect normal people's lives in meaningful ways. These members spent most of their time with me talking about big ideas and long-term visions. Then they threw in their votes with me. Without them, even if I had been chosen Speaker, I could not have achieved the measure of success I did.

The first thing we did was make a plan. This one was different than *100 Innovative Ideas* though. I had learned something since then. The ideas are the goal, but we could not get there without reforming the process. In addition, I used the plan to serve as a philosophical statement, a place to return to so we could all agree on our "why." The "why" was not the media or the special interests or even friends in the process. The "why" was to serve the people of Florida.

Blueprint Florida was a road map for how we would govern as a class once I was Speaker. It had three main points: our philosophy, ethics reform, and leveling the playing field so good ideas could rise to the top. The leadership team that was put into place in 2011 was the group that was the foundation for the accomplishments during my speakership from 2016 to 2018. With *Blueprint Florida* as a basis, we set about to enact its principles over the next several years while I waited to become Speaker.

STORMING THE IVORY TOWER

My class and I used our time in 2011 to 2015 to upend bad policy and challenge power when necessary—primarily against our own party, as it was the one in control. It was a party that far too often was part of the problem. As a result, even before my speakership started, I had established a reputation as someone willing to fight the power structure when necessary. Our biggest move of all was to shut down Medicaid expansion at a time Senate leadership was strongly behind the move. The beneficiaries of such expansion would have been primarily able-bodied, working-age men, as many others who needed it, such as children, were already covered under existing law. The hospital lobby—and other interest groups that would benefit financially—was spending millions trying to get this passed to increase their bottom lines. The Republican Senate was attempting to force the House to pass it by including it in the budget. I stood up on behalf of my class and told them there was no way the House—because of the members in my class—would approve this huge expansion of the budget to primarily able-bodied, working-age men. In the debate on the issue, I explained our stance.

> *[The Senate] want[s] us to come dance? We are not dancing. We are not dancing this session. We are not dancing next session. We are not dancing next summer. We're not dancing. And if you want to blow up the process because somehow you think you have the right that doesn't exist, have at it. But we are going to do what's right.*

I then pointed to the ideas my class had put into *Blueprint Florida* in 2012.

> *The enemy is the status quo, and the status quo is all the people who profit from the system...I will proudly declare war on the special interests. Every single one of which. All the Gucci-loafing, shoe-wearing, special interest powers that be. They are sitting in that hallway. Every single one of them want Medicaid expansion.... Come to war with us. I'll fight. And if it costs me my political career, or yours, so be it. That's where the fight should be had. That's who our enemy is. That's why our people don't have the health care they deserve.*

I got a bit carried away with this off-the-cuff speech and misspoke with the "Gucci-loafing, shoe-wearing" phrase, which then took on a life of its own. Someone even launched a Twitter account called @Gucciloafing. People got the idea though. Our class was going to change the game in Tallahassee.

• • •

Without the speakership gavel, though, there is only so much one can accomplish. When 2016 rolled around, I felt like a runner at the starting line who had finally heard the whistle blow to start the race. Or maybe Gelber had been right: I was like a character Jet Li played in a movie who had figuratively been locked in a cage, and now I was finally out. Or maybe I just never forgot what it felt like to have to force my way into the conversation about not raising taxes on average citizens, while serving as a staffer for a member who was sitting in the far back row of the legislature. I am not sure which example works best, but they probably all apply. I and my class were eager to get started and implement all the plans we had laid out in *Blueprint Florida*. Once I finally got the opportunity to be part of the process in a meaningful way, I did not want to waste it.

In the first few weeks of my speakership, we made rapid changes. We ousted the state's top tourism official after exposing his secret $1 million contract with the rapper Pitbull, demanded financial records from dozens of colleges and tourism boards, began impeachment of a judge over sexist and racist remarks, and refused to pay $13 million in legal fees amassed by a state agency whose director soon quit.

We also began work on what I saw as our most important fight, as it was central to most of the other legislation that would follow: ethics reform. I knew that without ethics reform, most of the rest of our agenda would be undermined. Therefore, we made it our goal to ban lawmakers from lobbying their branch of government for six years after their service. It would be the toughest lobbying ban in the country. This was met with immediate resistance by the Republican Senate, which refused to pass it. We then pivoted and put it into the House Rules. I knew, though, that there was one way to bypass the Senate: put it on the ballot.

I worked with former senate president Don Gaetz, who was a strong supporter of the idea while he was in the Senate. He and I had worked in 2016 to get it passed, but it had fallen short that year as well. The Florida Constitution Revision Commission was meeting in 2017, and I worked with former president Gaetz, who was on the commission, to get the idea to the voters, writing a letter stating that "[r]ecent legislative attempts to extend the lobby ban and impose stricter ethical requirements have been thwarted by the self-interested politicians we hope to regulate."

The amendment for the six-year lobbying ban was then placed on the ballot and passed in 2018. The Republican Senate also refused to pass other commonsense ethics reforms. Unable to control what the so-called upper chamber did with their own process, I put them into House Rules instead. These included requiring lobbyists to file notices of appearances on issues, prohibiting lobbyists from contacting legislators electronically during a public meeting, banning Florida House members from traveling on private jets owned by lobbyists, prohibiting members from entering into business deals or financial relationships with lobbyists, and requiring private contracts to be disclosed and noticed in advance if lobbyists were representing public entities or any institution receiving taxpayer funding.

In my time in and around the legislature, I had personally seen how these behaviors had corrupted the process too many times. It made all the hard work worth it when those reforms were enacted. Corruption happens when people are only there to serve their own goals, but these rules made it much harder for them to do so.

The Republican Senate also opposed our attempts to ensure fiscal transparency and accountability. These were then put into House Rules. These rules require every budget request to be filed as a standalone piece of legislation; compel members to disclose any new employment with a taxpayer-funded entity; and require lobbyists to specifically disclose which bills, which amendments, and which appropriations they are trying to influence.

We then turned to things that would affect the people of Florida, putting an amendment to increase the homestead exemption on the ballot and passing legislation requiring more price transparency from healthcare providers. We worked to expand school choice. We also were determined to end corporate welfare so that Republicans would no longer support the interests of big business over the interests of the average taxpayer. These were things I had dreamed of doing for years.

The legislative process is rare in its beauty and power for good—and frightening in its destructive power when it is misused. All the time I had spent in the process had given me a good vantagepoint to see both sides of it. Many espouse conservative ideals when they are running for office; only a few have the courage to be change agents on these issues once they are elected. The easiest and most comfortable path, and therefore the one most traveled, is to capitulate to the special interests or cave to the pressure of the liberal press—and oftentimes, both factor into why campaigning conservatives turn into governing moderates.

This results in the swamp. The elected officials, after a few years, want power and money, forgetting the people who elected them. The lobbyists get power because the elected officials delegate it to them. Term limits are the first step—first for elected leaders but also for leadership positions. Florida had both. While term limits passed in 1992, it was not until 2000 that the first wave came in, and it was another ten years before an earthquake occurred that ushered in a tsunami of groundbreaking members. The second step is to set up a process through ethics reform that makes corruption harder to take root. Florida had all these elements, and this was a big reason why Florida has been singularly effective in passing transformative policy as well as refusing to pass bad policy that would negatively affect its populace.

• • •

In 2018, Gov. Ron DeSantis was elected, and the legislature and he worked together to further propel Florida to being the number one state in the nation for enacting policy that positively impacts people's lives. They were like kerosene and a match.

However, my original plan was that I would be the match. I wanted to use the reforms we passed to clean out the swamp to run for governor in the statewide Republican primary dominated by conservative voters.

In the spring of 2017, I was in the middle of my term as Florida House Speaker, a position that ran from May 2016 until May 2018. I was planning to run as the conservative candidate, though the front-runner, and the person insiders thought was going to be the nominee, was Adam Putnam, the agriculture commissioner who had served in Congress eight years before. The other name I kept hearing was Congressman Ron DeSantis, but I was skeptical. I knew that the actual number of people that can stand up in an executive situation was scant, and I wondered if this untried young man would have the ability if he became governor. I had never met DeSantis, and had only seen him once, when he and I were both speaking at the same event in mid-2011.

However, I knew he would compete with me for the conservative voters that dominated primaries in Florida. I had brought Tony Fabrizio, one of the best pollsters in the conservative political space, onto my campaign team. An Italian from New York, Fabrizio is a former competitive body builder who has worked with the some of the biggest names in Republican campaigns, from Donald Trump in 2016 all the way back to Bob Dole in 1996. I mentioned to Tony that I had heard DeSantis might jump into the race. Tony was concerned, as this would put another "base conservative" in the picture. "Hey, if it's head-to-head versus Putnam, I don't think there's any way you can lose," Fabrizio would tell me. The problem was, it might not be just me and Adam Putnam. It might be me, Putnam, and DeSantis.

DeSantis worried me. He and I were aligned in our voting patterns and political stances. We were both stuck in the low digits, and we both had our eyes on an endorsement by Trump, but it was difficult for me working in the state rather than the federal government. On December 22, 2017, I returned from a day of fishing with my fifteen-year-old son. I had not had my phone, but my wife had received a text that Trump had tweeted in support of Ron. It was not an endorsement, but it came close.

I continued to work, but by May, I called a press conference and announced I was getting out of the race. It was a rainy, muggy day in Tallahassee, and at the press conference Adam Putnam was standing beside me because I was endorsing him for governor. Given DeSantis's ability to fight for conservative principles, it was the wrong decision. Adam was a known quantity whom I had been acquainted with for years. Almost all conservative leaders in the state supported him. When he reached out for my endorsement, I agreed. Soon after, Trump tweeted out his full endorsement of DeSantis.

DeSantis and Putnam had one debate. Putnam asked if I would be willing to be his spokesperson in the greenroom after the debate. I was his second choice. Pam Bondi—the state's conservative attorney general who had endorsed Adam earlier in the race—had originally been scheduled to represent him. Despite the polls showing Putnam with a sizeable lead, most people were starting to think the race was over.

I agreed to represent Putnam. My counterpart from the DeSantis campaign in the greenroom was Matt Gaetz. We had been friends for years, and Matt had been a vocal supporter of mine in my run for governor. However, when I dropped out, he immediately backed DeSantis. Therefore, while I was stumping for Putnam at this event, he was there as a surrogate for DeSantis.

We would be vying for the attention of the press pool as we spoke about the outcome of the debate that had just occurred, and the idea of a little friendly competition clearly appealed to both of us. A few reporters grabbed me as soon as I walked in the room, and I began answering their questions. From less than ten feet away, I could hear Gaetz rattling off his own talking points, effortlessly commanding an audience. I do not remember exactly what he said, but he was having fun making sure I heard it. So, I tried to bring a little color of my own to the conversation. "Ron has a bulldog mouth and a chihuahua ass," I said in response. "He might have talked tough, but he just rattled off talking points. He doesn't know Florida."

My wife was standing nearby, and I saw her grimace. "Where on earth did you come up with that phrase?" she asked after the reporter walked away.

It did the trick, though, and it made many news stories. It was not enough for Adam Putnam. Ron had exposed Adam's Achilles' heel in that debate: his voting record. Once Adam's voting record was exposed for all to see, Ron ran away with the conservative voters in the Florida Republican primary.

By the time the August 28th primary rolled around, everyone knew what was going to happen. It was Florida's Democrats who were in for the surprise that primary night—Tallahassee mayor Andrew Gillum upset Congresswoman Gwen Graham.

For Republicans, the inevitable became reality. DeSantis won by double digits. With all the excitement of the past year over, I was ready to return to private life—almost a decade older and, hopefully, somewhat wiser. I had held elected office for the last eight years. I was ready to return to one of my other loves: capitalism. Ron DeSantis had other plans. I was about to get one of the biggest shocks in my life.

The night after the primary election, I was with my kids at a sports event when I got a phone call from an unknown number. It had a 904 area code, which was from the Jacksonville area. As a rule, I do not answer calls from unknown numbers because it could be from a telemarketer or—even worse—a reporter. I let it go to voice mail, but when I saw the caller had left a message, I listened. The message was from a voice I had heard fairly often over the past few months. "Hey Richard, it's Ron DeSantis. Give me a call if you get a chance, I want to talk to you about a couple of things." That's interesting, I thought to myself.

I had no idea why he would be calling me, but I called him back immediately. He answered, and I congratulated him on his victory. He thanked me, then got right to the point.

"Hey, I've talked to Matt, and I've asked him to help cochair my transition," he said. "I'm pretty sure I'm going to win this race. And when I do, I want to hit the ground running. I'd like to get started right away. And so, I'd like to ask you to cochair my transition team as well."

I am fairly sure there was dead air for a few seconds while I processed this request. This was completely out of my realm of experience. Here was a former political opponent who was offering me a coveted top position. This was very outside the norm in politics.

I was also a former opponent who had also supported his main competitor. This made it even more unusual. Not to mention the disparaging remarks I had made about him in a roomful of reporters. For once in my life, I was speechless. I wondered: Did he know about that little exchange in the greenroom after the debate, which had been printed in numerous news outlets? "I'm honored," I told him. "I really appreciate it. But, before I say yes, there's something I want to make sure you are aware of. After the debate, when I was supporting Putnam in the greenroom, I did say that you had a bulldog mouth and a chihuahua ass." To my surprise, he burst out laughing.

"Yeah, I know all about that," he said when he finally stopped laughing. "My biggest regret is that I wasn't in the greenroom. I'd love to watch you and Gaetz go at it."

When I joined the transition team, I did not know Ron DeSantis well. The fact that he would even ask me to join his transition team spoke volumes though. Most other political leaders would not have done so. DeSantis, as I would learn over the next few years, was not your typical leader. He focused on the bigger picture.

• • •

Shortly after DeSantis was elected, while I was cochairing his transition team, he offered me the position as education commissioner. I thanked him, but I did not accept it. The idea of doing the type of work that consumed a typical education commissioner in Florida's days did not appeal to me.

In my head, I pictured myself spending my days trying to cut through bureaucracy and fighting to make even basic commonsense reforms. As Speaker, I had championed many reforms to help the school choice and charter school movement. While as Speaker I had the ability to do transformative policies in education, I doubted whether this would be the case as education commissioner. My interest in politics had always been directly related to how much I could move the needle to benefit people's lives. Traditionally, for the person running the Florida Department of Education—or any state DOE—the answer was: not much. After the post-Jeb Bush education transformation and after spending ten-plus years rebuilding Florida's economy post-2009 recession, Floridians seemed more concerned with economic prosperity than education. It was difficult to enact even the most incremental changes. At this point, having gone through the campaign with Ron, I had immense respect for his passion and intelligence.

Therefore, when the governor initially offered me the position, I volunteered to help him find someone else since I knew that world well. I initially suggested and we pursued Matt Gaetz's father, Don Gaetz, a former Senate president and someone who had been involved in Florida politics for decades. He was a man of principle and conviction. He also had the experience, having served as a district superintendent, and was well respected around the state for his knowledge, acumen, and statesmanship. I could not make the interview, but I heard afterwards that Don had been very impressive. However, Matt indicated it probably was not going to work out logistically on his father's end.

Matt called to talk about it, he said, "The governor told me, 'I want Richard for ed commissioner.'"

"Matt, I've already had a conversation with Ron that I was not interested."

"Well, that's what he said," Matt Gaetz replied. Matt's not always the easiest guy to argue with. Neither is the governor. I was flattered that someone as talented as the governor was continuing to offer me the position for a second time.

Leaders were usually just looking for a competent person to fill a position, and there were any number of qualified individuals interested in a high-profile appointment in the state of Florida. It would not have been hard to find someone else. Looking back, now knowing the governor and his leadership style better, I realize it was probably more than my well-known passion for educational reform that made him continue to offer me the job. He had a big list for transforming education—bigger than I could have imagined, and I have a big imagination—and he wanted someone who would not back down from a fight.

The next time I saw governor-elect DeSantis in our transition offices in Tallahassee, he brought up the position again.

"Richard, I really want you to be education commissioner."

"I really can't," I said. "However, I've got another great candidate for you: Mike Bileca. When I was Speaker, this guy was the head of education for me. He's a self-made man. He's a CPA. He built up a bunch of dental clinics, sold them for tens of millions of dollars, knows education, and he's super conservative. He's a great guy."

"All right, let me interview him," Ron said.

After he interviewed Bileca, Ron called me again. "What'd you think?" I asked. "He's great, right?"

"You're right," DeSantis replied. "He checked all the boxes. He's a great guy."

"Excellent," I said, somewhat relieved. "So, we're good?"

"No, we're not good," DeSantis said. "I still want you to think about taking the position."

I did not refuse immediately when he offered a third time. I said I would go home and talk about it with my wife. The fact that he kept coming back to offer me the commissioner position made me pause. I was now questioning my initial reasoning for declining: that the typical education commissioner's role was day-to-day management. I realized that this was probably not what the governor had in mind for the role if he was pursuing me for the position so doggedly. He knew my reputation as a disrupter. He probably had a very different agenda and vision for the role than anyone before had. When I went home and talked to Anne, she had the same thoughts. She was originally against me taking the job as well, mainly because she thought it was not a good fit for my personality. Now we were both realizing that the governor wanted to seriously move the needle with education. The only reason for him to offer someone like me the position three times was because he was gearing up to jump into the fray and make systemic changes. And in making changes to education, it would be a brawl. The liberal press and teachers' unions would absolutely not let their iron grip on the educational world go without epic battles.

I called him back and told him I would accept the position.

● ● ●

Florida for the last several years has accomplished infinitely more than other states with conservative legislatures and governors. Florida is Florida not by accident but because of bold leadership over twenty-five years.

CHAPTER 9

Road Map

Then it began to dawn on us: There was no miracle moment. Although it may have looked like a single-stroke breakthrough to those peering in from the outside, it was anything but that to people experiencing transformation from within. Rather, it was a quiet, deliberate process of figuring out what needed to be done to create the best future results and then simply taking those steps, one after the other.
—Jim Collins, Good to Great

In a mere ten months, New College of Florida went from one of the most progressively captured universities in the country to the freest university in the nation. It was not "so easy" as one author claimed recently. However, it did follow a road map: "It may have looked like a single-stroke breakthrough," but it was a "deliberate process...taking those steps, one after the other."

Here are the steps.

1. Leadership is everything.

To change an institution of public higher education, it is necessary to have alignment between strong leaders at three levels: governor, the board, and the president.

Governor

It all starts with the governor. DeSantis has made many courageous decisions as governor, particularly with COVID. However, the awareness of the issues at the core of higher education came toward the end of his first tenure. This is why only Florida has been successful at changing its public institutions.

Boards

In April 2021, I applied to be the president of Florida State University. At that time, I was still serving as education commissioner. I had approached the governor about the idea of applying for the position, and he was supportive. I made the cut to be in the second round of interviewees, which included nine applicants. The governor and his team indicated to members of the FSU presidential search committee that I was a strong candidate and many of those on this committee indicated that they would support me. However, despite giving their word to him and to me, it became apparent that several were actively working against me. My name had caused consternation among the Left—and even with some establishment Republicans who did not want to make any waves. Therefore, several members of this committee were nervous to support me as they did not want to challenge the status quo, and I was eliminated on May 15th during this round of interviews.

It was ostensibly because FSU's accreditation agency, SACSCOC, on May 13, 2021, had sent a letter to the chairman of the BOG and copied the current FSU president and chairman of the FSU board. The president of SACSCOC, Belle Wheelan, wrote that she had read stories in the press that I was being considered for the FSU presidency. In the letter, Wheelan noted that she was "concerned" that my application could affect FSU's accreditation. According to a news article at the time, "SACSCOC President Belle Wheelan said it was improper for Corcoran to seek the job while holding a seat on the Board of Governors. She also commented on Corcoran's fitness for the position and insinuated FSU's accreditation would be on the line if his application advanced."[1] I was on the BOG because I was required to be on its board as the commissioner of education. I had been prepared to recuse myself on a BOG vote, which would only take place if I was chosen by the FSU board. However, Wheelan's letter came before even the FSU vote.

On May 16th, Alan Levine, a member of the BOG, wrote a letter to the BOG president about his concern's with Wheelan's letter. Levine stated that Wheelan's letter prior to the FSU board vote on the candidates for president was an improper interference with the search process and that "members of the search committee for the next president of Florida State University were potentially influenced by the May 13 letter sent by...Wheelan." This was unacceptable, according to Levine.

Deeply concerning to me is that a letter which seemingly threatens the accreditation of a major state university was sent literally in the middle of the process we established as a governing body and was done so without even a cursory investigation into the facts... I will reserve my own judgment on that at such time as I hear the rationale directly from Dr. Wheelan as to why she felt it necessary to intrude into our process without even a hint of fact-finding.[2]

SACSCOC's interference in Florida's university system would be part of the reason a bill was passed in the next legislative session requiring public colleges to change accreditors every five years. In addition, the committee vote resulted in a discussion about what was happening at the leadership level at universities. The FSU experience in part led to the New College revolt because DeSantis became keenly aware that country-club donors who historically dominated board appointments in many cases did not have the fortitude to fight for what was needed to reform higher education. The new trustees had to be people who believed in free speech and civil discourse and were against ideological indoctrination, as well as have the courage to stand up against what would be great opposition.

Even after the success at New College, it has been hard to replicate the strength of the New College board. This is in large part because majority of the New College board was up for appointment, given that there had been some whose terms had technically expired but had not been replaced. Not only did he appoint six new people but—fortuitously—three of the four existing trustees were happy to finally have reinforcements to repair the school and the ability to finally start rebuilding the school. Therefore, with DeSantis's six new members, a seventh appointed shortly thereafter by the BOG, and three existing members on board with the vision, the New College board now had very quickly ten out of thirteen members who were in agreement about the need to fight against the cancel culture pervasive on campus—which resulted in members who were willing to vote for a disrupter like myself to be president. At other universities—such as Florida Atlantic University and Florida Gulf Coast University—both part of the 12-member Florida university system, presidential search processes unfolded but the boards still had a majority of traditional board members who had other agendas—many personal rather than for the organization—resulting in processes that unfolded in a similar manner to what occurred at FSU with the presidential search committee. Some members indicated they supported candidates who were willing to fight for free speech—but were actively working behind the scenes against these candidates.

For this reason, New College's board thus far has been at the tip of the spear in achieving systemic change. Florida is not alone in this struggle. Many college boards have been appointed by Republican governors throughout the nation, and often trustees tend to avoid difficult decisions if possible. It has been New College trustees who have led the way, taking the slings and arrows of the press and other liberal organizations that masquerade as objective players.

President

The board can make all the edicts it wants. If its policies are not instituted with fidelity by the administration—primarily through who it hires and fires as president—it will not make a difference. Here are two examples from strong conservative states.

Texas

Texas passed Senate bill 17 in May 2023. Aimed at state-funded colleges and universities, it prohibits them from: having DEI offices, hiring employees to perform duties related to DEI, requiring diversity training, or asking for DEI statements from job candidates.[3] It took effect on January 1, 2024.

On February 15, 2024, Accuracy in Media, a conservative news outlet, released video footage of employees from nine Texas universities who had done interviews with an undercover reporter posing as a prospective employee. Three of the university employees—from West Texas A&M, Texas State, and the University of Houston—told the undercover reporter that DEI was no longer promulgated at their institutions. Six, however, said they were merely calling it something different.

The employee at Texas A&M stated that, "They just rebranded. So we're still doing the same work. We just can't call it that."

At Tarleton State, the employee said that "you have all the same DEI people. They're just called something else…I'm not supposed to say that."

The same thing was happening at UNT Dallas. The undercover interviewee asked, "They're gonna keep a lot of the programs just not call it diversity, equity, and inclusion?" The employee nodded emphatically, then stated, "Yeah, just skirt the lines a little."

At the University of Houston, while one of the employees did state the school was doing away with DEI, a different one said that the work is now done through "a different lens. It's a different take on it. I would say it's DEI lite."

This philosophy continued when the undercover reporter went to the University of Texas at Tyler. The undercover reporter asked, "So there are loopholes in the new law?"

The employee said, "We carry on. We do the work. I plot and plan…You can still do it. You just have to be [long pause] creative."[4]

The employee at Texas Tech summed it up when she said that "we're just gonna call it different things, just like every university is going to do."[5]

Oklahoma

In December 2023, Oklahoma's governor joined other Republican governors who followed the lead of Gov. DeSantis in Florida, signing an executive order to review the DEI departments, staffing, and programs at the state's colleges. Later in January, two bills were filed in the Oklahoma Senate, one to prohibit DEI offices in higher educational institutions and one banning diversity statements and racial preferences as well as any requirement to disclose pronouns.

According to the *Chronicle of Higher Education*, "Oklahoma's recent moves are part of a wave of anti-DEI legislation sweeping the country. The movement builds off the advances conservatives made against DEI in 2023, when 49 bills were introduced across 23 states, and seven became law. As the 2024 state-legislative season kicks into gear, 29 new bills have been introduced."

The reporter then interviewed Belinda Higgs Hyppolite, vice president for diversity and inclusion and chief diversity officer at the University of Oklahoma, the state's flagship university. Hyppolite said her office was closing; however, the reporter stated that Hyppolite "and her team would work to create DEI

efforts in a way that would comply with the executive order."
Yes, that's right, she and her team will still be around doing
basically the same thing with a new coat of paint.

Hyppolite addressed the Staff Senate at OU in December,
stating that "[t]he big question right now is that, 'Is DEI going away?' Well, DEI in [its] current iteration, is absolutely going away...We will be complying with this executive order, but
we know that we have a responsibility to make sure that we
continue to increase access and to create opportunity for our
campus community." While no one disagrees about the general
words she spoke at the end, this is the same person who had
been in charge of DEI at the state's biggest university. It is likely
that whatever she and her team create will have similar issues to
those found in DEI programs.

The president of OU said something similar. President
Joseph Harroz Jr. stated in the student newspaper that "nobody's
losing their job. No one's losing their employment with the university because of these changes."

In an even more powerful statement of how the staff and
leaders in higher education in Oklahoma think, Kayse Shrum,
the president of the Oklahoma State University system, said that
the "institution's DEI work didn't need to cease because of the
governor's executive order, declaring that 'an initial review indicates that no significant changes to our processes or practices
are needed.'"[6]

Juxtapose that with New College. New College acted without any force of law upon us. Trustees, many of them newly
appointed by DeSantis, eliminated the DEI office because its
philosophy was flawed. I then terminated the director because I
understood the intent of the board to abolish the incursions on
free speech and equal protection. The employee, who had voiced

strong support for the beliefs underpinning the theories behind DEI, was not reassigned to another part of the university. Every other public university that has done what the New College board did has done so under force of law. That is the difference a strong board and president make. Gov. DeSantis knew this and chose trustees that understood the importance of their role in protecting free speech, civil discourse, equal protection, and academic freedom.

2. Litigate, litigate, litigate.

In the twelve months I have been interim president and now president, New College has been targeted in a federal lawsuit, state lawsuits, human resource complaints, Department of Education complaints, SACSCOC allegations, faculty censures, union grievances, and more. We have fought every single one. We have yet to lose, but it is not an easy fight. We are now approaching legal expenses of close to half a million dollars as well as many hours of staff time and research.

In my experience, the hard Left wields litigation as a weapon to wear down its opponents. It does not let up, using it as a cudgel to abuse and manipulate those who oppose its aims.

New College fought back. Few others do.

Take for example the Biden executive orders on DEI or gender identity. These were pure, unadulterated policy capture. The Right has yet to litigate these.

However, the Left has been unleashing massive fire power on tiny New College.

No wonder the radical Left is winning this war.

We do not just fight back. We proactively go on the offensive, such as when a group of New College alumni, faculty, and others started a group called Alt New College. We immediately filed an intellectual property dispute. They quickly capitulated because it was such an egregious offense and changed the name, but we were not done. We demanded that they publicly apologize, pay our attorneys' fees and costs, and turn over intellectual property, which they agreed to do.

On DEI, on gender identity, on the ideological capture of higher education, the Right holds the moral high ground. That is what the justice system exists to enforce. I think that sometimes the right is reticent to use the courts to enforce the law because there is a concern of engaging in "lawfare." It is important to realize there is a stark difference between using the law to punish, harass, and demoralize opponents for no strong legal reason—such as the left has engaged in often particularly of late—and using the legal system to enforce a constitutional or legal right. It is actually imperative that we as citizens utilize the courts when necessary to ensure that the Constitution and other legal principles are followed to protect our system of government.

The Right should be litigating these executive orders as well as any other time the hard Left encroaches on the constitutional system that exists. While it is nice to hear these arguments made within conservative media, that will not change anything. These points need to be made in a courtroom because, in the end, they are based on an appeal to justice and the ideals contained in the US Constitution.

The radical Left constantly brings their arguments in court and through other systems, but they do it to obfuscate and wear us down. We would do it to win on the merits.

I say this from experience. When I was preparing to take over as Speaker, I told my chief of staff to hire the best lawyers. He asked me why. I told him it was because "we are going to litigate and stop this corruption." The corruption I was referring to was that which was occurring in the many areas of government where people were infringing on the state and federal Constitution. No one was challenging these. These were cases I felt that literally could not be lost.

I was right. We won every single one.

There were a lot of them. I threatened to sue the state supreme court—which had a liberal majority at the time—for court packing. I sued local governments over illegal taxation. I sued the executive branch (which was in Republican hands for) trying to co-opt the legislature's appropriations power. I sued the management company of an international rap star to ensure full transparency of the use of public tax dollars. I brought impeachment proceedings against corrupt judges, some of which were appointed by Republicans. In every single case, I either won or the other side backed down.

I took this philosophy with me to New College. It is time for other Republicans to try this as well. If Republicans do not, we will continue to be railroaded at every agency and institution. There are always excuses for inaction—when, in reality, there is likely cowardice in the leadership at some level.

New College is the exception, not the rule.

3. Ensure actual shared governance.

While faculty tout the shared governance model in higher education, their unions do not actually support it in practice. In their minds, governance of the important areas of a college or university is 100 percent under the control of the faculty: which students are admitted, which faculty get to teach them, and what these students are taught. The main role of administration in the minds of faculty unions is fundraising and keeping the lights on.

Such an arrangement would be allowed in no other industry. What person would sign a contract or enter into a deal in which they fund the entire project—but had no input on hiring, products, or other metrics? This is what has happened in higher education. When we realize this, it is not surprising that things are in the current state of disarray.

At New College, we have taken steps to ensure that there is true shared governance. The New College board has said that admissions, hiring, and curriculum are under its auspices, though we will consult with faculty about decisions related to all of these things. The New College union contract actually supports this, though no one had tried to enforce it. This is the same at most universities. New College's collective bargaining agreement states there is shared governance and that administration is to consult with the faculty. I follow it to the letter. Yet this has never meant—and the contract does not read—that faculty are the only decision-makers. Boards and presidents fail in their fiduciary duty when they allow this type of behavior.

In addition to actually ensuring the faculty adhere to the union contract, the board and administration required that the university's faculty comply with SB 266 immediately upon its effective date of July 1, 2023. This bill states clearly that, while the faculty will be consulted, it is the trustees or their designee (usually the president) who has the final say in decisions.

4. Presidents should have CEO capabilities.

Universities are multibillion-dollar enterprises. It makes little sense to put someone at the helm whose main accomplishment is having climbed the ranks in academia. Most have never run a business or organization. In addition, they often view other members of faculty as their brethren. Therefore, it can be difficult for them to push back against this group, even if it is in the best interests of the institution.

The default for a president should be a significant background in an executive position. Bill Ackman shared a similar thought when he wrote a letter to the Harvard leadership on January 3, 2024, suggesting ways it could fix its culture.

> *I would suggest that universities should broaden their searches to include capable businesspeople for the role of president, as a university president requires more business skills than can be gleaned from even the most successful academic career with its hundreds of peer-reviewed papers and many books...The president's job—managing thousands of employees, overseeing a $50 billion endowment, raising money, managing expenses, capital allocation, real estate acquisition, disposition, and construction, and reputation management—are responsibilities that few career academics are capable of executing.*

When I delved into the past administrative decisions at New College, it became apparent how unprepared past presidents had been to make even the most basic decisions—such as ensuring the foundation was solvent each year in the midst of a bull market, negotiating a lease with a tenant that was at market value, or applying the law with regard to student conduct. Ackman also found specific instances at Harvard that had caused the institution to suffer because of the lack of an executive with experience at its helm. According to Ackman, he discovered that "Harvard is a massive business that has been mismanaged for a long time."

5. Enforce the rule of law

One of the first things we did at New College was set the expectation that the law and the Student Code of Conduct were now going to be enforced. With countries, uniform application of the rule of law is what separates great ones from those that struggle. What separates the US from other countries in history, more than anything else, is our adherence to the rule of law. Without laws that are enforced equally and with due process, a society will struggle to have successful financial, corporate, educational, or justice systems. An organization also will not be effective without fair and equally applied rules.

When I first started, it was impossible not to notice the graffiti, the stickers placed randomly throughout campus, and the chalk in front of entrances that was tracked all over buildings. Once I began to look into other areas, it was even more troubling. Students were allowed to be harassed and bullied without consequences. During one of my first weeks on campus, a student was caught on a news video committing an apparent assault and battery by spitting on Rufo. Our attorney began the process to convene the Student Conduct Board—which was required by the student handbook, the faculty handbook, and state rule—only to find it did not exist and never had in the collective memories of staff.

Therefore, as it was summer, it took about a month before the new conduct board could meet. This was inconvenient for everyone, including the student who was facing discipline. This student needed to make decisions but was in a holding pattern longer than she should have been because of the malfeasance of the past administration. Anarchy hurts everyone.

Once the conduct board met, the college then enforced discipline on two students who had violated both the law and the Student Code of Conduct. Both ended up withdrawing rather than have the discipline on their record. This was a game changer. Once this occurred, other more minor areas, such as the graffiti, chalk, and the stickers, ceased to be issues. This also freed up much of the maintenance employees' time because they could now spend their hours on maintaining the rest of the campus rather than cleaning up after students.

On November 4, 2023, Bill Ackman wrote a letter to Harvard about changes to make to push back against the current wave of anti-Semitism on campus following the October 7th attacks. Four of the seven changes he recommended related to the exercise of the rule of law. First, he advised that students who harassed and allegedly physically assaulted a Jewish student be suspended, as videos of the incident showed the students violated the Student Code of Conduct. Second, he recommended that students who had been seen on video shouting statements about eliminating the Jews should be referred to the disciplinary committee for review of each case. Third, he said that the student message board should be reviewed and students who had posted anti-Semitic statements and images should be referred for disciplinary review. Finally, he wanted the university to ask students if there were other incidents that they thought should be reviewed for possible violation of the Student Code of Conduct.

These were reasonable requests. They were similar to some of the actions taken at New College that worked to effectively set expectations for more respectful behavior in the future. Once the administration indicated it was going to enforce the Student Code of Conduct, the campus became a much more pleasant place for everyone.

6. Curriculum should teach students how to think, not what to think

Faculty unions have convinced almost every higher educational institution that shared governance means that faculty alone controls what students are taught. As the faculty at most schools is dominated by the hard Left, this ideology has overtaken the curriculum. There has been a concerted effort to teach one side, which results in attempted indoctrination. This is the opposite of what education should be in a democratic society. Rather, students should be prepared to be citizens who can make the complex decisions necessary for self-governance. For this reason, at least some part of higher education should have as its aim to teach students to think critically, to express themselves clearly, and to engage in civic life in a thoughtful manner.

On the day I started as interim president at New College, the local paper ran an interview with me that was published in a question-and-answer format. The reporter asked how I defined a traditional liberal arts education and what such a program could look like at New College. I said that the definition of the "liberal arts" has broadened over the years. Lacking clear vision, colleges have thrown together a "chaotic hodgepodge of courses that do not appear to be particularly related in a strategic way."

For students to learn to think, we do not have to reinvent the wheel. We just need to do what educators have done for hundreds of years: expose students to the conversation of the centuries. The current practice in higher education of focusing on whatever thoughts are popular at the moment is problematic. Albert Einstein describes such an education in this manner: "Somebody who only reads newspapers and at best books of contemporary authors looks to me like an extremely nearsighted person who scorns eyeglasses. He is completely dependent on the prejudices and fashions of his times, since he never gets to see or hear anything else." That is what higher education has become. It is an echo chamber of what everyone generally thinks right now. This needs to change, and we need to purposefully allow students to have "the clean breeze of the centuries blowing through [their] minds." I explained it to the reporter in this manner:

> *We are born into a conversation that has been happening for thousands of years. And in it there have been certain people—artists, authors, philosophers, scientists, mathematicians—whose works speak across cultures and times and social status to the biggest questions of existence. It is not a perfect conversation, but there are certain contributors... that have helped humanity "stitch together the patches of the universe." We are poorer as a society when we allow students to think that the only ideas that exist are the ones right in front of them.*

As I discussed earlier, at New College, we are working on building out a curriculum based on Logos—the best thoughts of humankind throughout the conversation of the centuries—and Techne—skills that are relevant at the present moment. This intersection of the liberal arts and technology, so well expressed by Steve Jobs, is a powerful combination.

At New College, I still have a small handful of faculty members who believe in leftist indoctrination. They are frustrated that New College is no longer among the most progressively leftist colleges in the country. They would like to see New College destroyed rather than have any faculty brought on board who are not from the hard Left of the political spectrum. However, also at New College, I have many faculty here who are self-described leftist liberals who are glad to bring in faculty from other perspectives in order to create balance. The board and I are committed to ensuring that the curriculum leads to the outcome of equipping students to be critical thinkers, thoughtful citizens, and lifelong learners, not easily manipulated sheep.

7. Personnel are policy.

Whenever I take over an existing organization—whether it is the Florida House, the Florida Department of Education, or New College—key positions are turned over because I bring people on board who share the vision. One year in, every leadership position has been replaced at New College, and of two hundred employees, we have replaced over one hundred. Long after I am gone, and the governor is no longer the governor, many of these employees will still be there. While as the day-to-day leader I give direction, it is the staff who make a myriad of daily

decisions that never trickle up. These small choices work together to determine the direction in which the organization will
go. Just as the board cannot achieve its goals without the president working to implement them, the president will not realize
objectives without employees who are aligned with the vision.

8. Do not abolish the US Department of Education.

The radical Left would never do that. They use the power of
agencies and institutions to effect change, and they have been
wildly successful. To push back on the radical Left's ideological
stranglehold, federal agencies can be utilized to legally, ethically,
and honorably bring about rapid change. In addition, imagine
the result of eliminating the US Department of Education. The
funds would now go straight to Gavin Newsom, Kathy Hochul,
and Gretchen Whitmer.

In Florida, we brought about rapid change through our own
department of education. For example, how did Florida open up
schools so quickly? Because of the power of the purse that was
given to the Florida Department of Education. We used that to
effectively achieve our goals, despite great pushback from certain
local superintendents. How did Florida stop masking in schools?
In the same way—the power of the purse that was given to
the Florida Department of Education. The governor and I used
this mechanism to force school districts to fall in line, and we
were backed up by the courts when I did so. The powers were
already provided to FDOE. We decided to use them. We need
a president who will do the same with the federal Department
of Education.

9. Give no quarter.

Since much of academia is overrun by ideologues who believe there is only one "correct" way to think on many intellectual matters, since the mainstream press is inclined to believe any spin put on a story from that side, the fight for me as a college president trying to return an institution to ideals of free speech and equal protection is not every day. It is every hour. Everything is a fight. If we want to fix moldy dorms, if we want to add sports, if we want to choose a mascot, if we want to add turf to areas where grass does not grow, every one of these have been actual fights that take up hours of time. They fight us on these things because they want to ensure our time is taken up with trivialities so we cannot address the big things. We do not give in on anything because we want excellence across the board. We will not give up on a fight because we will achieve the goal. But it is all-consuming. In addition to the internal struggle, there is the constant stream of misinformation coming from the media.

In 2015 when I was in line for the speakership, a television reporter came to interview me in my legislative office. He noted that I had lined the lobby with "framed headlines of critical newspaper articles calling [Corcoran] names such as 'immoral.' " I told him that I did that for a reason. "I frame those to remind myself I'm here to serve the constituents and not the press."

"Look, I'll take a thousand more (negative) headlines if it really is helping the people of Florida. If it's a headline that's bad and I've done something that's not beneficial to the people of Florida then I should walk away." I have to have internal checks all the time. Was the crux of the article that I made a move that was positive for the institution? Then it does not matter what the press says. I would encourage anyone getting into this fight to have some type of way to keep the perspective on the goal of serving the institution.

The reason we lose when we have the moral high ground—free speech and equal protection—is because those opposing these ideals fight so much harder and smarter. We can do that too. We just have to determine not to give up inches of ground, because eventually one will realize that one has given up miles and is so off course that it is impossible even to see where one started from.

• • •

On Nov. 16, 2023, the *Chronicle of Higher Education* published an article entitled "Dear Administrators: Enough with the Free-Speech Rhetoric!" It was written by Richard Amesbury and Catherine O'Donnell, both professors at Arizona State University.[7] The authors were concerned that people were daring to question DEI or the necessity of having rules about who could speak on campus. The timing of the article, six weeks after the Hamas attacks, was a clear pushback against the uncomfortable spotlight now on academia based on the shocking behavior being witnessed by the public.

The authors supported the idea that views that did not align with the current ideological orthodoxy in academia should be excluded from "free speech." Therefore, "Enough with the Free Speech Rhetoric!" (The subtitle was: "It concedes too much to right-wing agendas.")

The article began by questioning the premises that "free speech is a cardinal virtue of higher education, and that colleges should aspire to a diversity of opinions." The authors asked darkly, "Are these goals in their own rights, as college administrators often seem to think, or means for achieving something else altogether?" They then warn against these "calls for greater freedom of speech on campuses" because "however well-intentioned, [they] risk undermining colleges' central purpose, namely the production of expert knowledge and understanding, in the sense of disciplinarily warranted opinion."

Accordingly, the authors suggest there be a "winnowing and refinement that is premised on the understanding that not all opinions are equally valid." Therefore, they "urge[d] administrators toward caution before uncritically endorsing calls for intellectual diversity in place of academic expertise."

• • •

It was exactly the kind of thinking that Orwell addressed in his introduction to *Animal Farm*.

> *At any given moment there is an orthodoxy, a body of ideas which it is assumed that all right-thinking people will accept without question. It is not exactly forbidden to say this, that or the other but it is "not done" to say it, just as in mid-Victorian times it was "not done" to mention trousers in the presence of a lady. Anyone who challenges the prevailing orthodoxy finds himself silenced with surprising effectiveness. A genuinely unfashionable opinion is almost never given a fair hearing, either in the popular press or in the highbrow periodicals.*

The intelligentsia in Orwell's time, like today, included the press and academia acting to gate-keep by peer pressure dissonant ideas, including, in his time, *Animal Farm*. It would likely have shocked those fighting the changes at New College to realize who disagreed with the publication of the book.

> *But now to come back to this book of mine. The reaction toward it of most English intellectuals will be quite simple: "It oughtn't to have been published."* ... *The issue involved here is quite a simple one: Is every opinion, however unpopular—however foolish, even—entitled to a hearing? Put it in that form and nearly any English intellectual will feel that he ought to say "Yes." But give it a concrete shape, and ask, "How about an attack on Stalin? Is that entitled to a hearing?" and the answer more often than not will be "No." In that case, the current orthodoxy happens to be challenged, and so the principle of free speech lapses.*

Say, for example, that gender is related to biology. Then the answer is no. Or that DEI statements should not be required. Then the answer is no. This is how the peer-pressure of the intelligentsia functions. It frightens people into silence, much as Ackman describes in his three letters to Harvard President Gay after the Hamas attacks.

• • •

Currently, the liberal intellectual elite have taken over academia, the mainstream press, major publishing houses, and many

STORMING THE IVORY TOWER

institutions of higher education. They believe it is righteous to suppress ideas to protect the public from diverse viewpoints.

The irony of this stance is summed up by the response of a college president in 2017 to students who wanted to shout down his state of the university address. Michael H. Schill, the president of the University of Oregon, wrote about students attempting to block him from speaking. In part, they were protesting his support for "free speech on campus—a stance they said perpetuated 'fascism and white supremacy.'"[8]

> *It is...ironic that they would associate fascism with the university during a protest in which they limit discourse. One of the students who stormed the stage during my talk told the news media to "expect resistance to anyone who opposes us." ... Fundamentally, fascism is about the smothering of dissent. ...Fascist regimes rose to power by attacking free speech, threatening violence against those who opposed them, and using fear and the threat of retaliation to intimidate dissenters.*

> *Undoubtedly, the term "fascism" has an effective anti-authoritarian ring to it, so perhaps that is why it is thrown around so much these days. But from what I can tell, much of what students are protesting, both at the University of Oregon and elsewhere, is the expression of viewpoints or ideologies that offend them.*

At New College in 2023, the reality was that the people who accused the governor, the board, and me of "fascism" were the ones who were silencing speech, including by preventing the promulgation of diverse viewpoints through the use of DEI programs and gender studies departments.

• • •

There are two endings to this book. Both are true.

There is a positive ending. New College was turned around quickly, revealing that this is possible at a public university. A higher educational institution can be returned to its principles of free speech and civil discourse, no matter how many distortions are printed in the media or propounded by the radical Left.

There is also an ending that is disheartening, namely that I do not see it happening elsewhere. While I hear people championing the need to fight for free speech in higher education, I see little effective action being taken on the ground. As usual, many Republican elected officials are just performative enough that they can tell voters they "did something." They give speeches to crowds who already agree with them and go on Fox News to thump their chests. And that is about it. There is little follow-through to ensure results happen. This is not unique to higher education. Republicans often run on a conservative platform, do a bit of virtue signaling, appear on a few friendly outlets throwing out catch phrases voters agree with, but do little in actuality to make their constituents' lives better.

I have bad news for these types of leaders. This book is called *Storming the Ivory Tower* for a reason. To ensure free speech and civil discourse exist in higher education, it will require more than knocking politely on the door and asking, "Please, may we come in and be part of the conversation?" It will even require more than banging a bit loudly. Bureaucrats will merely look down from their superior height—as those in Oklahoma and Texas did when DEI was eliminated—and smile and move the furniture around a bit.

However, there is still time to stop being talkers and start being doers. While I believe this second ending is true for the moment, it does not have to continue to be. We can ensure that New College is not just a blip on the screen. We can take its lessons and apply them throughout public institutions.

On that graduation evening in May of 2023, Dr. Atlas painted a bleak picture of where we were as a nation in higher education.

> *If our democracy, with its defining freedoms, is to survive, we need good people, individuals with integrity, and there are many, to rise up—meaning speak up, as we are allowed, as we are expected to do in free societies—or it has no chance…. We cannot have a civil society if it's filled with people, led by people, who refuse to allow discussion of views counter to their own…or this country, as an ethical society, as a virtuous society, as a free and diverse society, is in serious trouble.*

The sun was slowly setting over Sarasota Bay as he ended, and a question hung in the air. It was a question that did not have an answer that night—and does not to this day: Do we have the courage to storm the ivory tower and ensure that free speech and civil discourse will exist in higher education for the next generation?

When I was a practicing attorney who did jury trials, I would often begin my closing argument by telling a story to the jurors, attributed to the famous trial attorney Gerry Spence, to emphasize the importance of the task before them. It was about a young boy who held a bird hidden between his two cupped hands. He went up to a wise old man and asked, "Wise old man, do you think the bird in my hands is living or dead?"

The old man looked at the boy and said, "The answer my son lies firmly in your hands."

The story applies to the choice before us today. What will be the answer to whether free speech will continue to exist in our nation's system of higher education? The answer lies firmly in our hands.

ENDNOTES

Chapter 1

[1] Hodgson, Ian. "A Difficult Year at New College Ends with a Tense Official Graduation," *Tampa Bay Times*, May 20, 2023, https://www.tampabay.com/news/education/2023/05/19/new-college-of-florida-commencement-desantis-scott-atlas-trump-graduates-trustees/.

[2] Walker, Steven. "New College of Florida Graduates Turn Backs, Wear Masks in Protest of Leadership Changes," *Sarasota Herald-Tribune*, May 20, 2023, https://www.heraldtribune.com/story/news/education/2023/05/19/new-college-of-florida-graduates-protest-desantis-appointees-at-commencement/70232553007/.

[3] Wolfe, Sophia. "Amid a Conservative Takeover of a Conservative Liberal Arts College, Graduation Attendees Boo a Former Trump Advisor Giving a Keynote Speech," CNN, May 20, 2023, https://www.cnn.com/2023/05/20/us/scott-atlas-new-college-florida-keynote-speech-boos/index.html.

[4] Walker, "New College."

[5] Hodgson, "Difficult Year."

[6] Art & Science Group LLC and David Strauss, "New College of Florida. Institutional Strategy: Research, Modeling, and Consultation," October 21, 2019, https://drive.google.com/file/d/1MB5RsMcrJC2vV27LqBYh53IOxe3ykb7Z/view?pli=1; Anderson, Zac. "Bill Would Abolish Sarasota-Based New College as Independent School and Make It Part of FSU," *Tallahassee*

287

Democrat, February 11, 2020, https://www.tallahassee.com/story/news/2020/02/11/bill-would-abolish-new-college-make-part-fsu-sarasota/4722011002/; "2022 Accountability Plan New College of Florida," April 19, 2022, https://www.ncf.edu/wp-content/uploads/2022/04/2022_NCF_Accountability_Plan.pdf.

7 "Scott William Atlas, MD," https://docs.house.gov/meetings/IF/IF14/20191210/110313/HHRG-116-IF14-Wstate-AtlasS-20191210-SD001.pdf.

8 Thomas, Elizabeth. "The New Doctor in Trump's Pandemic Response Briefings: Scott Atlas Agrees with Him on Masks, Opening Schools," ABC News, Aug. 14, 2020, https://abcnews.go.com/Politics/doctor-trumps-pandemic-response-briefings-scott-atlas-agrees/story?id=72376728.

9 Joner, Josiah. "Dr. Scott Atlas Shouted Down at New College of Florida Commencement Speech," *Stanford Review*, May 21, 2023, https://stanfordreview.org/dr-scott-atlas-shouted-down-at-new-college-of-florida-commencement-speech/.

10 "Rufo is among six people who were appointed to New College's board...setting the stage for what many think will be a conservative overhaul of an institution known for an LGBTQ-friendly ethos and a carefree student body." Stripling, Jack. "DeSantis Trustee Appointees Face Skeptical Crowd at New College of Florida," *Washington Post*, January 26, 2023, https://www.washingtonpost.com/education/2023/01/25/rufo-new-college-of-florida/; "While the authority of the new trustees is limited to one small college of about 700 students, their appointment—and provocative agenda—represent the broader aim of DeSantis's push into higher education, serving as a laboratory for a conservative experiment to reshape academe in the Sunshine State." Moody, Josh. "The DeSantis Takeover Begins," *Inside Higher Ed*, January 31, 2023, https://www.insidehighered.com/news/2023/02/01/desantis-puts-action-his-plan-end-woke-activism; "A slate of new board members installed by DeSantis earlier this month replaced college President Patricia Okker...

turbo charging a dramatic conservative culture shift." Anderson, Zac. "New College Board Fires President, Installs Former GOP House Speaker, DeSantis Ally," *Sarasota Herald-Tribune*, February 1, 2023, https://www.heraldtribune.com/story/news/local/sarasota/2023/01/31/richard-corcoran-becomes-interim-president-of-sarasotas-new-college/69858928007/; "The small liberal arts college in Sarasota whose student enrollment is approximately 700 has been the focus of Gov. Ron DeSantis' efforts to create a more conservative education model for Florida's public colleges and universities." APNews, "New College Gets Interim President Amid Conservative Push," February 13, 2023, https://apnews.com/article/ron-desantis-politics-education-sarasota-florida-c548e63d139856caba179a5593285e87; "Gov. Ron DeSantis's plan to transform New College of Florida into a beacon of conservatism has left students and faculty members at the tight-knit progressive school reeling." Mazzei, Patricia. "DeSantis's Latest Target: A Small College of 'Free Thinkers,'" *New York Times*, February 14, 2023, https://www.nytimes.com/2023/02/14/us/ron-desantis-new-college-florida.html; Carter, Cathy. "At New College of Florida, A New Leader Is In and Diversity Initiatives Are Out," WFSU News, March 1, 2023, https://news.wfsu.org/state-news/2023-03-01/at-new-college-of-florida-a-new-leader-is-in-and-diversity-initiatives-are-out; "DeSantis very much seems to want to raze New College and replace it with a Hillsdale of the South, and he's well on his way to getting away with it...The irony is off the charts, replacing a politically left, but intellectually diverse, and open-minded student body with a conservative monoculture." Warner, Josh. "Stopping the DeSantis Wrecking Ball," *Inside Higher Ed*, Jan. 31, 2023, https://www.insidehighered.com/blogs/just-visiting/stopping-desantis-wrecking-ball; "Reid scrolled through messages...She learned that the governor...planned to turn Florida's progressive honors college into a conservative institution." DeGregory, Lane. "A Semester Inside the Siege: New College Professor Is Trapped in the Takeover," *Tampa Bay Times*, August

21, 2023, https://www.tampabay.com/narratives/2023/08/16/
semester-inside-siege-new-college-professor-is-trapped-takeover/.

[11] Stuart, Tessa. "Inside the Fight to Keep a Florida
College Queer," *Rolling Stone*, May 19, 2023, https://
www.rollingstone.com/culture/culture-features/
ron-desantis-takeover-florida-queer-new-college-1234732975/.

[12] Achumba, Adaure. "Students, Faculty at New College Rally
against New School Leadership," WTSP, February 28, 2023,
https://www.wtsp.com/article/news/local/sarasotacounty/
new-college-florida-rally-interim-president-corcoran-board-of-
trustees/67-44b563a6-618f-43f4-b6dc-f6cdf2f30d57; Stancil,
Kenny. "New College of Florida Students and Faculty Protest
DeSantis' Right-Wing Assault on Education," *Common Dreams*,
February 28, 2023, https://www.commondreams.org/news/
new-college-florida-protest-desantis-attack; Teh, Cheryl. "Ron
DeSantis Posed with a Handmade Snowflake. It Had the Word
'Fascist' Written All Over It," *Business Insider*, March 13, 2023,
https://www.businessinsider.com/ron-desantis-fascist-snowflake-
iowa-2023-3; Carbonaro, Giulia. "Ron DeSantis Called 'Fascist'
by College Director in Resignation Letter," *Newsweek*, April 11,
2023, https://www.newsweek.com/ron-desantis-called-fascist-
college-director-resignation-letter-1793380; Stuart, Tessa. "Inside
the Fight to Keep a Florida College Queer," *Rolling Stone*, May
19, 2023, https://www.rollingstone.com/culture/culture-features/
ron-desantis-takeover-florida-queer-new-college-1234732975/;
"What the DeSantis Agenda Means for Higher Education in
Florida," May 23, 2023, NPR, https://www.wwno.org/2023-05-23/
what-the-desantis-agenda-means-for-higher-education-in-florida;
Canfield, David. "'It's Been Weird and Scary': On the Front Lines
of New College's Student-Led Rebellion against Ron DeSantis,"
May 24, 2023, https://www.vanityfair.com/news/2023/05/
new-college-student-rebellion-against-ron-desantis.

[13] Hodgson, "Difficult Year."

[14] Strauss, "New College of Florida."

[15] Stevens, S. T. "2024 College Free Speech Rankings: What Is
the State of Free Speech on America's College Campuses?,"

The Foundation for Individual Rights and Expression (FIRE), September 4, 2023, https://www.thefire.org/research-learn/2024-college-free-speech-rankings.

[16] McLaughlin & Associates. "National Undergrad Study 2023."

[17] Joner, "Atlas Shouted Down."

[18] Yanovskiy M. and Socol Y. "Are Lockdowns Effective in Managing Pandemics?," *Int J Environ Res Public Health* 19, no. 15 (July 29, 2022):9295, doi: 10.3390/ijerph19159295; Magness, Phillip W. and Earle, Peter C. "The Origins and Political Persistence of COVID-19 Lockdowns," *The Independent Review* 25, no. 4 (Spring 2021): 503-520; Jefferson T. et al. "Physical Interventions to Interrupt or Reduce the Spread of Respiratory Viruses," *Cochrane Database of Systematic Reviews* no. 1. (January 30, 2023), doi:10.1002/14651858. CD006207.pub6; Joffe, Ari R. "COVID-19: Rethinking the Lockdown Groupthink," *Frontiers in Public Health*, February 25, 2021, https://www.ncbi.nlm.nih.gov/pmc/articles/PMC7952324/.

[19] Cadelago, Christopher. "'We Would've Done Everything Differently,' Newsom Reflects on COVID Approach," *Politico*, September 10, 2023, https://www.politico.com/news/2023/09/10/newsom-covid-california-00114888.

[20] Editorial Board. "Randi Weingarten's Incredible COVID-19 Memory Loss," *Wall Street Journal*, April 30, 2023, https://www.wsj.com/articles/randi-weingartens-incredible-covid-memory-loss-teachers-union-pandemic-education-reopen-1015ce21.

[21] O'Shea, Donal. "State of the College Report," New College of Florida, September 8, 2018, https://www.ncf.edu/wp-content/uploads/2020/10/2018-19_SotC.pdf.

[22] "New College of Florida 2022–2023 Fact Book," https://www.ncf.edu/wp-content/uploads/2023/07/2022-2023-Fact-Book-PDF.pdf.

[23] Dodd, Colt. "Efforts to Improve Retention Yielding Positive Results," *Catalyst*, October 29, 2014, https://ncfcatalyst.com/efforts-to-improve-retention-yielding-positive-results/.

[24] Dodd, "Efforts to Improve."

[25] Espinosa, Emiliano. "Retention Rates on Campus," *Catalyst*, March 6, 2019, https://ncfcatalyst.com/retention-rates-on-campus/.

26   Miles, Izaya. "In the Midst of the Growth Problem, New College Is Shrinking," *Catalyst*, March 14, 2019, https://ncfcatalyst.com/in-the-midst-of-the-growth-plan-new-college-is-shrinking/.

27   Head, Michala. "Student Focus Groups to Be Held on Social Media Use," *Catalyst*, March 28, 2019, https://ncfcatalyst.com/student-focus-groups-to-be-held-on-social-media-use/.

28   Miles, "Growth Problem."

29   Ibid.

30   Head, "Focus Groups."

31   Ibid.

32   Ibid.

33   Miles, "Growth Problem."

34   Ibid.

35   Ibid.

36   Ibid.

37   Bryan, Haley. "Art & Science Group Presents Findings on Enrollment," *Catalyst*, September 19, 2019, https://ncfcatalyst.com/art-science-group-presents-findings-on-enrollment/.

38   Espinosa, "Retention Rates."

39   Strauss, "New College of Florida."

40   Winfrey, Anna Lynn. "Campus Hot Takes on the Retention Rate," *Catalyst*, May 8, 2019, https://ncfcatalyst.com/campus-hot-takes-on-the-retention-rate/.

41   Ingraham, Christopher. "The Dramatic Shift among College Professors That's Hurting Students' Education," *Washington Post*, January 11, 2016, https://www.washingtonpost.com/news/wonk/wp/2016/01/11/the-dramatic-shift-among-college-professors-thats-hurting-students-education/.

42   Langbert, Mitchell. "Homogenous: The Political Affiliations of Elite Liberal Arts College Faculty," National Association of Scholars, Academic Questions, no. 31 (Summer 2018):186–197, https://www.nas.org/academic-questions/31/2/homogenous_the_political_affiliations_of_elite_liberal_arts_college_faculty.

43 Klein, Daniel B. and Charlotta Stern. "Groupthink in Academia: Majoritarian Departmental Politics and the Professional Pyramid," *The Independent Review* vol. 13, no. 4 (Spring 2009): 589.

44 Klein and Stern, "Groupthink in Academia."

45 Krugman, Paul. "The Conscience of a Liberal: Academics and Politics" *New York Times*, January 4, 2016, https://archive. nytimes.com/krugman.blogs.nytimes.com/2016/01/04/ academics-and-politics/.

46 Schaffer, Michael. "The Right Is Dancing on Claudine Gay's Grave. But It Was the Center-Left That Did Her In," *Politico*, January 5, 2024, https://www.politico.com/news/magazine/2024/01/05/ claudine-gay-resignation-battle-column-00133820.

47 "Governor DeSantis Delivers Inaugural Address, Sets Priorities for Second Term," January 3, 2023, https://www.flgov. com/2023/01/03/governor-desantis-delivers-inaugural-address-sets-priorities-for-second-term/.

48 Moody, Josh. "DeSantis Aims to Turn Public College into 'Hillsdale of the South,'" *Inside Higher Ed*, January 10, 2023, https://www.insidehighered.com/news/2023/01/11/desantis-seeks-overhaul-small-liberal-arts-college; Nelson, Joshua Q. "DeSantis Shakes Up Liberal University, Appoints Six Board Members to the New College of Florida," Fox News, January 6, 2023, https:// www.foxnews.com/media/ron-desantis-shakes-liberal-university-appoints-six-new-members-new-college-florida.

49 "Governor DeSantis Elevates Civil Discourse and Intellectual Freedom in Higher Education," January 31, 2023, https://www. flgov.com/2023/01/31/governor-desantis-elevates-civil-discourse-and-intellectual-freedom-in-higher-education/.

50 Saul, Stephanie, Patricia Mazzei, and Trip Gabriel. "DeSantis Takes on the Education Establishment, and Builds His Brand," *New York Times*, January 31, 2023, https://www.nytimes. com/2023/01/31/us/governor-desantis-higher-education-chris-rufo.html.

51 WTSP, "Governor's Press Conference on Higher Education Reform" (quoted remarks begin around 16:20), January 31, 2023,

The Florida Channel, https://thefloridachannel.org/videos/1-31-23-governors-press-conference-on-higher-education-reform/.

52 Rufo, Christopher L. "Laying Siege to the Institutions," *Imprimis*, April/May 2022.

53 Stripling, "Skeptical Crowd."

54 Carter, Cathy. "DeSantis Appointees to New College of Florida Lay Out Their Visions to Faculty and Students," WUSF, January 26, 2023, https://www.wusf.org/education/2023-01-26/desantis-appointees-new-college-of-florida-lay-out-visions-faculty-students.

55 Ibid.

56 Wallace-Wells, Benjamin. "What Is Ron DeSantis Doing to Florida's Public Liberal-Arts College?," *The New Yorker*, February 22, 2023, https://www.newyorker.com/news/the-political-scene/what-is-ron-desantis-doing-to-floridas-public-liberal-arts-college.

57 Brown, Sophia. "Inside the 'Hostile Takeover': An Autopsy of the Jan. 31 Board of Trustees Meeting," *Catalyst*, February 4, 2023, https://ncfcatalyst.com/inside-the-hostile-takeover-an-autopsy-of-the-jan-31-board-of-trustees-meeting/.

58 Ibid.

59 Later, in April 2023, Gov. DeSantis would go to Hillsdale College and say during a speech, "[New College could] be like a little Hillsdale down in Florida. Can you imagine how good that would be?" This was after three months of messaging clearly that the goal was to have New College be a public college that modeled free speech. The reference was to its successful traditional liberal arts model.

60 Anderson, Zac. "Richard Corcoran Q & A: New College Interim President Outlines Vision, Defends Salary," *Sarasota Herald-Tribune*, February 27, 2023.

61 Goldberg, Michelle. "DeSantis Allies Plot the Hostile Takeover of a Liberal College," *New York Times*, January 9, 2023, https://www.nytimes.com/2023/01/09/opinion/chris-rufo-florida-ron-desantis.html.

62 Wood, Graeme. "DEI Is an Ideological Test," *The Atlantic*, February 10, 2023, https://www.theatlantic.com/ideas/archive/2023/02/christopher-rufo-manhattan-institute/673008/.

63 Hodgson, Ian, Divya Kumar, and Lane DeGregory. "Change Comes Swiftly to New College as DeSantis Appointees Replace President," *Tampa Bay Times*, January 31, 2023, https://www. tampabay.com/news/education/2023/01/31/change-comes-swiftly-new-college-desantis-appointees-replace-president/.

64 Staff Reports. "Florida Politics' Definitive List of Florida Politicians of the 2010s," Florida Politics, January 4, 2020, https://floridapolitics.com/archives/314532-introducing-florida-politics-definitive-list-of-florida-politicians-of-the-2010s/.

65 Bridges, C. A. "Who Is Richard Corcoran, The New Interim President of New College?," *Sarasota Herald-Tribune*, February 14, 2023.

66 Dixon, Matt. *Swamp Monsters: Trump vs. DeSantis* (Boston: Little, Brown and Company, 2024), 23–24.

67 Bousquet, Steve. "How Richard Corcoran Stormed Florida's Capital and Made Some People Angry," *Tampa Bay Times*, March 6, 2017, https://www.tampabay.com/news/politics/stateroundup/heres-how-richard-corcoran-stormed-floridas-capital-and-made-some-people/2315176/; Staff Writer, "Fox in the Henhouse," *Ocala StarBanner*, December 19, 2018, https://www.ocala.com/story/opinion/editorials/2018/12/19/editorial-corcoran-is-fox-in-henhouse/6607688007/.

68 Henderson, Joe. "Richard Corcoran: 2017 Politician of the Year," Florida Politics, December 30, 2017, https://floridapolitics.com/archives/251183-richard-corcoran-2017-florida-politician-year/.

69 Bousquet, "Richard Corcoran."

70 Ibid.

71 Krishnaiyer, Kartik. "In Begrudging Praise of Speaker Richard Corcoran," The Florida Squeeze, May 9, 2018, https://thefloridasqueeze.com/2017/05/04/in-begrudging-praise-of-speaker-richard-corcoran/.

72 Wood, "Ideological Test."

73 Garcia, Jason. "Heavy Hitter: Florida Speaker Richard Corcoran Wields Power," *Florida Trend*, February 27, 2017, https://www.floridatrend.com/article/21579/heavy-hitter-florida-speaker-richard-corcoran-wields-power.

74   WTSP, "Governor's Press Conference" (19:45).

75   Joner, "Atlas Shouted Down."

76   Ibid.

Chapter 2

1   Executive Order on Further Advancing Racial Equity and Support for Underserved Communities through the Federal Government. February 16, 2023.

2   Lowry, Rich. *The New York Post*. *"Biden's shocking push to radicalize the federal bureaucracy."* February 20, 2023.

3   *The Journal of Contemporary Legal Issues*. Maimon Schwarzschild. "Goodbye to All That: Three No-Longer-Quite-Contemporary Theories of Equality and Something More Up-To-Date (and Worse)." Vol. 23, Issue 2, Article 10. (2022).

4   Jeffrey J. Pyle, Boston College Law Review. "Race, Equality and the Rule of Law: Critical Race Theory's Attack on the Promises of Liberalism." 40. B.C.L. Rev. 787 (1999)]

5   Henry Louis Gates Jr., "Critical Race Theory and the First Amendment." 1993

6   "Glossary of Diversity, Inclusion and Belonging (DIB) Terms," Harvard Human Resources. https://edib.harvard.edu/files/dib/files/dib_glossary.pdf.

7   Seth Boden, "Start Here: A Primer on Diversity and Inclusion (Part 1 of 2)." *Harvard Business Publishing Corporate Learning*, July 23, 2020. https://www.harvardbusiness.org/start-here-a-primer-on-diversity-and-inclusion-part-1-of-2/.

8   New College of Florida. "New College of Florida—Board of Trustees," YouTube, February 28, 2023, https://www.youtube.com/watch?v=PoA8Ac2ZhUs.

9   Hodgson et al., "Change Comes Swiftly."

10   Save New College, "NCF Protect Educational Freedom Rally against Hostile Political Takeover," YouTube, January 31, 2023, https://www.youtube.com/watch?v=nZf2-993ltk.

11   Hodgson et al., "Change Comes Swiftly."

12   Anderson, "Board Fires President."

13 Beltran, Ruth, Jack Wallace, and Karla Correa. "Minutes for January 31, 2023," New College of Florida Board of Trustees, January 31, 2023, https://www.ncf.edu/wp-content/uploads/2023/04/1-31-23-DRAFT-BOT-minutes1.pdf; New College of Florida, "New College of Florida—Board of Trustees," YouTube, January 31, 2023, https://www.youtube.com/watch?v=z679xI57zIY.

14 Lerner, Carol. "Minutes for January 31, 2023," New College of Florida Board of Trustees, January 31, 2023, https://www.ncf.edu/wp-content/uploads/2023/04/1-31-23-DRAFT-BOT-minutes1.pdf; New College of Florida, "New College of Florida—Board of Trustees," YouTube, January 31, 2023, https://www.youtube.com/watch?v=z679xI57zIY; Lerner, Carol. "Fighting for Inclusive Schools," *Learning for Justice* no. 5 (Fall 2023).

15 Williams, Robin. "Minutes for January 31, 2023," New College of Florida Board of Trustees, January 31, 2023, https://www.ncf.edu/wp-content/uploads/2023/04/1-31-23-DRAFT-BOT-minutes1.pdf; New College of Florida, "New College of Florida—Board of Trustees," YouTube, January 31, 2023, https://www.youtube.com/watch?v=z679xI57zIY.

16 Atterbury, Andrew. "Conservative Trustees Oust President at Florida's New College amid Leadership Overhaul," *Politico*, January 31, 2023, https://www.politico.com/news/2023/01/31/florida-new-college-conservative-trustees-00080541.

17 Brown, Sophia. "Board of Trustees Abolish Office of Outreach and Inclusive Excellence, Welcomes New Interim President Corcoran to Campus," *Catalyst*, March 3, 2023, https://ncfcatalyst.com/board-of-trustees-abolish-office-of-outreach-and-inclusive-excellence-welcomes-new-interim-president-corcoran-to-campus/.

18 Manz, Cassandra. *Catalyst*. "New Director of Diversity and Inclusion Talks Goals." March 8, 2017. https://ncfcatalyst.com/new-director-of-diversity-and-inclusion-talks-issues-goals/

19 https://www.ncf.edu/departments/institutional-research-assessment/

20 New College of Florida, Florida Equity Report, Report Year: 2022. Page 13. https://www.ncf.edu/wp-content/uploads/2022/09/NCF_2022_Equity_Report.pdf

21 Frank Dobbin, Alexandra Kalev. "Why Diversity Training Doesn't Work: The Challenge for Industry and Academia". *Anthropology Now*. http://anthronow.com/uncommon-sense/why-doesnt-diversity-training-work https://scholar.harvard.edu/dobbin/publications/why-diversity-training-doesn't-work-challenge-industry-and-academia

22 Frank Dobbin and Alexandra Kalev. "Why Doesn't Diversity Training Work? The Challenge for Industry and Academia." *Anthropology Now*, September 2018, Vol. 10, no. 2 (48–55). https://scholar.harvard.edu/files/dobbin/files/an2018.pdf.

23 Michelle Penelope King, "Who Benefits From Diversity and Inclusion Efforts?" *Forbes*, May 16, 2023. https://www.forbes.com/sites/michelleking/2023/05/16/who-benefits-from-diversity-and-inclusion-efforts/?sh=51f726e76c7e.

24 Patricia G. Devine and Tory L. Ash, "Diversity Training Goals, Limitations, and Promise: A Review of the Multidisciplinary Literature," Annual Reviews: *Annual Review of Psychology*, January 2020, Vol. 73 (403–429). https://www.ncbi.nlm.nih.gov/pmc/articles/PMC8919430/.

25 Elizabeth Levy Paluck, Roni Porat, Chelsey S. Clark, and Donald P. Green, "Prejudice Reduction: Progress and Challenges," Annual Reviews: *Annual Review of Psychology*, January 2021, Vol. 72 (533–560). https://www.annualreviews.org/docserver/fulltext/psych/72/1/annurev-psych-071620-030619.pdf?expires=1715372339&id=id&accname=guest&checksum=5E12ADBA1B146EEB37F384ECC6D05BA8.

26 William Taylor Laimaka Cox. "Developing scientifically validated bias and diversity trainings that work: empowering agents of change to reduce bias, create inclusion, and promote equity." PMC 2023 Apr 21. 61(4): 1038-1061. https://www.emerald.com/insight/content/doi/10.1108/MD-06-2021-0839/full/html

27 Singal, Jesse. *New York Times.* "What if diversity training is doing more harm than good?" January 17, 2023. https://www.nytimes.com/2023/01/17/opinion/dei-trainings-effective.html

28 Ibid.

Chapter 3

1 Wallace, David Foster. "Authority and American Usage," *Consider the Lobster* (New York: Back Bay Books, 2005), 121.

2 Bari Weiss, "Resignation Letter," Bari Weiss, https://www.bariweiss.com/resignation-letter.

3 Bari Weiss, "An Update on Our Newsroom From Bari," The Free Press, August 22, 2022. https://www.thefp.com/p/an-update-on-our-newsroom-from-bari.

4 Katie Herzog, "Med Schools Are Now Denying Biological Sex," The Free Press, July 27, 2021. https://www.thefp.com/p/med-schools-are-now-denying-biological.

5 "Academic Freedom Conference," Stanford University, Stanford Business, 2022. https://cli.stanford.edu/events/conference-symposium/academic-freedom-conference.

6 Luana Maroja, "An Existential Threat to Doing Good Science," The Free Press, November 7, 2022. https://www.thefp.com/p/an-existential-threat-to-doing-good.

7 Zurie Pope, "'A Lot to Handle': Ohio Professor at Center of Tiktok Controversy Speaks Out," The Columbus Dispatch, June 9, 2023. https://www.dispatch.com/story/news/2023/06/09/olivia-krolczyk-professor-university-cincinnati-assignment-failed-women-studies-ohio/70305781007/.

8 Joshua Q. Nelson, "University Rescinds Reprimand for Professor Who Failed Student for Using Term 'Biological Woman,'" *New York Post,* July 8, 2023. https://nypost.com/2023/07/08/university-rescinds-reprimand-for-professor-who-failed-student-for-using-term-biological-woman/#:~:text="UC%20is%20affirming%20that%20professors,professional%20manner%2C"%20Krolczyk%20said.

[9] "Weather in Sarasota, August 10—Detailed Weather Forecast for August 10 in Sarasota, Florida, United States," World Weather, August 10, 2023, https://world-weather.info/forecast/usa/sarasota/10-august/.

[10] Samsel, Stephanie. "New College of Florida Moves to Abolish Gender Studies Program," Campus Reform, August 22, 2023, https://www.campusreform.org/article/new-college-florida-moves-abolish-gender-studies-program/23840.

[11] Allen, Robert Jr. "New College's Critics Are Running Out of Arguments. Why Won't They Admit It?," *Sarasota News Herald*, July 20, 2023.

[12] Ibid.

[13] Fiamengo, Janice. "New College of Florida Is Right to Abolish Gender Studies," *Spectator*, September 18, 2023, https://www.spectator.com.au/2023/09/new-college-of-florida-is-right-to-abolish-gender-studies/.

[14] Jones, Sarah. "DeSantis's New College Minions Want to Ax Gender Studies: The Latest Battle in the Conservative War on the American Mind," *New York Magazine*, August 11, 2023, https://nymag.com/intelligencer/2023/08/desantiss-new-college-minions-want-to-ax-gender-studies.html.

[15] Dove-Viebahn, Aviva. "Florida Fights to Preserve the Future of Gender Studies: 'This Is About to Be the Entire Country's Problem,'" *Orlando Weekly*, August 11, 2023, https://www.orlandoweekly.com/news/florida-fights-to-preserve-the-future-of-womens-and-gender-studies-this-is-about-to-be-the-entire-countrys-problem-34828967.

[16] Donegan, Moira. "Florida's Attacks on Academic Freedom Just Got Even Worse," *Guardian*, August 16, 2023, https://www.theguardian.com/commentisfree/2023/aug/16/florida-ron-desantis-academic-freedom.

[17] Jolley, Veronica. "Uncertainty Looms over NCF's Gender Studies Program," *Catalyst*, September 13, 2023, https://ncfcatalyst.com/uncertainty-looms-over-ncfs-gender-studies-program/.

18 Butler, Judith, *Gender Trouble*. 1999 Preface. Pg. xv. (originally published 1990) Routledge Classics ed.

19 Id. Page 9-10.

20 The New Statesman. "Judith Butler on the culture wars, JK Rowling and living in 'anti-intellectual times'." Ferber, Alona. September 22, 2020. https://www.newstatesman.com/long-reads/2020/09/judith-butler-culture-wars-jk-rowling-living-anti-intellectual-times

21 Gleeson, Jules. *The Guardian*. "Judith Butler: We need to rethink the category of woman." Sept. 7, 2021. https://www.theguardian.com/lifeandstyle/2021/sep/07/judith-butler-interview-gender

22 Rustin, Susanna. *The Guardian*. "Feminists like me aren't anti-trans—we just can't discard the idea of 'sex'." Sept. 30, 2020. https://www.theguardian.com/commentisfree/2020/sep/30/feminists-anti-trans-idea-sex-gender-oppression

23 Burns, Katelyn. *Vox*. "The rise of anti-trans, 'radical' feminists, explained." Sept. 5, 2019. https://www.vox.com/identities/2019/9/5/20840101/terfs-radical-feminists-gender-critical

24 Fradella, Henry F. *William & Mary Journal of Race, Gender, & Social Justice*. "The Imperative of Rejecting 'Gender-Critical' Feminism in the Law." Vol. 30, Issue 2 (2023) https://papers.ssrn.com/sol3/papers.cfm?abstract_id=4419750

25 Hooven CK. Academic Freedom Is Social Justice: Sex, Gender, and Cancel Culture on Campus. Arch Sex Behav. 2023 Jan;52(1):35-41. doi: 10.1007/s10508-022-02467-5. Epub 2022 Nov 7. PMID: 36344790. https://pubmed.ncbi.nlm.nih.gov/36344790/

26 Lanum, Nicholas. Fox News. "Former Harvard lecturer who defended biological sex claims school failed to support her as career crumbled." Jan. 15, 2024. https://www.foxnews.com/media/former-harvard-lecturer-defended-biological-sex-claims-school-failed-support-career-crumbled

27 Carole Hooven, "About," Carole Hooven. http://www.carolehooven.com/about.html#:~:text=As%20a%20result%20of%20the,position%20in%20Harvard's%20Psychology%20department.

28 "The Cancellation of Carole Hooven," Why Evolution is True, November 11, 2022. https://whyevolutionistrue.com/2022/11/11/the-cancellation-of-carole-hooven/.

29 Favaro, Laura. Times Higher Education. "Researchers are wounded in academia's gender wars." September 15, 2022. https://www.timeshighereducation.com/depth/researchers-are-wounded-academias-gender-wars

30 Ibid.

31 Grove, Jack. "Laura Favaro: 'Gender Studies 'Groupthink Is Forcing Scholars Out,'" *Times Higher Education*, August 30, 2023, https://www.timeshighereducation.com/news/laura-favaro-gender-studies-groupthink-forcing-scholars-out.

32 Wyckoff, Alyson Sulaski. "AAP Reaffirms Gender-Affirming Care Policy, Authorizes Systematic Review of Evidence to Guide Update," *AAP News*, August 4, 2023, https://publications.aap.org/aapnews/news/25340/AAP-reaffirms-gender-affirming-care-policy?autologincheck=redirected.

33 Ghorayshi, Azeen. "Doctors Debate Whether Trans Teens Need Therapy Before Hormones," *New York Times*, January 13, 2022, https://www.nytimes.com/2022/01/13/health/transgender-teens-hormones.html.

34 Ibid.

35 Ibid.

36 Ibid.

37 Ibid.

38 Terhune, Chad, Robin Respaut, and Michelle Conlin. "As More Transgender Children Seek Medical Care, Families Confront Many Unknowns," Reuters, October 6, 2022, https://www.reuters.com/investigates/special-report/usa-transyouth-care/.

39 Leibowicz, Scott. "Gender-Affirming Care for Adolescents: Separating Political Polarization from Medicine," *Psychiatric Times*, June 16, 2023, https://www.psychiatrictimes.com/view/gender-affirming-care-for-adolescents-separating-political-polarization-from-medicine.

40 Owermohle, Sarah and Eugene Daniels. "Biden Launches
    Plan to Protect Transgender Youths' Health Care," *Politico*,
    June 15, 2022, https://www.politico.com/news/2022/06/15/
    biden-plan-transgender-youth-health-care-00039844.

41 Ibid.

42 Simmons-Duffin, Selena. "Rachel Levine Calls State Anti-LGBTQ
    Bills Disturbing and Dangerous to Trans Youth," *NPR: All Things
    Considered*, April 29, 2022, https://www.npr.org/sections/health-
    shots/2022/04/29/1095227346/rachel-levine-calls-state-anti-lgbtq-
    bills-disturbing-and-dangerous-to-trans-you.

43 Kaltiala-Heino, R. et al. "Gender Dysphoria in Adolescence:
    Current Perspectives," *Adolescent Health, Medicine and Therapeutics*
    9 (March 2, 2018): 31–41, doi: 10.2147/AHMT.S135432;
    Steensma, Thomas D. et al. "Factors Associated with Desistence
    and Persistence of Childhood Gender Dysphoria: A Quantitative
    Follow-Up Study," *Journal of the American Academy of Child and
    Adolescent Psychiatry* vol. 52, no. 6 (June 2013).

44 Ghorayshi, Azeen. "Medical Group Backs Youth Gender
    Treatments, but Calls for Research Review," *New York Times*,
    August 3, 2023, https://www.nytimes.com/2023/08/03/health/aap-
    gender-affirming-care-evidence-review.html.

45 Levine, S. B. and E. Abbruzzese. "Current Concerns about Gender-
    Affirming Therapy in Adolescents," *Current Sexual Health Reports*
    15 (2023): 113–123, https://doi.org/10.1007/s11930-023-00358-x.

46 Ibid.

47 Tracy, Kailey. "Lawsuit Claims Clay County Schools Withheld
    Information about Child's Well-Being before Student
    Attempted Suicide," First Coast News, January 28, 2022,
    www. firstcoastnews.com/article/news/education/parents-file-
    lawsuitagainst-clay-county-schools-say-administrators-didnt-
    disclosemeetings-about-gender-identity-confusion-district-denies-
    claims/77-e2a135bd-ef65-4c35-999e-6b39ece496dd.

48 Clarkson, Nicholas. Letter of Resignation (via Ms.), August 17,
    2023, https://msmagazine.com/wp-content/uploads/2023/08/
    clarkson-resignation.pdf.

49   Clarkson, Nicholas. "Teaching Trans Students, Teaching Trans Studies," *Feminist Teacher: A Journal of the Practices, Theories, and Scholarships of Feminist Teaching* vol. 27, nos. 2–3 (2017): 233–252, https://www.jstor.org/stable/10.5406/femteacher.27.2-3.0233.

50   Suissa, Judith and Alice Sullivan. "The Gender Wars, Academic Freedom and Education," *Journal of Philosophy of Education* vol. 55, no. 1, (February 2021): 55–82, https://doi.org/10.1111/1467-9752.12549.

51   Ibid.

Chapter 4

1   Orwell, George. "In 1945, George Orwell wrote an introduction to 'Animal Farm.' It was not printed and remained unknown till now. It appears here under Orwell's title: The Freedom of the Press," *New York Times*, October 8, 1972.

2   Greene, Jay P. and James D. Paul. "Diversity University: DEI Bloat in the Academy," *Backgrounder*, July 27, 2021, https://www.heritage.org/sites/default/files/2021-07/BG3641_0.pdf.

3   Greene, Jay P. and James D. Paul. "Inclusion Delusion: The Antisemitism of Diversity, Equity, and Inclusion Staff at Universities," *Backgrounder*, December 8, 2021, https://www.heritage.org/education/report/inclusion-delusion-the-antisemitism-diversity-equity-and-inclusion-staff.

4   Center for Strategic & International Studies. "Hamas October 7 Attack: Visualizing the Data," December 19, 2023, https://www.csis.org/analysis/hamass-october-7-attack-visualizing-data.

5   TOI Staff. "14 Kids under 10, 25 People over 80: Up-to-Date Breakdown of Oct 7 Victims and What We Know about Them," *Times of Israel*, December 4, 2023, https://www.timesofisrael.com/14-kids-under-10-25-people-over-80-up-to-date-breakdown-of-oct-7-victims-we-know-about/.

6   Karchmer, Mauricio. "Why I Quit My Dream Job at MIT," The Free Press, January 9, 2024, https://www.thefp.com/p/resigned-mit-october-7-antisemitism.

7   "Ackman, William." Open Secrets, accessed February
    9, 2024, https://www.opensecrets.org/donor-lookup/
    results?name=William+ackman.

8   Cadenhead, Rebecca E. J. and Miles J. Herszenhorn. "Steven
    Pinker and the Fight Over Academia's Future," *Harvard
    Crimson*, October 27, 2022, https://www.thecrimson.com/
    article/2022/10/27/steven-pinker-scrut/.

9   Steven Pinker (@sapinker), X (formerly Twitter),
    September 9, 2023.

10 Burleigh, Nina. "It's Time for Presidential Candidates to Talk
    about Science," *Newsweek Magazine*, August 12, 2015, https://
    www.newsweek.com/2015/08/21/presidential-candidates-should-
    talk-science-362063.html.

11 2022 NTSE Public Tables--Endowment Market Values-
    -FINAL.pdf.

Chapter 5

1   Shepherd, Lauren Lassabe. "The History Behind the Right's Effort
    to Take Over American Universities," *Time*, October 23, 2023,
    https://time.com/6319108/conservative-universities/. (Calling the
    New College changes a "sinister development.")

2   Cineas, Fabiola. "Conservatives Have Long Been
    at War with Colleges," *Vox*, February 1, 2024,
    https://www.vox.com/politics/2024/2/1/24056238/
    conservatives-culture-war-colleges-universities.

3   Ogles, Jacob. "A New Boss for New College," *SRQ Magazine*,
    May 2023, https://www.srqmagazine.com/articles/1837/
    New-Boss-For-New-College.

4   Anderson, Zac. "New College Student Enrollment 'A Little Bit
    Down,' President Tells Board Members," *Sarasota Herald-Tribune*,
    April 18, 2023, https://www.heraldtribune.com/story/news/
    politics/2023/04/18/new-college-struggling-with-enrollment-after-
    ron-desantis-overhaul/70124227007/.

5   Anderson, Zac. "Florida Legislature Pumps $50 Million into
    New College after DeSantis Takeover," *Sarasota Herald-Tribune*,

May 1, 2023, https://www.heraldtribune.com/story/news/
politics/2023/05/01/new-college-of-floridas-budget-getting-big-
boost-from-ron-desantis/70170654007/.

6 Nonprofit Explorer, "Ringling College of Art and Design
Inc," ProPublica, https://projects.propublica.org/nonprofits/
organizations/590637903.

7 "New College Foundation Incorporated," ProPublica: Nonprofit
Explorer, April 24, 2024. https://projects.propublica.org/nonprofits/
organizations/590911744.

8 Nonprofit Explorer, "New College Foundation Incorporated,"
ProPublica, https://projects.propublica.org/nonprofits/
organizations/590911744.

9 "Hired and Fired from New College of Florida since Jan.
6,",NCF Freedom, June 27, 2023, https://ncffreedom.org/f/
hired-and-fired-from-new-college-of-florida-since-jan-6.

10 Ogles, Jacob. "David Rancourt Joins New College as Dean of
Students," Florida Politics, April 15, 2023, https://floridapolitics.
com/archives/629209-david-rancourt-joins-new-college-as-dean-
of-students/.

11 Allan, Nathan. "When Lilacs Last in the Palm Court Bloom'd,"
Medium, October 26, 2021, https://nathan-a-allen.medium.com/
when-lilacs-last-in-the-palm-court-bloomd-d4185dbb474.

12 Anderson, "Enrollment 'Down.'"

13 Walker, Steven. "What to Know from New College of Florida
Board of Trustees Meeting Thursday," *Sarasota Herald-Tribune*,
June 2, 2023, https://www.heraldtribune.com/story/news/
education/2023/06/01/new-college-of-floridas-board-of-trustees-
met-thursday-heres-3-things-to-know/70268651007/.

14 Walker, Steven. "New College of Florida Sees
Record Enrollment after DeSantis Shake-Up but at
Academic Cost," *USA Today*, July 27, 2023, https://
www.usatoday.com/story/news/nation/2023/07/27/
new-college-of-florida-enrollment-up/70477277007/.

15 Knox, Liam. "Seeking an Enrollment Hail Mary,
Small Colleges Look to Athletics," *Inside Higher Ed*,

December 4, 2023, https://www.insidehighered. com/news/admissions/traditional-age/2023/12/04/ small-colleges-bet-new-sports-boost-enrollment.

16 Walker, Steven. "New College of Florida to Add Softball, Soccer, Basketball in Athletics Expansion," *Sarasota Herald-Tribune*, May 2, 2023, https://www.heraldtribune.com/story/news/ education/2023/05/02/new-college-of-florida-to-expand-athletics- to-soccer-softball-and-basketball/70158635007/.

17 Walker, Steven. "New College of Florida Approved to Join NAIA Athletic Association, Will Compete in 2024–25," *Sarasota Herald- Tribune*, October 2, 2023, https://www.heraldtribune.com/story/ news/education/2023/10/02/new-college-of-florida-officially-joins- naia-athletic-association-corcoran/71030145007/.

18 Walker, "What to Know."

19 Suarez, Carlos. "New College of Florida Enters Agreement with US Department of Education over Alleged Civil Rights Violation," CNN, September 23, 2023, https://www.cnn.com/2023/09/29/ us/new-college-florida-us-department-of-education-agreement/ index.html.

20 Walker, Steven. "New College Campus Café Re-Opens with Vendor Tied to Interim President Corcoran," *Sarasota Herald- Tribune*, May 12, 2023, https://www.heraldtribune.com/story/ news/education/2023/05/12/new-college-of-florida-re-opens- campus-cafe-with-corcoran-tied-vendor/70183046007/.

21 Walker, Steven. "New College Student Orientation Leaders Push Back When Told to Remove Pride, BLM Pins," *Sarasota Herald- Tribune*, August 23, 2023, https://www.heraldtribune.com/story/ news/education/2023/08/22/new-college-of-florida-tells-student- workers-to-remove-pride-blm-pins/70649925007/.

22 Moody, Josh. "New College Board Denies Tenure for Five Professors," *Inside Higher Ed*, April 27, 2023, https://www. insidehighered.com/news/governance/trustees-regents/2023/04/27/ new-college-board-denies-tenure-5-professors.

23 Ibid.

24 Anderson, Curt. "DeSantis-Backed New College Board Scraps 5 Professors Tenure," AP News, April 26, 2023, https://apnews.com/article/new-college-florida-tenure-conservatives-desantis-ce711c9169ebe84e9d062ebbb281ebce.

25 Bartlett, Tom. "'Shame on You': Over Fiery Protests, Florida's New College Trustees Deny 5 Tenure Bids," Chronicle of Higher Education, April 26, 2023, https://www.chronicle.com/article/shame-on-you-over-fiery-protests-floridas-new-college-trustees-deny-5-tenure-bids?sra=true.

26 Ogles, "New Boss"; Corcoran, Richard. "First 100 Days," *SRQ Magazine*, June 10, 2023, https://www.srqmagazine.com/srq-daily/2023-06-10/21911_First-100-Days; Gordon, Mark. "One-on-One with New College Interim President Richard Corcoran," Business Observer, June 13, 2023, https://www.businessobserverfl.com/news/2023/jun/13/one-on-one-with-new-college-interim-president-richard-corcoran/; Corcoran, Richard. "New College a Beacon to Attract Elite Faculty to Florida," SRQ Magazine Perspectives, August 19, 2023, https://www.srqmagazine.com/srq-daily/2023-08-19.

27 Walker, "Record Enrollment."

28 Perry, Mitch. "Richard Corcoran Says He's Never Compared New College of Florida to Hillsdale College," Florida Phoenix, September 15, 2023, https://floridaphoenix.com/2023/09/15/richard-corcoran-says-hes-never-compared-new-college-of-florida-to-hillsdale-college/.

29 Tampa Tiger Bay Club, "The NEW New College," video, 52-minute mark, September 15, 2023, https://tigerbay.tbae.net/m/VSoSP7fb/the-new-new-college-with-richard-corcoran?list=M8yM0k3n.

Chapter 6

1 United States Department of Education Office for Civil Rights, letter to Richard Corcoran, September 8, 2023, https://cdn01.dailycaller.com/wp-content/uploads/2023/09/New_College_Civil_Rights_Complaint.pdf.

2   Golgowski, Nina. "Director at Florida Liberal Arts College Likens Ron DeSantis' Takeover to 'Fascism,'" *HuffPost*, April 11, 2023, https://www.huffpost.com/entry/ron-desantis-fascism-new-college-resignation_n_64355d5ce4b0de24724a 95c7.

3   Aaron Hillegass (@AaronHillegass). "I have been getting some requests for clarification, so I will give those in this thread," Twitter, April 10, 2023, https://twitter.com/AaronHillegass/status/1645410585696256002.

4   Walker, Steven. "New College of Florida Faculty Votes to Censure Board of Trustees," Sarasota Herald-Tribune, May 23, 2023, https://www.heraldtribune.com/story/news/education/2023/05/23/new-college-of-florida-faculty-votes-to-censure-board-of-trustees/70247213007/.

5   Ibid.

6   Achumba, Adaure. "New College Faculty Push Back on New Online Degree Program," WTSP, January 18, 2024, https://www.wtsp.com/article/news/local/sarasotacounty/new-college-online-degree-program/67-50474ecb-63bf-4be9-ae6d-61fa2fa3ed54.

7   Christopher Rufo (@realchrisrufo). Twitter (now X), June 6, 2023, https://twitter.com/realchrisrufo/status/1666212614605799424.

8   Anderson, Zac. "California Gov. Newsom Rips DeSantis during Sarasota Visit with New College Students," *Sarasota Herald-Tribune*, April 5, 2023, https://www.heraldtribune.com/story/news/politics/2023/04/05/gavin-newsom-rips-ron-desantis-during-new-college-florida-visit/70083923007/.

9   Richard Corcoran (@richardcorcoran). X (formerly Twitter), August 21, 2023.

10 Fitzsimmons, Emma. "Maya Wiley Has 50 Ideas and One Goal: To Make History as Mayor," *New York Times*, May 19, 2021, https://www.nytimes.com/2021/05/19/nyregion/maya-wiley-mayor-nyc.html.

11 Williams, Robin. "New College Leaders Botched New Mascot Process," *Sarasota Herald-Tribune*, June 18, 2023, https://www.heraldtribune.com/story/opinion/columns/your-voice/2023/06/18/

new-college-mascot-is-yet-another-poor-decision-by-schools-leaders-racial-stereotypes-corcoran-rufo/70300998007/.

12 Christopher Rufo (@realchrisrufo). Twitter (now X), June 19, 2023.

13 Anderson, Chris. "If New College Turns to Sports the School Will Be Thrown for a Loss," *Sarasota Herald-Tribune*, February 11, 2023, https://www.heraldtribune.com/story/opinion/columns/2023/02/11/new-college-addition-of-sports-would-set-school-up-for-certain-failure/69890054007/.

14 Anderson, Chris. "Opinion: Sports at New College Won't Bring New Students," *Sarasota Herald-Tribune*, June 16, 2023, https://www.heraldtribune.com/story/opinion/columns/2023/06/16/sports-at-new-college-sounds-good-but-will-have-little-impact/70324744007/.

15 Brown, Danielle J. "FL's Education Commissioner Encourages 'Everyone' Never to Read The Washington Post and The New York Times," Florida Phoenix, September 23, 2020, https://floridaphoenix.com/2020/09/23/fls-education-commissioner-encourages-everyone-never-to-read-the-washington-post-and-the-new-york-times/.

16 Atterbury, Andrew. "University of Florida, New College Stumble in National Rankings," *Politico*, September 18, 2023, https://www.politico.com/news/2023/09/18/university-of-florida-college-national-rankings-00116589#:~:text=But%20there%20was%20bad%20news,campus%2C%20Florida's%20smallest%20state%20university.

17 Walker, Steven. "New College of Florida Plummets in National Rankings amid DeSantis Conservative Overhaul," *Sarasota Herald-Tribune*, September 18, 2023, https://www.heraldtribune.com/story/news/education/2023/09/18/amid-desantis-overhaul-new-college-drops-double-digits-in-rankings/70889485007/.

18 Morse, Robert and Eric Brooks. "A More Detailed Look at the Ranking Factors," *US News & World Report*, September 17, 2023, https://www.usnews.com/education/best-colleges/articles/ranking-criteria-and-weights.

19 Strauss, Valerie. "DeSantis Moves to Turn a Progressive Fla. College into a Conservative One," *Washington Post*, January 7, 2023, https://www.washingtonpost.com/education/2023/01/07/new-college-florida-desantis-rufo/.

20 Mazzei, "DeSantis's Latest."

21 Mazzei, Patricia. "Sports Are In, Gender Studies Are Out at College Targeted by DeSantis," *New York Times*, September 23, 2023, https://www.nytimes.com/2023/09/22/us/new-college-florida-desantis.html.

22 Walker, Steven. "New College of Florida Nets Record Number of New Students, but at Academic Cost," *Sarasota Herald-Tribune*, August 18, 2023, https://www.heraldtribune.com/story/news/education/2023/07/27/new-college-of-florida-pursues-student-athletes-at-academic-cost-richard-corcoran/70445567007/.

23 Mazzei, "Sports Are In."

24 "It's unclear what facilities they will use or who they will compete against, because New College doesn't have any athletic facilities and hasn't yet been accepted to the [NAIA]." Walker, "Record Enrollment"; "The college has yet to get approval to play in the National Association of Intercollegiate Athletics (NAIA), it doesn't have a baseball field of its own, and batting cages are just going up." LaGrone, Katie. "Housing Woes, Canceled Classes among Issues Students at New College Report as New Year Begins," ABC Action News, August 28, 2023, https://www.abcactionnews.com/news/state/housing-woes-canceled-classes-among-issues-students-at-new-college-report-as-new-year-begins; "How student athletics will actually work is far from clear. For one thing, NCF does not have the athletic facilities needed. Nor has it yet been accepted into the [NAIA]. Nevertheless, NCF has signed off on employment contracts for coaches of baseball, softball, men's and women's basketball and women's soccer." Greenfeld, Nathan M. "Fears for College at Centre of DeSantis' War on 'Woke,'" University World News, August 5, 2023, https://www.universityworldnews.com/post.php?story=20230805142028126; "Despite the surge in student-athletes and its consequences on New College's traditional

student body, the college has yet to gain approval to play in the National Association of Intercollegiate Athletics (NAIA)." Donadel, Alcino. "New College of Florida Facing a 'Dumpster Fire' Start to the Academic Year," *University Business*, August 28, 2023, https://universitybusiness.com/new-college-of-florida-facing-a-dumpster-fire-start-to-the-academic-year/.

25 Anderson, Zac. "New College Could Lose $29 Million in Donations after DeSantis' Takeover, Alum says," *Sarasota Herald-Tribune*, March 10, 2023, https://www.heraldtribune.com/story/news/politics/2023/03/10/florida-governor-ron-desantis-new-college-takeover-drying-up-alumni-donations/69984607007/.

26 Gecker, Jocelyn. "Desantis War on 'Woke' Colleges Sparks Fear among Professors, Students," PBS NewsHour, March 30, 2023, https://www.pbs.org/newshour/education/desantis-war-on-woke-colleges-sparks-fear-among-professors-students.

Chapter 7

1 Hassell, Hans, John Holbein, and Matthew Miles. "Journalists May Be Liberal, but This Doesn't Affect Which Candidates They Choose to Cover," *Washington Post*, April 10, 2020, https://www.washingtonpost.com/politics/2020/04/10/journalists-may-be-liberal-this-doesnt-affect-which-candidates-they-choose-cover/.

2 "Media Bias: Pretty Much All of Journalism Now Leans Left, Study Shows," *Investor's Business Daily*, November 16, 2018, https://www.investors.com/politics/editorials/media-bias-left-study/.

3 Rubenstein, Adam. "I Was a Heretic at the New York Times," *Atlantic*, February 26, 2024, https://www.theatlantic.com/ideas/archive/2024/02/tom-cotton-new-york-times/677546/.

4 Cadelago, Christopher. "'We Would've Done Everything Differently': Newsome Reflects on Covid Approach," *Politico*, September 10, 2023, https://www.politico.com/news/2023/09/10/newsom-covid-california-00114888.

5 Cabrera, Tony. "Coronavirus: SoCal Parents Sue Gov. Gavin Newsom over School Closure Order," ABC7 News, August 14, 2020, https://abc7news.com/

governor-gavin-newsom-school-closures-coronavirus-california-socal-parents-sue/6371086/.

6   Mays, Mackenzie. "Newsom Sends His Children Back to Private School Classrooms in California," *Politico*, October 30, 2020, https://www.politico.com/states/california/story/2020/10/30/newsom-sends-his-children-back-to-school-classrooms-in-california-1332811.

7   Gecker, Jocelyn. "California Governor and Unions Clash over School Openings," AP News, February 1, 2021, https://apnews.com/article/san-francisco-health-coronavirus-pandemic-california-gavin-newsom-6c64b0c63102b341cf7ba3ff46 7df330.

8   NBC News. *Meet the Press.* "Full Newsom: 'I'm not convinced we've learned the lessons from' Covid." Sept. 8, 2023. https://www.nbcnews.com/meet-the-press/video/full-newsom-i-m-not-convinced-we-ve-learned-the-lessons-from-covid-192566853729

9   Hanes, Tim. RealClear Politics. "Gov. Gain Newsom on Covid Response Mistakes: 'It was hardly I, It was we, collectively." September 11, 2023. https://www.realclearpolitics.com/video/2023/09/11/gov_gavin_newsom_on_covid_response_mistakes_it_wasnt_i_it_was_we.html

10 Sforza, Lauren. The Hill "Newsom worries about 'fetishness for 'autocray' in the U.S." September 10, 2023. https://thehill.com/homenews/4196689-newsom-worries-about-fetishness-for-autocracy-in-the-us/

11 Falcon, Gabriel. "Andrew Cuomo and Daughters on Life during the Pandemic," CBS News, October 11, 2020, https://www.cbsnews.com/news/andrew-cuomo-and-daughters-on-life-during-the-pandemic/.

12 Ibid.

13 Olen, Helaine. "Opinion. Gavin Newsome, Andrew Cuomo and the Perils of Pandemic Stardom," *Washington Post*, November 20, 2020, https://www.washingtonpost.com/opinions/2020/11/20/gavin-newsom-andrew-cuomo-pandemic-stardom-perils/.

14 Handler, Chelsea. "Dear Andrew Cuomo, I Want to Be Your First Lady," *Vogue*, March 31, 2020, https://www.vogue.com/article/chelsea-handler-andrew-cuomo-love-letter.

15 Kornick, Lindsay. "'Trevor Noah Mocked as 'Cuomosexual' Clip Resurfaces Following Cuomo's Resignation," Fox News, August 10, 2021, https://www.foxnews.com/media/trevor-noah-mocked-cuomosexual-clip-cuomos-resignation.

16 Carras, Christi. "Gov. Andrew Cuomo Approves of People Who Identify as 'Cuomosexuals,'" *Los Angeles Times*, April 28, 2020, https://www.losangelestimes.com/entertainment-arts/story/2020-04-28/andrew-cuomo-sexual-ellen-degeneres-youtube.

17 Kornick, "Trevor Noah Mocked."

18 Carras, "Cuomo Approves."

19 Dwyer, Colin. "Andrew Cuomo to Receive International Emmy for 'Masterful' COVID-19 Briefings," NPR, November 21, 2020, https://www.npr.org/sections/cornavirus-live-updates/2020/11/21/937445923/andrew-cuomo-to-receive-international-emmy-for-masterful-covid-19-briefings.

20 Wulfsohn, Joseph. "Gov. Cuomo Pummeled Online for Selling Poster Touting New York's COVID Response," Fox News, July 14, 2020, https://www.foxnews.com/politics/gov-cuomo-pummeled-for-selling-poster-touting-new-yorks-covid-response.

21 Ibid.

22 Andrew Donovan (@AndrewDonovan). "IMAGE: @NYGovCuomo releases a 'New York Tough' political poster…," Twitter (now X), July 13, 2020, https://twitter.com/AndrewDonovan/status/1282724478871580674.

23 Cuomo, Andrew. "American Crisis: Leadership Lessons from the COVID-19 Pandemic," Amazon, October 13, 2020.

24 Ibid.

25 Tobin, Jonathan. "Despite Media Narrative, DeSantis Was Right and Cuomo Was Wrong," *Newsweek*, May 28, 2020, https://www.newsweek.com/despite-media-narrative-desantis-was-right-cuomo-was-wrong-opinion-1506950.

26 Ibid.

27   Levine, Jon. "Top Navy Admiral Begged Melissa DeRosa to Fill
      Comfort Ship during COVID: Emails," *New York Post*, February
      18, 2023, https://nypost.com/2023/02/18/top-navy-admiral-
      begged-melissa-derosa-to-fill-comfort-ship-during-covid-emails/.

28   Condon, Bernard, and Jennifer Peltz. "AP: Over 9,000 Virus
      Patients Sent into NY Nursing Homes," AP News, February 11,
      2021, https://apnews.com/article/new-york-andrew-cuomo-us-
      news-coronavirus-pandemic-nursing-homes-512cae0abb55a55f375
      b3192f2cdd6b5.

29   Ibid.

30   Ashford, Grace, and Luis Ferre-Sadurni. "Cuomo Is Ordered to
      Forfeit Earnings from $5.1 Million Book Deal," *New York Times*,
      December 14, 2021, https://www.nytimes.com/2021/12/14/
      nyregion/andrew-cuomo-book.html.

31   Goodman, J. David, Alexandra Alter, Rachel Abrams, and
      Luis Ferre-Sadurni. "Cuomo Set to Receive $5.1 Million from
      Pandemic Book Deal," *New York Times*, May 17, 2021, https://
      www.nytimes.com/2021/05/17/nyregion/cuomo-tax-returns-
      pandemic-book.html.

32   Task Force on COVID-19 in New York Nursing Homes and
      Long-Term Care, New York State Bar Association. "Report
      and Recommendations of the Task Force on Nursing Homes
      and Long-Term Care," New York State Bar Association, June
      2021, https://nysba.org/app/uploads/2021/06/11.-Task-Force-on-
      Nursing-Home-and-Long-Term-Care-Report-staff-memo-and-
      comments-6.11.2021.pdf.

33   Ibid.

34   McCarthy, Tom. "What Is It about New York Governors?
      Cuomo Is the Latest in String of Scandals," *Guardian*, March
      20, 2021, https://www.theguardian.com/us-news/2021/mar/20/
      new-york-governors-scandals-cuomo.

Chapter 8

[1] "Florida Amendment 9, Term Limits Initiative
     (1992)," Ballotpedia, https://ballotpedia.org/
     Florida_Amendment_9,_Term_Limits_Initiative_(1992).
[2] Moritsugu, Ken. "Leaner Budget Proposed," *Tampa Bay Times*,
     March 21, 1992, https://www.tampabay.com/archive/1992/03/21/
     leaner-budget-proposed/.
[3] Ibid.
[4] Ibid.
[5] Ibid.
[6] Goldschmidt. "Legislature Back at Work," *Fort Myers News-Press*,
     March 24, 1992; O'Neal, Donna. "Democrats Rip Budget Cuts
     Proposed by Republicans," *Orlando Sentinel*, March 26, 1992.
[7] Moss, Bill, Charlotte Sutton, and Diane Rado. "Chiles Approves
     $31-Billion Budget," July 2, 1992, https://www.tampabay.com/
     archive/1992/07/02/chiles-approves-31-billion-budget/.

Chapter 9

[1] Wilson, Drew. "Halt and Review FSU Presidential Search,
     BOG Member Says," Florida Politics, May 18, 2021, https://
     floridapolitics.com/archives/430490-halt-and-review-fsu-
     presidential-search-bog-member-says/.
[2] Atterbury, Andrew. "BOG Member Raises Alarm
     over Accreditation Board's Role in FSU Search,"
     Politico, May 18, 2023, https://www.politico.com/
     states/f/?id=00000179-7bb4-d60d-a9f9-ffb75aae0000.
[3] Welch, Monica. *Houston Landing*. "Explainer: Texas' DEI ban
     is in full effect. Here's how it impacts colleges, universities."
     August 24, 2023.
[4] Mangan, Katherine. "After Texas' DEI Bans, Administrators
     Got 'Creative.' Then They Got in Trouble," *Chronicle of Higher
     Education*, March 4, 2024, https://www.chronicle.com/article/after-
     texas-dei-bans-administrators-got-creative-then-they-got-in-trouble.

5   Accuracy in Media (@AccuracyInMedia). "Shocking new video reveals how radical Texas university officials are circumventing state law to implement DEI," X (formerly Twitter), February 15, 2024, https://twitter.com/AccuracyInMedia/status/1758123006444835299?s=20.

6   Charles, Brian J. "The Rise and Fall of DEI at the University of Oklahoma," *Chronicle of Higher Education*, February 16, 2024, https://www.chronicle.com/article/the-rise-and-fall-of-dei-at-the-university-of-oklahoma.

7   Amesbury, Richard and Catherine O'Donnell. "Dear Administrators: Enough with the Free-Speech Rhetoric!," *Chronicle of Higher Education*, November 16, 2023, https://www.chronicle.com/article/dear-administrators-enough-with-the-free-speech-rhetoric.

8   Schill, Michael H. "The Misguided Student Crusade against Fascism," *New York Times*, October 23, 2017.

ACKNOWLEDGMENTS

This book would not have been possible without Governor Ron Desantis and First Lady Casey Desantis. They invited me to be a part of their dream to make Florida the greatest state in the nation. I was certainly an unconventional choice to be a part of this vision given my past as a primary opponent. Their trust in me to be a part of the team to achieve their goals for the state of Florida has truly been the honor of a lifetime for which I will be forever grateful.

I would also like to thank Dr. Jonathan Bronitsky, cofounder and CEO of the literary public relations firm Athos, for his support and encouragement, as well as the publishing team at Bombardier Books. They believed this was a story that needed to be told, and their combined efforts helped bring this book to fruition.

Thanks also to Eric Eggers for his outstanding work in organizing, researching, reporting, and editing material in this book, as well as to Peter Schweizer for introducing me to Eric.

I am also grateful for the colleagues who I worked with during events in this book whose friendship and professional competence were a ballast during many a storm, including Bill

Galvano, Alex Kelly, James Uthmeier, Taryn Fenske, James Blair, and Mat Bahl.

Many thanks are also due to Carmen and Carlos Trujillo and the teams at Continental PLLC and Continental Strategy. In between my stint and education commissioner and my appointment as interim president at New College of Florida, I spent a year joining one of my closest friends, Carlos Trujillo, in starting three companies, including a law firm and a government consulting firm. These businesses became very successful very quickly. Then, right in the middle of brainstorming how to hire more quality people to handle the volume of work in early 2023, I decided to consider accepting the interim presidency at NCF. Carlos didn't hesitate to leave the decision up to me, though I know he could easily have asked me to stay. While our business partnership has ended, Carlos, Carmen, and the teams at the Continental companies still feel like family and will always have my and Anne's immense respect and deep friendship.

I would also be remiss if I didn't thank the Corcoran family. First, I am thankful to my mother and father who, though no longer with us, always put their family first—despite growing up in families who were not able to be present much for them. Their advice and wisdom are the bedrock on which I have built much of my life. Second, to my siblings and their children, I am so grateful for our relationships and the way we stay present and involved in loving and supporting each other.

Thanks also to my six children—Kate, Jack, Caroline, Luke, Major, and Evangeline. They have grown up surrounded by politics. Sometimes this world intruded upon their lives in ways that were not always pleasant, but they accepted this with aplomb and grace. They have developed thick skins and adaptability as humans, and I think also empathetic hearts that hopefully will remind them throughout their lives to treat others with kindness and dignity despite difficult situations. One of the best parts of any day is the time I get to hang with them.

And, to my wife, Anne. She does a lot. She's a mom of six who prioritizes her relationship with each of them, a talented lawyer, a community volunteer who donated her time to start a school for our children, and— on top of all that—she is also fully involved in any endeavor I have going. We have a non-stop conversation starting in the morning before we leave, during the day on the phone, and at night when we get home. I am always wanting to know what she thinks and why she thinks it. In this book, she has been a writing and thought partner, and wherever life takes us, the best part is always the time I get to spend with her.